HTML for Fun and Profit

3rd edition

Mary E. S. Morris
John E. Simpson

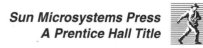

Sun Microsystems Press
A Prentice Hall Title

The publisher offers discounts on this book when ordered in bulk quantities. For more information, con-
tact Corporate Sales Department, Prentice Hall PTR, One Lake Street, Upper Saddle River, NJ 07458.
Phone: 800-382-3419; FAX: 201-236-7141.
E-mail: corpsales@prenhall.com

Editorial/production supervision: *Eileen Clark*
Cover designer: *Anthony Gemmellaro*
Cover design director: *Jerry Votta*
Manufacturing manufacturer: *Alexis R. Heydt*
Marketing manager: *Miles Williams*
Acquisitions editor: *Jeffrey Pepper*
Sun Microsystems Press publisher: *Rachel Borden*

10 9 8 7 6 5 4 3 2 1

ISBN 0-13-079672-7

Sun Microsystems Press
A Prentice Hall Title

Contents

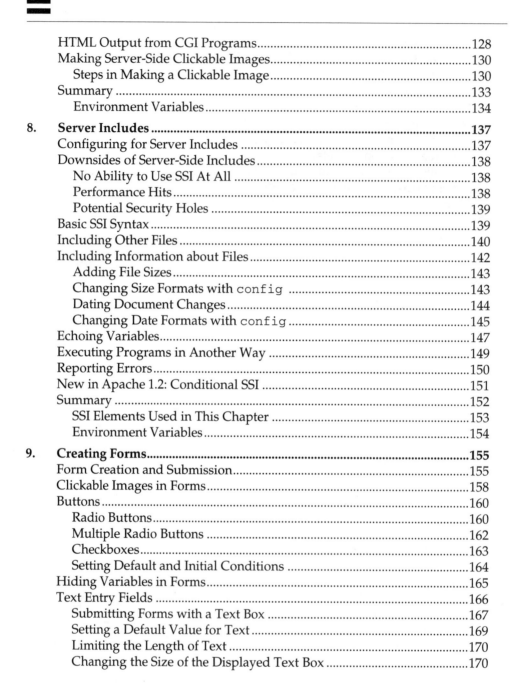

HTML for Fun and Profit

Preface

HyperText Markup Language (HTML) is the language of the World Wide Web, the fastest growing part of a very quickly evolving phenomenon called the Internet. This new edition of *HTML for Fun and Profit* covers basic HTML authoring and emphasizes the use of CGI scripts and forms to create customized and interactive web pages. Information is also included on some of the newest features, like cascading style sheets, that have at last brought HTML into the real publishing world.

Third Edition Preface

The third edition now includes a Microsoft Windows 95 web server. In addition, the text contains many updates to reflect the most recent version of the HTML standard, version 3.2, client-side processing, and a wide variety of other new enhancements to web page makeup, such as cascading style sheets. New media types, such as streaming audio, are covered. The bulk of Appendix B is now included on the CD-ROM as a hypertext document for easier reference.

Who Should Use This Book

If you want to make a home page to list your musical preferences, this book is for you. If you want to make a high-tech career out of building storefronts for the newest commercial ventures, this book is for you also. No matter what your ambitions, if you want to be a producer of information instead of just a consumer on the Web, this book will help you learn HTML and related technologies.

Furthermore, if you're already an experienced web designer and HTML author, this book can take you to new levels of professionalism by introducing you to current standards and practices in this fast-changing field.

How This Book Is Organized

Part I: The Static Web

This section gives you a sound basis for developing most of the information you will be placing on your website.

Chapter 1, "Getting Started," provides an overview of the history of the World-Wide Web and lays out some of the authors' basic assumptions and philosophies.

Chapter 2, "The Basics," introduces the concept of a tag and demonstrates the use of several simple tags.

Chapter 3, "Hypertext — Linking Documents," describes hypertext and document interaction in HTML. Here we'll also cover non-text forms of hyperlinking, such as image maps.

Chapter 4, "Multimedia — Going Beyond Text," explains the full range of data beyond plain text and shows how to incorporate multimedia into your web creations.

Chapter 5, "Tables," teaches how to create basic tables and identifies table components.

Chapter 6, "Frames," covers the most effective ways to use this still-novel way of structuring complex documents.

Part II: The Dynamic Web

This section covers approaches to interacting with your website's users and generating web documents "on the fly" to respond to changes in data or the context in which the user views your site.

Chapter 7, "Using the Common Gateway Interface (CGI)," introduces the Common Gateway Interface which enables developers to tie scripts to web pages.

Chapter 8, "Server Includes," demonstrates the use of commands that are included or embedded in web pages to customize web pages.

Chapter 9, "Creating Forms," details the variety of form elements and implements several forms.

Chapter 10, "Processing Data from Forms," discusses input and output handling from the CGI and implements a feedback form.

Chapter 11, "Client-Side Processing," offers basic information about handling user interaction without server intervention through scripting tools such as JavaScript and other means.

Chapter 12, "Cascading Style Sheets," demonstrates the use of style sheets to simplify HTML document maintenance and control and improve your pages' user interface.

Part III: Design, Style, Production, Professionalism

In this section you will move beyond the nitty-gritty details of simply creating web documents into the realm of organizing and presenting your site for maximum impact.

Chapter 13, "Style Guide," outlines common-sense guidelines to make web pages more intuitive to use and more appealing to all audiences.

Chapter 14, "Work-Saving Tools," explains the classes of available tools that make HTML authoring less tedious.

Chapter 15, "Testing/Quality Assurance," describes the steps necessary to ensure that your web site as a whole and its component documents can withstand the rigors of use in the real world.

Chapter 16, "Publishing to the Web," shows you how to move your existing documents to the Web without re-creating them all from scratch.

Chapter 17, "Putting Data on the Internet," discusses the issues involved in putting your data out for public consumption.

Chapter 18, "Future Directions," highlights the trends and directions of the World-Wide Web.

Appendices

Appendix A, "References," provides a complete list of the tags, environment variables, and special characters listed throughout the book.

Appendix B, "More Information," lists pointers to additional resources. (Most of this material is also provided in hypertext form on the accompanying CD-ROM.)

Typographic Conventions

Table PR-1 describes the typographic conventions used in this book.

Table PR-1   Typographic Conventions

Typeface or Style	Description	Examples
AaBbCc123	The names of commands, files, tag attributes, and directories; on-screen computer output	Edit your `.login` file. Use `ls -a` to list all files. `system% You have mail.`
AaBbCc123	What you type, contrasted with on-screen computer output	`system%` **su** `password:`
AaBbCc123	Command-line placeholder: replace with a real name or value	To delete a file, type **rm** *filename*.
Abc Def	Labels which appear in on-screen buttons	Click the Submit button to send the form's date to the server.

Other notes on this book's formatting conventions:

- Screen shots depict Web documents as viewed using the Netscape Communicator browser, Netscape Navigator 4.03.

- URLs, those strings beginning with `http://` which indicate a Web document's location, may occasionally break at the end of a line. In such cases, to avoid confusion, there will be *no* hyphen at the end of the line which breaks.

- Names of Internet services (e.g., TELNET, Archie, FTP) will be capitalized and displayed in a normal typeface. Many of these services have command or protocol equivalents (e.g., **telnet, archie, ftp**); these will be displayed in lowercase boldface font.

- The terms "web" (lowercase) and "Web" (uppercase) will be used to refer to, respectively, a particular site (as in the phrase "designing your web") and to the World-Wide Web as a whole ("when browsing the Web").

Are You Being Served?

If you have done any work at all with HTML already—even simply experimented with some of your browser's capabilities—you know that you can view a *local file* (that is, a file located on whatever machine you're using) simply by opening it directly. To open a *remote file* you specify its location using a Universal Resource Locator, or URL, which includes a reference to the identity of the machine on which the remote file resides. For example, `http://www.w3c.org/somefile.html` points to a file at the Web address "www.w3c.org". (More information about URLs is provided in Chapter 2, and especially in Chapter 3).

Once you've installed the server software provided on this book's accompanying CD-ROM, you have two options to view the sample files discussed throughout the book:

- You can open the sample files as you would any local files—that is, by entering in the browser's Location field the path and filename to be browsed. (For example, on a Windows 95 PC, `file:///D:\Win95\somesample.html`.)

- You can start the server software you've installed and open the file to be viewed *through the medium of that server*. For example, after starting the WebSite 2.0 server for Windows 95, you can enter `http://localserver/somesample.html` in the browser's Location field.

In most cases, either of these approaches yields the same result in your browser window. Fonts, paragraphs, headings, images, and other elements will appear identically regardless of whether you've opened the sample directly (as a true local file) or as a "pseudoremote" file (by passing it through the server software to your browser).

However, particularly in the case of some more advanced features (such as forms which use CGI programs), you *must* use the "pseudoremote" option in order to view the page properly. In these cases, the name of the file to be opened will be designated in this book using an `http://{server}/` prefix. In all cases where this prefix does not appear, you can safely assume that the sample page can be viewed as either a local file or as a "served" file.

HTML for Fun and Profit

Getting Started

Our experiences in learning HTML have led us down many strange and unusual paths. We have spent many hours reading news groups and mailing lists just to find starting points for our learning. Until the last few years, such learning has been limited by the bootstrapping problem: You must have at least a browser in order to find most documentation on the subject, and you must be on the Internet to get anything (including a browser). Needless to say, no bedtime perusing for us.

We found documentation in some unusual sources, including web-document source code itself. It has become a habit for us now to `grep` or search all source code that we get for the string `http`. Tutorials for HTML are spread across the Internet. It is the nature of the Web that people publish locally and a few souls then publish hotlists or lists of pointers to items of interest on a topic. Unfortunately, there is no single master list, so you can spend many hours following dozens or hundreds of links in the hope of finding new material or a different perspective on design. In this edition of *HTML for Fun and Profit*, as in the previous, we hope to change this state of affairs and give HTML authoring—and web development in general—a new beginning.

Begin at the Beginning

The story of HTML is the story of the medium that uses it, the World-Wide Web. Then again, the story of the World-Wide Web is a story about the evolution of tools to manage the vast sea of data that is the Internet.

The Internet

The Internet was born sometime in the early 1980s after a 14-year gestation period as the research and development network called ARPAnet, originally a brainchild of the U.S. Defense Department's Advanced Research Projects Agency (hence the acronym). Its growth has equaled that of a child by almost doubling in size every year. So far this child shows no sign of slowing its rampant growth.

1

The data available to casual users on the Internet have grown as fast as the Internet itself and easily measure in the terabytes. Products have been developed to manage the information about data and provide a way of finding the document or program—in general, the bytes—that are wanted.

Early information was shared via e-mail and FTP. E-mail is powerful and moderately easy to use, but it is transitory. Information could be passed from one person to another, or groups of people could form a mailing list to avoid the hassle of forwarding the information to Sam that you got from Sara. Even today, if you aren't on the mailing list when the e-mail is sent, your only recourse is to hope that there is an archive where you can search for the data (assuming you know about the mailing list in the first place).

Originally e-mail consisted entirely of plain text; it lacked the capability to include (or attach) programs and data files. In some cases, this is still true. Data and programs were stored and retrieved by using additional features of the UNIX mail transfer software, uucp (the *UNIX*-to-*UNIX* *c*opy *p*rogram). FTP (File Transfer Protocol) was developed to move files from place to place on systems that lacked uucp capabilities. Files were stored at anonymous FTP sites. ("Anonymous" here simply refers to the fact that you don't have to be known to the FTP site, via username and password, in order to acquire files from it—you can be anonymous.) For those familiar with the command syntax, FTP provides an efficient method of acquiring data, with only one drawback—you have to know that the data exist and where they can be found.

A program called Archie was then developed at McGill University to canvass anonymous FTP sites and create a database of what is available. This made for two-stop shopping: one stop at the Archie server to locate the data, and another stop to pick up the data.

This method was fine for storing programs and information files at a site. However, the Internet is a little like the stone soup myth. One person contributes a script here, another offers some documentation there, and a third offers a cute little add-on utility which in turn winds up documented by yet another third party. Together these pieces make up the tools that the Internet offers. This development method does little for the two-stop shopping model.

Some enterprising students at the University of Minnesota created a tool that could tie together the pieces of a tool and make them accessible from a common menulike access point in the form of a tree. This humanly logical organizer was called Gopher (after the school's mascot) and was a significant breakthrough in ease of use. Now users could walk Gopher trees to find related information stored at different sites.

For some people, even this level of organization wasn't enough. They wanted to be able to compose an entire document, not just one-line descriptions, complete with pointers to other papers and reference documents, even to point to software when available. This concept had previously been baptized *hypertext*.

Hypertext

Consider what happens when you encounter a footnote in text, like this.[1] Without thinking about it, your eye jumps to the bottom of the page or end of the chapter, reads the note which corresponds to the footnote, and jumps back. In short, you've just participated in a simple demonstration of the principle of hypertext.

Look at the following two paragraphs. The underlined word *hypertext* in the first paragraph links logically to the boldfaced version of the word in the second one, without breaking the flow of the document for those who don't require the additional information.

> Gopher menus resemble hypertext documents in that they are links to other information, but Gopher menus are quick information blips instead of a document that presents a master theme or top-level discussion.

> The word **hypertext** was coined many years ago. In essence, hypertext documents are a set of documents where various parts of the text can be selected to follow a specific thread or concept other than the topic under discussion.

Document Publication

Once the concept of hypertext was born, people needed a language to describe hypertext documents. The publishing world was already employing a document-formatting language called Standard Generalized Markup Language (SGML) that could consistently be implemented on different platforms, to address this need. SGML is unfortunately a large and complex language. Furthermore, the tools created to use this formatting language were also large and usually commercial (which is to say, expensive). These factors have continued to limit the use of SGML.

A few scientists at CERN (the European Particle Physics Laboratory in Geneva, Switzerland) needed to share their documents with cohorts in various places. They needed the platform variety that SGML promised, but they also needed something much less complex than SGML, something that could be distributed over wide areas, such as the Internet, and something that supported hypertext.

---

1. So you found the footnote, eh?

These scientists designed a TCP/IP-based protocol to share hypertext information and called it *http*, or *hypertext transfer protocol*. To write the documents that this tool would convey, they developed an SGML-derivative language that used hypertext linking conventions and a reduced set of formatting codes that worked with the new hypertext protocol. This language became HyperText Markup Language, or HTML.

"Standard" HTML

If all page designers or browser-software vendors on the World-Wide Web used their own conventions for such document elements as headers, bulleted lists, and tables, the Web would be even more chaotic than it already sometimes seems. For this reason, HTML's development has taken place under the jurisdiction of an international standards body, the World-Wide Web Consortium (W3C).

The first "approved" version of HTML, suitably enough, was dubbed HTML 1.0. It allowed for rudimentary markup of text that could be rendered as paragraphs, standard heading styles, and so on. HTML 2.0 added support for forms.

Then things got complicated, thanks (if that's the word) primarily to the influence of commercial browser vendors. The standards process, which necessarily involves complex discussion of the pros and cons of every proposed change, was seen as too sluggishly paced for the business needs of vendors (although these were usually disguised as their customers' needs). We'll discuss browsers more in a moment. For now, suffice it to say that the browser vendors began a process—still continuing to this day—of devising their own sometimes baroque extensions to and subsets of the very HTML "standards" they profess to support.

This has led on one hand to confusion among web authors: should I follow Browser X's lead, or Browser Y's? Should I make up duplicate pages covering both browsers' standards, or should I follow the straight-and-narrow but somewhat duller officially sanctioned standard? On the other hand, it has made things confusing for *consumers* of World-Wide Web content, who cannot know for certain that the browser they've opted to use will be able to open and display any given page.

After version 2.0, HTML was moving in the direction of becoming—logically enough—version 3.0 (also called "HTML+"). However, so many changes in so many elements were deemed essential that the new version was released as 3.2, the current level. (Note that HTML 3.2 is actually a *subset* of 3.0. If we'd had to wait until version 3.0 were approved in full, we might never have gotten it.) W3C declared HTML 3.2 to be the current official version in January 1997.

Remember, by the way, that the World-Wide Web was first and foremost a document-*distribution* application, and only secondarily a document-*publishing* medium. This means that some features which most publishing systems have had for a long time are still developing in HTML. Tables, for example, have become part of the formally recognized HTML standard only recently; methods of precisely placing graphic elements such as illustrations are still awaiting standardization as of this writing.

Mosaic, the "Sexy App"

Back to our history.

Early versions of World-Wide Web tools were text-based, just like Gopher. The most common client tool or browser was the text-based Lynx. Methods were eventually developed, though, to handle images externally for the times when the images could actually be viewed. Yet this was only possible when using a windowing system, such as X-Windows, the Macintosh interface, or Microsoft Windows. Windowing systems, or GUIs (graphical *user* *interfaces*), use point-and-click methods to enable the user to move around in a file.

It didn't take too long before the wonders of the GUI were incorporated into a browser itself. NCSA, the National Center for Supercomputing Applications in Illinois, developed the next most popular browser, Mosaic. Mosaic not only became a popular browsing tool; it also became the darling of the media, who christened it the "sexy app." This popularity brought the World-Wide Web (WWW) to the attention of the general public.

Mosaic and other second-generation browsers that supported HTML 2.0 conventions brought the WWW community out of the library and document-handling world and into the interactive application realm with forms.

In recent months, the phrase "browser wars" has become a drumbeat among the media. This phrase refers to the ongoing competition primarily among browsers from Netscape Communications and Microsoft, although there are other GUI-based browsers available. Sadly, NCSA decided in early 1997 that it could no longer support development of Mosaic; the Web's first cross-platform GUI browser has stopped at version 3.0.

Note – Browser screen shots in this book, except where otherwise noted, all depict the current release of Netscape Communications' browser, Netscape Navigator (part of the Netscape Communicator 4.0 suite). This is largely an arbitrary decision; with the lapsing of Mosaic into a historical footnote, there is no longer a "neutral" browser. For reasons that will become obvious, however, you should attempt to view your newly created pages using as many browsers, on as many platforms, as possible.

The WWW is considered to be interactive because the user chooses what to view next by clicking on hypertext links. The current versions of HTML and http servers (the network computers that deliver web pages to your browser) have significantly extended that interactivity. Now, web pages can be customized and built on-the-fly. Other tools such as WAIS (Wide Area Information Server) can be used to locate specific words within an entire document set, like an index for a book. Scripts can be used to access databases as well. With the addition of these capabilities, not only can users choose their own path through the web, but a server can generate a custom path for that specific person's wishes. This extended level of interactivity creates even more versatile HTML applications, including help systems, cyberspace shopping malls, and surveys.

Future Directions

HTML 3.2 has brought the Web into something closely resembling more traditional library and document-production environments. HTML 3.2 focuses on the features that most document-publishing systems have but that the WWW previously did not have. These features include tables, the ability to wrap text around images and figures, mathematical notation, text alignment, and more ways to format text to add structure to the information.

Version 4.0 of HTML, formerly code-named Cougar, is expected to include support for such enhancements as "rich" forms and truly interactive documents, the use of scripting languages such as JavaScript and VBScript, frames and subsidiary windows, improved access to HTML features for people with disabilities, and multimedia objects.

Some of these features are outside the scope of HTML evolution and will only be touched on in Chapter 18. Others, although not yet finalized, can be said to have "stabilized" to the point where this book can cover them as the need arises—especially in Part II.

WWW Miscellany

The World-Wide Web is a generalist's dream and a specialist's nightmare. The person who flourishes in producing for this environment is part technical professional, part writer, part layout designer, part information analyst, and part visionary. Information about WWW technology, culture, and tradition hasn't always been conveyed in the formal documentation. However, with the rich medium that the WWW is becoming, it is time to place the oral tradition into print.

WWW Naming

Most multiple-word terms in the computing field become acronyms. Unfortunately, taking the first letter of each word in World-Wide Web yields WWW, which when spoken becomes *double-you double-you double-you*—a mouthful for anyone this side of Elmer Fudd, indeed more of a mouthful than the term itself. Therefore, WWW is usually referred to as *double-you-three*. It is also sometimes written as W3.

WWW Culture

The Internet evolved as a culture very different from the standard Western in-your-face and hype-based communications. A certain morality evolved that is now known as *netiquette*. The basic concepts are to maintain a high signal-to-noise (or relevant-to-irrelevant information) ratio, conserve resources, and give back to the Internet community.

The original WWW project contributed to these values by deploying a set of tools that served data in a stripped-down, text-based way that focused on content rather than on appearance and hype. At the start, the WWW conserved resources by sending text instead of bulky, preformatted PostScript files. It provided the means for thousands of people to give back to the Internet the very lifeblood of the Internet—information.

The popularity of Mosaic, Netscape Navigator, Microsoft Internet Explorer, and other GUI browsers has taken the Web away from its roots. Images now add flash, sex appeal, and bulk. In some cases the flash has led people astray from the concept of providing content. As long as the Web gives back to the Internet community and brings Internet access and understanding to more people, the shortcomings aren't all hopeless. But it remains important to understand the guiding principles of the Web and hopefully make a positive contribution.

Emotags

One of the most significant inroads that the WWW has made into the Internet culture is the HTML-ization of *emotags*. Recent e-mail has gone beyond the initial smiles and limited quantities of emoticons. E-mail now uses HTML-style emoticons, for example, `<smirk>` and `</smirk>`. Luckily, this type of communication was found on a WWW mail alias where it was recognized for what it was. This type will evolve to the point that `<flame>` and `</flame>` will become as common as `*flame on*` and `*flame off*` warnings. If only the browser developers would figure out how to format emotags, we may yet find a way to add new depth to the information that is being published.

1

Page Formatting Philosophy

For many years the term *WYSIWYG* (pronounced *wizzy-wig*, short for What You See Is What You Get) has dominated the desktop publishing world. This usually means that there is different software for each hardware platform. The only thing that these Desktop Publishing, or DTP, systems had in common was paper. HTML was originally designed to be not a WYSIWYG publishing tool, but a universal document distribution and publishing medium.

This makes sense when you think about it. Browser users can stretch the window until it fills up the entire screen. They can change and enlarge the fonts until even the near-blind can see. For this reason, the HTML author traditionally could not say that all text would be right-justified or that a page break would occur here, because the author doesn't control the browser—the user does.

Ingenious webmasters (some a bit too ingenious) have developed various ploys over time to create the semblance of a printed page in an HTML document and to control not only what the user sees, but also the form in which he or she sees it. Recent additions to the HTML standard—such as cascading style sheets, covered at greater length in Chapter 12—have at last given web authors significant standardized control of the appearance of their pages. Margins, text colors and sizes, and other enhancements now make it possible for a page's design to support its content (at least assuming the user's browser supports these advanced features as well).

Nonetheless, content (as the saying goes) remains king; appearance can at best only provide strong reinforcement of the content. Regardless of the tools available to authors and users, what the author always does control—and should pay greatest attention to—is the conceptual organization. The author can add emphasis when it is needed. The words can be *strong* or **bold**. Titles, headings, and list structures can be defined. Many, however, feel that this is still not enough, even counting the latest and greatest additions to the HTML specification. In consequence, many of the current structures are used in ways for which they weren't designed, such as employing glossary or list definitions in order to indent text. Where advanced HTML features have been implemented in the most common browsers, they are heavily used.

Perhaps the current HTML isn't enough. Maybe we'll do better with HTML 4.0—or whatever comes after it.

People

WWW document management and creation remains a new field. The people in this field now wear many hats. One day the person may be a technical writer, the next a programmer, and that night become a system administrator when the server logs overflow.

Many uninitiated clients with dreams of their own Web site are looking for HTML programmers, which is something of a misnomer. HTML is not a programming language; it is a formatting language. However, the use of scripts along with the documents requires generalists instead of the technical specialists who can't reach beyond their specific field.

Within the Web community, webmaster is the term commonly used to refer to the person who manages the technical administration and integrates new web pages. Since most webmasters previously wrote the information on the server, a title hasn't been created for the writer of HTML material. We propose that the title become HTML Author. (However, in deference to common usage, we will employ the familiar "webmaster" more often than not.)

Where's the Fun? Where's the Profit?

If you have purchased *HTML for Fun and Profit*, or are simply browsing this chapter in the bookstore, you might wonder what seemingly dull matters like protocols, markup language, and web servers have to do with profit, let alone fun.

Let's address the *profit* question first.

Given the Web's history as recounted above, in the early days (all of five or so years ago) anyone who had anything professional to do with the WWW could be expected to be a computer scientist, an academic, or other researcher. While such professions are not necessarily poorly paid, their chief rewards are commonly understood to be intangible. Indeed, a too-strong profit motive often undercuts success for researchers.

Since the Web's explosion as a mass medium, this has been turned upside down. Salary surveys of computer professionals conducted by such trade publications as *ComputerWorld* consistently place Web-related skills at or near the top in terms of salary, benefits, and other perks. It is not quite true that a web professional can write his or her own job description, but it *is* true that skill with HTML, web page design, and Java and other Internet technologies does a resumé no harm at all. In fact this is so much the case that it seems as though everyone in the neighborhood—from the middle-school whiz next door, to the mailman, to the $80,000-a-year CIO across the street—now professes proficiency as a web developer and is perhaps even charging clients in an effort to prove it. If you were looking to hire a *real* web professional, how would you separate the wheat from the chaff?

One strong indicator of true professionalism is *certification*: the validation, by a neutral third party, of one's web-development skills. While we do not directly address certification in HTML for Fun and Profit, this book—and others like it—can give you a solid foundation in preparing you for it.

As for the fun...

There is nothing quite like seeing your first web page (even one saying no more than "Hi, Mom!") inside a browser display. Take that thrill a notch further: Imagine seeing your company's annual report on the screen, exactly as an investor on the far side of the world will experience it—replete with tables, graphs, photographs of the corporate headquarters and key personnel, perhaps even an audio message from the president—and knowing that *you* made that happen. Imagine finding your site listed on Yahoo! or another search engine's "Best of the Web" list. Imagine, for that matter, the day when you receive the first e-mail message addressed to webmaster@yourown.com.

Need we say more?

Plow on into the meat of this book. Scratch your head if necessary when something doesn't come out quite as you expected; fiddle with the HTML or other code until it's just right, indeed beyond anything we could have imagined (let alone prepared you for). But whether you're after a career as a web professional—profit—or just trying to figure out what all this World-Wide Web stuff is all about, we're sure that one thing you'll come away with is lots of fun.

The Basics

The chapter covers formatting basics, including formatting paragraphs, section headings, titles, italics, bold text, special characters (8-bit letters), other formatting codes, indenting, blocking text, and creating both numbered and unnumbered lists.

Starting Out

What you see on your screen when using a word processing program is actually a combination of the text (and other visible elements) that you can enter and modify and hidden formatting commands. With most WYSIWYG word processors, you never see the formatting codes. (WordPerfect is a notable exception; its "Reveal Codes" feature exposes these codes for examination and even manipulation.) WYSIWYG HTML editors are covered in Chapter 14. For now, let's consider WYSIWYG displays and the HTML-equivalent formatting codes, which are called *elements* or *tags*.

Formatting Text in Word Processing

Some word processing products break formatting into classes such as character or paragraph formatting. Character formatting refers to formatting that is applied to a single character or set of contiguous characters, such as in a word or phrase. Paragraph formatting refers to formatting all text in the same group or paragraph. Usually, paragraphs are ended by a carriage return.

If you were to look behind the scenes of a word processor, it would look like Example 2-1:

Example 2-1   *Behind the Scenes—Formatting Text with a Word Processor*

> *(hidden formatting information: 8pt Helvetica type)* This is the text of the document itself. It is important to remember that you normally see only the text here. The *(hidden formatting information: start italics)* format *(hidden formatting information: end italics)* in this document is not usually displayed for you to see. *(Carriage Return)*

In the above example, the hidden information that instructs the display to italicize the word format has a start format block and an end format block. A pair of formatting instructions like this is called a *container* in HTML. On the other hand, the paragraph information *8pt Helvetica* doesn't have an end format block to match the start format block. This is called an *empty element* since it doesn't have an end instruction to match the start instruction. In HTML, these strings of format information—both the ones that have start-and-stop instructions, and the ones that turn a formatting option on but don't turn it off—are called *tags*.

Opening the First Document

1. **If you want to use a server to view your samples, start up the server.** In any case, open the client browser of your choice.

2. **Open the document on the CD-ROM** Chapter2/example1.html, which should look like the document in Figure 2-1. (If you've modified your browser's default font, the display will of course be in your own choice of fonts rather than the Times New Roman shown here.)
    Notice that when displayed in the browser, this document is all text, and nothing but text—one long paragraph without headings or breaks between ideas and concepts. If you resize the browser window, the wrapping of lines adjusts automatically to match the window's new dimensions. This is the raw material; by adding HTML formatting instructions, a finished product will be created.

Note – With some older browsers, if you loaded this document as http://{*server*}/Chapter2/example1.html/ (note closing "/"), the browser displays the document as it is typed in rather than as shown in Figure 2–1. This is a problem with documents that are improperly, or incompletely, marked as HTML documents. (Document identification is described in the Naming the Document section, later in this chapter.) Newer browsers either display the document correctly or generate an error message that the requested document could not be found.

---

3. **Start up a text editor for your specific platform. Load the file** Chapter2/example1.html (i.e., the same document you just viewed in your browser). (Note: You will be making changes to this and other files throughout this book. In order to save your changes, you will have to use your text editor's "save as" feature to save the file to a drive and directory to which you have write access, as CD-ROMs are by definition read-only devices.)

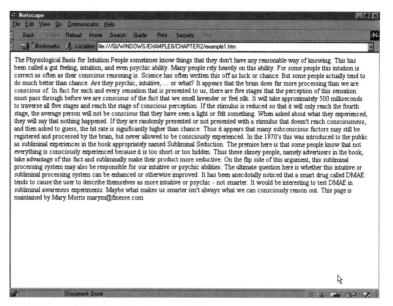

Figure 2-1   A Document as One Continuous Block

Notice that the actual text (as in Example 2-2) has carriage returns all over the place. The WWW browser, on the other hand, ignores the carriage returns in the actual text and inserts a carriage return only where the line should wrap on that specific display.

HTML Example 2-2   Text of First HTML Example

```
The Physiological Basis for Intuition
People sometimes know things that they don't have any reasonable
way of knowing. This has been called a gut feeling, intuition,
and even psychic
ability.
Many people
rely heavily on this ability. For some people this
intuition
is correct as
often as their conscious reasoning is.
Science has often written this off as luck or chance. But some people
actually tend to do much better than chance. Are they psychic,
intuitive, ... or what?
It appears that the brain does far more processing than we are
conscious
```

HTML Example 2-2   Text of First HTML Example (Continued)

```
of. In fact for each and every sensation that is presented to us,
there
are five stages that the perception of this sensation must pass
through
before we are conscious of the fact that we smell lavender or feel
silk. It will take approximately 500 milliseconds to traverse all
five stages and reach the stage of conscious perception. If
the stimulus is reduced so that it will only reach the fourth
stage, the average person will not be conscious that they have
seen a light or felt something. When asked about what they
experienced,
they will say that nothing happened. If they are randomly presented
or not presented with a stimulus that doesn't reach consciousness,
and then asked to guess, the hit rate is significantly higher than
chance.
Thus it appears that many subconscious factors may still be
registered and processed by the brain, but never allowed to be
consciously experienced. In the 1970's this was introduced
to the public as subliminal experiences in the book appropriately
named Subliminal Seduction. The premise here is that some people
know that not everything is consciously experienced because it is
too short or too hidden. Thus these slimy people, namely advertisers
in the book, take advantage of this fact and subliminally
make their product more seductive.
On the flip side of this argument, this subliminal processing system
may also be responsible for our intuitive or psychic abilities.
The ultimate question here is whether this intuitive or subliminal
processing system can be enhanced or otherwise improved.
It has been anecdotally noticed that a smart drug called DMAE tends
to cause the user to describe themselves as more intuitive or
psychic - not smarter. It would be interesting to test DMAE in
subliminal awareness experiments.

Maybe what makes us smarter isn't always what we can consciously
reason out.

This page is maintained by
Mary Morris
marym@finesse.com
```

4. Switch back to the browser and change the font size on the browser display to Large.

How you do this varies according to your browser. In the current release of Netscape Navigator in a Windows environment, the simplest way to temporarily increase the font size as displayed is by pressing the `Ctrl-]` (right bracket) keys. If you are using a different WWW browser, refer to the documentation for that browser for changing the size of the font.

Notice (see Figure 2-2) that when the text became larger, the lines wrapped at different places. To repeat: *WWW browsers are not WYSIWYG.* They display the document differently, depending on the display configuration of the browser.

Another important point to note here is that by simply altering the browser's font characteristics, you have *not* changed any of the underlying HTML formatting as supplied (or in this simple case, not supplied) in the HTML file. You have just changed the way in which you're viewing the page at the moment.

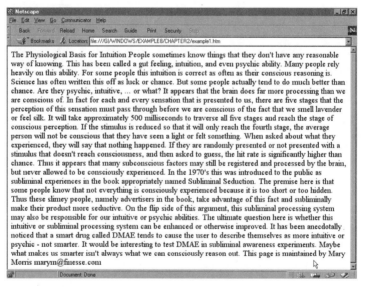

Figure 2-2   Different Fonts with the Same Continuous Block

Adding Paragraphs — A Start Tag without an End Tag

HTML tags are formatting codes surrounded by < > (less-than and greater-than signs, also referred to as angle brackets). For example, the tag <p> tells the WWW browser to start a new paragraph. Note that tags (and other elements of HTML) are case-insensitive: <P> is treated the same as <p>, <BODY> the same as <Body> and <body>, and so on.

In word processing, paragraphs are broken into reasonably sized ideas, perhaps with titles or headers for each group of concepts, and important words and phrases are made to stand out by either bold or italicized text. In the exercise below, you will add tags to format the text in the document, example1.html.

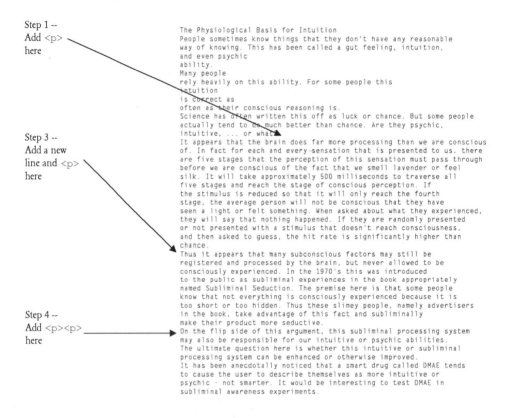

Step 1 --
Add <p>
here

Step 3 --
Add a new
line and <p>
here

Step 4 --
Add <p><p>
here

```
The Physiological Basis for Intuition
People sometimes know things that they don't have any reasonable
way of knowing. This has been called a gut feeling, intuition,
and even psychic
ability.
Many people
rely heavily on this ability. For some people this
intuition
is correct as
often as their conscious reasoning is.
Science has often written this off as luck or chance. But some people
actually tend to do much better than chance. Are they psychic,
intuitive, ... or what?
It appears that the brain does far more processing than we are conscious
of. In fact for each and every sensation that is presented to us, there
are five stages that the perception of this sensation must pass through
before we are conscious of the fact that we smell lavender or feel
silk. It will take approximately 500 milliseconds to traverse all
five stages and reach the stage of conscious perception. If
the stimulus is reduced so that it will only reach the fourth
stage, the average person will not be conscious that they have
seen a light or felt something. When asked about what they experienced,
they will say that nothing happened. If they are randomly presented
or not presented with a stimulus that doesn't reach consciousness,
and then asked to guess, the hit rate is significantly higher than
chance.
Thus it appears that many subconscious factors may still be
registered and processed by the brain, but never allowed to be
consciously experienced. In the 1970's this was introduced
to the public as subliminal experiences in the book appropriately
named Subliminal Seduction. The premise here is that some people
know that not everything is consciously experienced because it is
too short or too hidden. Thus these slimey people, namely advertisers
in the book, take advantage of this fact and subliminally
make their product more seductive.
On the flip side of this argument, this subliminal processing system
may also be responsible for our intuitive or psychic abilities.
The ultimate question here is whether this intuitive or subliminal
processing system can be enhanced or otherwise improved.
It has been anecdotally noticed that a smart drug called DMAE tends
to cause the user to describe themselves as more intuitive or
psychic - not smarter. It would be interesting to test DMAE in
subliminal awareness experiments.
```

Figure 2-3   First Steps in Creating Paragraphs

1. **Using your text editor, add the paragraph formatting code <p> to the text so that it resembles step 1 of Figure 2-3.**

2. **Save the changes to your document; update your changes to the document by pressing the** Reload **button at the top of the Navigator window.** If you are using a different WWW browser, refer to the appropriate documentation for equivalent instructions. Most browsers cache a few documents locally to save the time of retrieving a new copy. To view the changes you made to the

document, you must force a reload of it.

Notice the blank line which appears in the browser display at the point where you inserted the <p> tag.

3. **Now add <p> on a line by itself, as noted in step 3 of Figure 2-3.** Save and reload the image.

   There is no difference between placing the <p> code at the start of the line, at the end of the line before it, or on a line by itself. (For the UNIX `troff`-literate, this is a notable item.)

4. **Add <p><p> as noted in step 4 of Figure 2-3.** Save and reload the image.

   Note that there is no difference between one or more <p> codes. This is *not* the way to add more than one blank line.

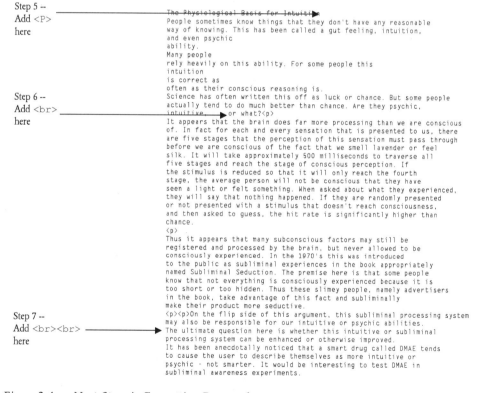

Figure 2-4   Next Steps in Formatting Paragraphs

2

5. **Add <P> (using a capital "P" rather than the lowercase used in earlier steps) as noted in step 5 of Figure 2-4.** Save and reload the image.

   There is no difference between lower- and uppercase tags.

6. **Add <p align=center> as noted in step 6 of Figure 2-4.** Some tags can have additional information within the left and right angle brackets and to the right of the tag itself, referred to as an *attribute*. Save and reload the image.

   New in HTML3.2: The align= attribute of the <p> tag specifies that this paragraph should be rendered in a particular alignment—left (the default), center, or right.

7. **Add <br> as noted in step 7 of Figure 2-4.** Save and reload the image. Note that <br> starts a new line but doesn't place a blank line between adjacent blocks of text.

   New in HTML3.2: The <br> tag now includes an optional attribute, clear=. This attribute specifies that the new line should begin below some other "floating" element on the page, such as an image. This attribute has the value left, right, or both, depending on where the browser should "look for" the first unoccupied margin. More information about the clear= attribute appears later in this book.

8. **Add

 as noted in step 8 of Figure 2-4.** Save and reload the image.

   Two <br> tags in a row equal a <p> tag.

Adding Italics—A Start and End Tag Pair

Where the formatting information needs a definite start and end place as in the example of italics below, there are two tags: a start tag and an end tag—together forming a *container*, as mentioned above. The start tag is the formatting command between the < and > characters. The end tag is a slash placed before the command, </*tag*>. An example of this is <i> and </i> to start and stop a string of italicized text.

9. **Add the paragraph formatting codes <i> and </i> to the text so that it resembles step 8 of Figure 2-5.** Save and reload the image.
   Note that the end tag is the same as the start tag except for the addition of the /.

Step 8 --
Add <i> here

Step 8 --
Add </i> here

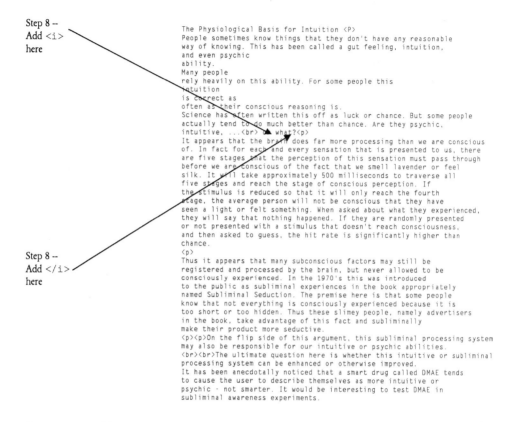

```
The Physiological Basis for Intuition <P>
People sometimes know things that they don't have any reasonable
way of knowing. This has been called a gut feeling, intuition,
and even psychic
ability.
Many people
rely heavily on this ability. For some people this
intuition
is correct as
often as their conscious reasoning is.
Science has often written this off as luck or chance. But some people
actually tend to do much better than chance. Are they psychic,
intuitive, ...<br> what?<p>
It appears that the brain does far more processing than we are conscious
of. In fact for each and every sensation that is presented to us, there
are five stages that the perception of this sensation must pass through
before we are conscious of the fact that we smell lavender or feel
silk. It will take approximately 500 milliseconds to traverse all
five stages and reach the stage of conscious perception. If
the stimulus is reduced so that it will only reach the fourth
stage, the average person will not be conscious that they have
seen a light or felt something. When asked about what they experienced,
they will say that nothing happened. If they are randomly presented
or not presented with a stimulus that doesn't reach consciousness,
and then asked to guess, the hit rate is significantly higher than
chance.
<p>
Thus it appears that many subconscious factors may still be
registered and processed by the brain, but never allowed to be
consciously experienced. In the 1970's this was introduced
to the public as subliminal experiences in the book appropriately
named Subliminal Seduction. The premise here is that some people
know that not everything is consciously experienced because it is
too short or too hidden. Thus these slimey people, namely advertisers
in the book, take advantage of this fact and subliminally
make their product more seductive.
<p><p>On the flip side of this argument, this subliminal processing system
may also be responsible for our intuitive or psychic abilities.
<br><br>The ultimate question here is whether this intuitive or subliminal
processing system can be enhanced or otherwise improved.
It has been anecdotally noticed that a smart drug called DMAE tends
to cause the user to describe themselves as more intuitive or
psychic - not smarter. It would be interesting to test DMAE in
subliminal awareness experiments.
```

Figure 2-5   Adding Italics

Now that you have learned how to add tags, it is time to learn what the tags do. There are tags for many purposes. As shown above, some tags create breaks in text, but there is no such thing as an HTML "page break" (since that is a concept with meaning for a printed page but not for display on a computer or terminal screen). The tags discussed so far are only a sample of the tags available for formatting text. In addition, there are yet other tags which define the different parts of an HTML document—its overall *structure*.

2

Sections of a Document — Tour of an HTML Document

A document is usually broken down into parts. First, it should be defined as an HTML document. Then, the head to the document includes a *title*; this is followed by a *body* that can be broken into subtopics with different levels of headings. Comments and other nondisplayable information can be included in a document. Finally, it is always good practice to "sign" your documents at the bottom.

Parts of a Page

The following sections describe the basic tags that a document should have. The ten steps in this section will help you visualize and experiment with an HTML page. HTML Example 2-3 shows a template that can be used when designing new documents.

HTML Example 2-3   template.html for Designing New Documents

```
<html>
<head>
<title>

</title>
</head>
<!-- this is a comment -->
<body>

<address>

</address>
</body>
</html>
```

Naming the Document

WWW browsers differ in how they determine what to do with incoming data. Most browsers look at the extension of the filename (that is, the portion of a filename after the last "."—typically htm or html for basic HTML documents) to determine what type it is. The UNIX-based XMosaic browser uses a combination of the filename extension and the .mailcap file to determine the viewer or display system to use. A list of common file types and their associated extensions can be found in Chapter 4.

In the first example of this chapter, if the name of the document that was opened had a trailing /, it wasn't recognized by some older browsers as an HTML document, even though it had the .html extension. This problem was introduced when the / became an optional character. Since the document wasn't known as an HTML document by its extension, the document itself was checked for internal clues as to what type of document it was.

Another way in which browsers determine the data type is to look for information at the start of the data to see if it matches a recognizable pattern. Since you can't control what browsers will be used, it is always a good idea to label your documents as HTML inside the document itself. This is done by placing the <html> and </html> tags at the start and the end of a document.

Note – It is important to label your documents fully in this way to avoid having the server or browser *guess* at the data type. Most browsers have routines that try to guess what document type a web page is if the page doesn't have an obvious type. Pure 7-bit ASCII text pages will be declared by some older browsers as <PLAINTEXT> (i.e., rendered with their contents exactly as they appear in the file, in a fixed font such as Courier); but multipart pages, such as multimedia pages, can contain 8-bit references. If the web page's contents cannot be identified, the browser treats it as a binary file and offers the user the option of saving the file to disk. This default treatment of unknown data types is sometimes referred to as *dropping* or *falling into the magic bucket*.

New in HTML3.2: To be strictly "correct," a document formatted conforming to the HTML 3.2 standard should contain this line at the very top, before the <html> tag itself:

```
<!DOCTYPE HTML PUBLIC "-//W3C//DTD HTML 3.2 Final//EN">
```

No code police will arrest you for omitting this identifier. Furthermore, including it by rote in all your pages may not actually be correct, especially if you have incorporated any HTML extensions not officially sanctioned under the HTML 3.2 standard.

Note that the above DOCTYPE directive is specific to HTML 3.2. Earlier versions of the HTML specification used a similar directive, with the appropriate version number and, perhaps, the term DRAFT instead of FINAL.

2

Defining the Head

HTML documents should have a clearly defined head and body. Many of the documents on-line today label the body of a document, but not the head. This practice works for most browsers, but it is usually better to define the head of a document as well as the body.

The head of a document is delimited by the <head> and </head> tags. Ideally, the head of a document will contain information about the document, such as the title and an index if used. This information is generally not displayed as part of the document itself, but as text in the title bar of a browser window. One part of the head that *will* be displayed in the browser is an index. If the <ISINDEX> tag is used, then an "index prompt" such as "This is a searchable index. Enter search string:" is presented at the top of the page, along with a text field in which the user can enter a search string.

New in HTML3.2: A prompt= attribute has been added to the <ISINDEX> tag. This attribute, as you might expect, defines the prompt string that will appear to the left of the user-editable text field. For example, <isindex prompt="You can enter a search term in the box at the right:">. Note the use of double quotes, which should be used whenever any tag attribute contains spaces or other special characters.

Indexes are covered in Chapter 10, in the section Search For Data.

Adding the Title

As noted, the title of a document doesn't appear in the body of a document. It is displayed in the window's title bar and in the user's bookmarks and the hotlist. It is a good idea to title your documents, so that if someone bookmarks your page, the bookmark will show a reasonable name. (The bookmark name can be edited in most browsers, but the default is to use the page's title if one is present.) If the document is left untitled, the Universal Resource Locator (URL) of the document appears in the hotlist instead. How many people are going to remember that they wanted to go back to http://www.somewhere.com/NeatStuf/Ocean/ Scubagear/NoGutsNoGlory.htm, especially if the URL is too long to show completely in their bookmarks or hotlist?

The title will be plain text, reproduced exactly as entered. Formatting information such as bold and italics doesn't appear in a browser title bar. The title is indicated by the <title> and </title> tags, as in this example:

```
<head>
<title>Nilsson Fan Club: The Point</title>
</head>
```

Defining the Body

The body of a document contains all the displayed information for a document. Unlike the head, the body of a document can contain format information. The start and end of the document body is indicated by <body> and </body> tags, respectively. Some of the key components of the body of a typical document are the text of the document itself, section titles or headings, and an address or author-contact information.

New in HTML3.2: The new HTML standard formally endorses several popular optional attributes of the <body> tag which have for some time been supported by Netscape Navigator and other browsers. These attributes are:

- background= sets a particular image file as the background for the document as displayed in the browser. This can be used to give an apparent background texture to the display. The value of the attribute is the URL of the desired image file. If the image file is smaller than the browser's window, the image is *tiled* (i.e., repeated as a pattern across and down the page).

- bgcolor= sets the background color to be used for the page as displayed. If both the background= and bgcolor= attributes are specified, most GUI browsers will first display the background color, then overlay it with the (possibly tiled) background image. The background color in this case will "show through" certain other page elements, such as horizontal rules (covered later in this chapter) and table borders.

- text= defines the color in which to display the text on the page, including headings.

- alink=, vlink=, link= define the colors to be used for hyperlinks that appear in the document. Respectively, the attributes apply to an *active link* (a link which is in the process of being activated, i.e., clicked on); a *visited link* (one which the user has previously activated); and an *unvisited link* (one which the user has never activated, or which was activated earlier than some user-defined time).

More information about images can be found in Chapter 4. How to specify colors for the bgcolor, text, and hyperlink color attributes is covered at greater length later in this section.

These attributes can all be overridden/suppressed by the user, using the browser's own properties or options menu. Note too that none of these attributes have any effect on non-GUI browsers.

The various color attributes are set in one of two ways: either by using one of sixteen standard color names, or by using a numeric string which identifies the mix of red, green, and blue colors (the *RGB value*) used by the browser to render the color on the user's screen. If you use the latter option, the six-digit numeric string (two hexadecimal digits for each of the three color components) is preceded by a # sign.

Why would you use the relatively arcane RGB value instead of the easier to remember color names? Because the names limit you to 16 available colors. (The colors chosen were the ones in the original Microsoft Windows VGA color palette.) With RGB values, on the other hand, you can specify any of up to 256 colors, from #000000 (pure black) through #FFFFFF (pure white). Also note that older browser versions, even ones that support the basic bgcolor= attribute, may not support the color names as standardized in HTML 3.2.

Table 2-1 summarizes the 16 standard color names and their RGB equivalents. (Note especially that "0" represents the digit zero, not the capital letter "oh.") To use a value from this table in one of the new attributes of the <body> tag, simply enter either the name or the RGB value to the right of the = sign.

We leave it as an exercise for industrious readers to determine from Table 2-1 how the mix of hexadecimal RGB values translates to equivalent color displays on the screen, even for the many "in-between" colors unnamed by the HTML 3.2 specification.

Table 2-1   Standard HTML 3.2 Color Specifications

Color Name	RGB Value
Black	#000000
Silver	#C0C0C0
Gray	#808080
White	#FFFFFF
Maroon	#800000
Red	#FF0000
Purple	#800080
Fuchsia	#FF00FF
Green	#008000
Lime	#00FF00
Olive	#808000
Yellow	#FFFF00
Navy	#000080
Blue	#0000FF
Teal	#008080
Aqua	#00FFFF

Headings

HTML supports six levels of headings. It is important to note that headings are actually logical formatting directives; that is, each browser implements the headings as appropriate for that platform. What may be 14-point Helvetica Bold on one system may be 20-point Times Roman Bold on another platform. Headings are indicated by <h#> and </h#>, where # is the level of the heading. For example, heading-level three is <h3> and </h3>. *The lower the value of the level, the larger the heading is rendered.*

Note – The text in heading-levels five and six is actually smaller than standard text in the document on many GUI browsers. Some HTML authors tend to take advantage of this font size difference by designating footer information as heading-level six. Especially with the addition in HTML 3.2 of the <font> tag, as discussed later in this chapter, this "creative" use of heading sizes in an attempt to control the size of what is actually body text should be avoided.

By convention, heading-level one is usually a repeat of the title line (with the addition of <h1> and </h1> codes) so that a document actually has a title visible in the document. This is important if you are writing documents that may be printed at a future date, since unlike the heading, the document title may or may not be displayed on the printed page (depending on the browser and, possibly, user preferences).

Figure 2-6 shows a good example of what each heading looks like in a browser display.

This is what Heading 1 Looks Like

This is text in between.

This is what Heading 2 Looks Like

This is text in between.

This is what Heading 3 Looks Like

This is text in between.

This is what Heading 4 Looks Like

This is text in between.

This is what Heading 5 Looks Like

This is text in between.

This is what Heading 6 Looks Like

This is text in between.

Figure 2-6   Samples of Headings

1. **Load** `Chapter2/heading_examples.html`.
    See what the different headings look like on your own browser's display.

Adding Comments

There may be times when you need to insert a comment in order to document your code or to incorporate information that you don't want the end user to see. There is no specific HTML comment tag, but the SGML comment tag can be used. A comment line looks like:

```
<!-- text here -->
```

Note that this simply prevents the code from being displayed in the browser's main window—it does *not* hide the comment when displayed in the browser's "View Page Source" (or equivalent) window.

Also note that the comment (as with other HTML tags) can span more than one line, with the closing --> not appearing until many lines after the opening <!--. However, prudent coding practice would be to "comment out" each line separately in order to avoid "losing" either the opening comment code and/or the closing should you at some point decide to remove the comment.

(An exception to this general rule is the use of SGML comments to hide in-line scripts from browsers that don't support the particular scripting language, such as JavaScript. See Chapter 11 for more information about such scripting languages.)

Adding the Author/Responsible Party

It is a good practice to list a contact who maintains the page. In some cases, this may be the author of the document itself (as opposed to the HTML code used to display it). However, many companies are now setting up websites on the Internet. Since a large corporate server usually contains work from several people, and still other people may provide administration services, the term *webmaster* has come into use. The webmaster is the person or group of people ultimately responsible for keeping the web site operational; under common usage, the terms "webmaster" and "HTML author" refer to the same person, who is responsible for integrating new work and referring content-related problems and questions back to the original author of the page's contents.

Regardless of whether you maintain the pages yourself or whether a corporate entity does that work, every page should have an address to contact for both questions and problems. The author or contact for the page is identified with the <address> and </address> tags.

New in HTML 3.2: The `<DIV>` Container

The new `<DIV>` tag may be used to structure your document into a hierarchy of divisions or subsections. In later versions of the HTML specification, this new tag is expected to acquire special significance in regard to formatting different sections in different ways; however, under version 3.2 it has only a single attribute, `align=`. As with the same attribute of the `<p>` tag, values of this attribute may be `left` (the default), `right`, or `center` for left-justified, right-justified, and centered divisions, respectively.

All text and other elements within the surrounding `<DIV>` and `</DIV>` container acquire the specified justification (except for embedded `<p>` or `<div>` elements which specify that their contents are to be aligned otherwise).

Note that HTML 3.2 also officially includes the widely used `<center></center>` container, which functions identically to `<div align=center>`. This has been done in order not to "break" browsers which support the `<center>` tag. Where possible, you should avoid further use of `<center>` as it may be made obsolete in later versions of the HTML specification.

Adding Document Tags to the Example

Now that you have seen the basic tags for all documents, use a text editor to put the tags into example1.html.

2. **Add the start and end tags that define this document to be type HTML.**

3. **Label the head and body of the document with the appropriate tags.**

4. **Label the title of the document.**
   The line that reads *The Physiological Basis for Intuition* was meant to be the title of the document. Label it as such.

5. **Make a level-one heading that matches the title.**

6. **Identify the author's address in the document. Reload the document.**

7. **Compare your results to** `Chapter2/example1d.html`.
   What you see in your browser should look like Figure 2-7.

8. **Optional: Experiment with the new HTML 3.2 document tags and attributes.**
   As a reminder, these might include:

   • Adding a `<!DOCTYPE>` directive to identify this as a fully compliant HTML 3.2 document.

   • Adding an `<ISINDEX>` tag to appear on the page with a customized prompt string.

- Adding one or more of the following attributes to the `<BODY>` tag to change the colors of the page: `background=`, `bgcolor=`, `alink=`, `link=`, `vlink=`, and/or `text=`

- Setting a section of the document in an alignment other than left-justified, using the `<div></div>` container. Do not use the `<center></center>` container if you opt for centered text!

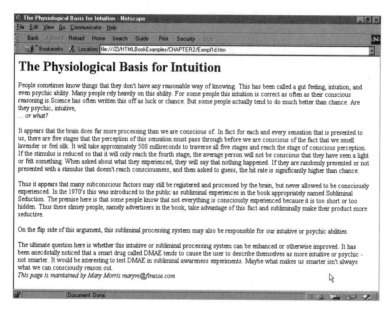

Figure 2-7   A Finished Product

Paragraph Formatting

Whitespace in HTML documents, such as carriage returns, tabs, and one or multiple spaces is ignored by browsers. Special types of tags create and control whitespace. These tags include paragraph and line breaks, headings (discussed above—a line break occurs after the closing `</h#>` tag), horizontal rules, list elements, address elements, and blockquotes.

HTML allows different browsers to display the information to the best of their ability. A browser that is sized to display only 30 columns of text will not display text with the same layout as a browser sized to display 60 columns. Consider the following two lines of text in Example 2-4. When the lines are entered in a text editor, or otherwise displayed in a fixed (monospace) font such as Courier, they appear to be about the same length.

Example 2-4   Monospace Font Display

```
mmmmmmmmmmmmmmmmmmmmmmmmmmmmmmmmmmmmmmmmmmmmmmmmmmm
iiiiiiiiiiiiiiiiiiiiiiiiiiiiiiiiiiiiiiiiiiiiiiiiii
```

However, when these lines are displayed using a kerned or proportional font, as most GUI displays do by default, the second line is only half the length of the first because the proportional space taken up by a lowercase "i" is significantly less than that taken up by a lowercase "m" (see Example 2-5).

Example 2-5   Kerned Font Display

```
mmmmmmmmmmmmmmmmmmmmmmmmmmmmmmmmmmmmmmmmmmmmmmmmmmm
iiiiiiiiiiiiiiiiiiiiiiiiiiiiiiiiiiiiiiiiiiiiiiiiii
```

This example illustrates that text can't be consistently formatted for both GUI and text-based displays if the formatting is controlled in the text. Therefore, HTML leaves the determination of where lines should wrap to the browser. That is, the text must have tags to indicate where carriage returns and other mandatory whitespace formatting should be used. These tags are as follows:

- **Paragraph** – <p> — This tag was introduced in the initial example in this chapter. The paragraph starts a new line and places a blank line between the text before the tag and the text after the tag. Under HTML 3.2, you can optionally specify the alignment of the paragraph's text.

- **Break** –
 — This tag was also introduced above. Like the paragraph, this tag starts a new line, but it does not place a blank line between the two sections of text. Under HTML 3.2, you can optionally specify that the new line is to begin on the line below an adjacent floating element, such as an image.

- **Horizontal Rule** – <hr> — This tag starts a new line and places a horizontal graphic line between the sections of text instead of a blank line.

  New in HTML 3.2: In HTML 2.0, it was not possible to specify the format of the horizontal rule; it was always rendered as a single line, of a single thickness, which ran from the left to right margins of the browser window. Starting in HTML 3.2, however, the <hr> tag comes with four optional attributes:

  - **align=** specifies that the rule is to be either flush with the left margin (the default), flush with the right, or centered (values left, right, and center, respectively). Note that this attribute will have visible effect only if the width= attribute (see below) specifies that the rule is to be shorter than the width of the window.

- **noshade**: If this attribute (which has no value, hence no = sign) is not specified, the rule is rendered as under HTML 2.0—that is, as a quasi-3D line which appears either embossed or incised (depending on the browser) on the display. Under HTML 3.2, if you specify the noshade attribute, the rule appears as a flat rectangle (i.e., with no shading).

- **size=** specifies the thickness of the rule, in pixels.

- **width=** specifies the length of the rule. Its value can be expressed either *absolutely*, in terms of pixels (e.g., `width=175`), or *relatively*, as a percent of the distance between the left and right margins (e.g., `width="75%"`—note the double quotes surrounding a value with the special "%" character).

- **Preformatted Text** – `<pre>` and `</pre>`— This set of tags defines a section of text that must be presented as it is typed in. The text is rendered in a fixed font. Prior to the introduction of HTML 3.2, such definition was the only way to make tabs and other whitespace characters appear within a line. (HTML 3.2 supports tables, which provide a simple means of accomplishing the same goal—especially when you do not want the preformatted text to appear in a fixed font. See Chapter 5 for information about creating tables with HTML.)

- **Blocktext** – `<blockquote>` and `</blockquote>` — This set of tags indents the text as if it were a quotation. This is a logical formatting method. Alternative methods for indenting text are discussed in the Lists section of this chapter. These methods were not designed for indent formatting and offend many HTML purists. In the absence of alternatives to date, they are, however, widely used.

Refer to Figure 2-8 to see how each of the formatting codes looks in the Netscape browser.

1. **Load** `Chapter2/paragraph_format_examples.html` **to see how the different formats look on your display.**

2. **View the HTML text by pulling down the View menu and selecting Page Source (or other menu choice as appropriate for your browser).**
   Note that only the preformatted text retains the whitespacing of the original material.

This is text that is terminated by a paragraph. What does that mean? The text will wrap on it own. Whitespace is not maintained. Notice how much space is between this text and the next line.

This is text that is teriminated by a line break. What does that mean? The text will wrap on it own. Whitespace is not maintained. Notice how much space is between this text and the next line.
This is text that is teriminated by a horizontal rule. What does that mean? The text will wrap on it own. Whitespace is not maintained. Notice how much space is between this text and the next line.

This is text that is in block quote. What does that mean? will the text wrap on its own? Will the text be in a specific format? Are tab and other whitespace characters conserved?

```
This is text that is in pre. What does that mean?
will the text wrap on its own? Will the text be in a specific format?
     Are tab and other whitespace characters conserved?
```

Figure 2-8   Samples of Various Paragraph Formats

Character Formatting

If you haven't read Page Formatting Philosophy in the Introduction, please do so now. As we have stated there and since, it is important to remember that HTML is not designed to be a WYSIWYG document system. HTML was designed for logical formatting. For example, if you define a section of text with the <code> tag, the browser will use some type of formatting to set off the text from other types of formatting. It *will probably* make the code monospace type, but if the browser display is already monospace type, that won't serve to distinguish the code text from surrounding regular text; in this case the text marked as code may appear as bold instead. With *physical* formatting, the browser renders the text exactly as you specify, if it can. With *logical* formatting, the browser renders the text based on the modifications that it can make for the environment that it is in.

There are significantly more tags for logical formatting of text than for physical formatting. Physical formatting tags have been provided to accommodate people who want to physically force bold or italics on a document; as GUI-based browsers continue to increase market share over non-GUI, it's likely that the physical formatting tags will come to predominate.

Note – HTML provides methods for both physical and logical formatting. In physical formatting, text is specified as being in *italics*. Logical formatting would declare the text to have *emphasis*. On most GUI-based browsers (as, indeed, in the printed version of the preceding two sentences), this means the same thing. However, a text-based browser doesn't have the display capabilities that would enable it to render italicized text, so it is good practice to use logical formatting instead of physical formatting. Then, a wider range of client browsers can see the special formatting. See Figure 2-9 for an example of how a text-based browser renders (or fails to render) the different kinds of character formatting; this particular screen shot shows the example page below as displayed in the DOSLynx browser for MS-DOS systems.

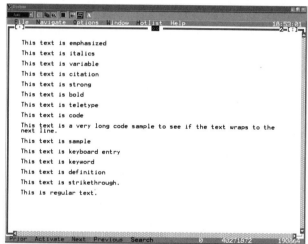

Figure 2-9   Sample of Non-GUI Browser Display

Font Sizes under HTML

If you've made any use at all of word processors—even typewriters with interchangeable font wheels—you know about varying text size, usually expressed in *points*. (A point is a common unit of measurement borrowed from traditional typesetting; one point equals 1/72 of an inch. A line of type in 72-point size measures one inch from the top of the tallest letter to the bottom of the lowest "descender," such as a lowercase g.)

One difference between text on the Web as opposed to text produced in a word processor—a difference that comes as a genuine shock to many HTML newcomers—is that there is currently no "official" way to specify, for example, that you want text on your page to be rendered in 18-point type. (Most GUI browsers, on the other hand, *can* specify a particular font size as the default. That's because the browser "knows about" the display characteristics of the user's environment. A web page can't yet—again, at least officially—assume any particular display characteristics.)

Instead, font sizes are specified either as absolute numbers from 1 to 7 (with 3 as the default), or as plus or minus sizes relative to the current size (like +1, -2, and so on). The exact size in points of a size-3 font, as rendered on the user's display, will vary depending on the font characteristics set in the browser's preferences. As a rule of thumb, each font size specified in the HTML code will be about 20 percent larger than the size just below it.

Font Changes

The initial example in this chapter showed how to put text in italics by surrounding the text with the start and stop tags `<i>` and `</i>`. All character formatting is done in the same way, only the tags are different. Table 2-2 outlines the different types of character formatting available.

1. **Load** `Chapter2/char_ex.html` **in your browser.**
   Compare your results with Figure 2-10, which is a sample of how each of these formatting tags looks on the Netscape Navigator browser, and with Figure 2-9 (discussed in the Note above).

This text is emphasized

This text is italics

This text is variable

This text is citation

This text is strong

This text is bold

`This text is teletype`

`This text is code`

`This text is a very long code sample to see if the text wraps to the next line.`

`This text is sample`

`This text is keyboard entry`

This text is keyword

This text is definition

~~This text is strikethrough.~~

This is regular text.

Figure 2-10   Samples of Character Formats

Note – When characters are formatted using any of these character formatting tags, they will still wrap when they reach the end of a line. Only paragraph formatting with <pre> can keep text on the same line if the line is too long.

Table 2-2   HTML Character Tags

Name	Start Tag	Stop Tag	Logical or Physical
citation	<cite>	</cite>	Logical
code	<code>	</code>	Logical
definition*	<dfn>	</dfn>	Logical
emphasized	<em>	</em>	Logical
keyboard entry	<kbd>	</kbd>	Logical
keyword	<key>	</key>	Logical
sample	<samp>	</samp>	Logical
strong	<strong>	</strong>	Logical
variable	<var>	</var>	Logical
bold	<b>	</b>	Physical
italics	<i>	</i>	Physical
strike-through*	<strike>	</strike>	Physical
teletype	<tt>	</tt>	Physical

* Although they appeared in this table in the previous edition of this book, these two tags were actually officially ratified only with HTML 3.2. See below for descriptions.

New in HTML 3.2: The character formatting tags listed in Table 2-2 were the only ones available under HTML 2.0. With the new HTML specification, the following tags and attributes have been added:

- **<big>** increases the current font size by one; the nesting of <big> tags has a cumulative effect (i.e., successively nested tags force the text to grow increasingly larger, a step at a time). Browsers have an upper limit to the font size they'll display; beyond this limit additional <big> tags have no effect.

- **\<small\>** decreases the current font size by one; the nesting of \<small\> tags has a cumulative effect (i.e., successively nested tags force the text to grow increasingly smaller, a step at a time). Browsers have a lower limit to the font size they'll display; beyond this limit additional \<small\> tags have no effect.

- **\<strike\>** displays the text enclosed with a horizontal line through it (known as "strike-through" text in most word processors). The HTML 3.2 specification notes that this tag may in the future be replaced by the \<s\> tag which was defined in the interim HTML 3.0 version and which is indeed supported by many browsers.

- **\<sub\>** and **\<super\>** render the enclosed text as, respectively, subscripts and superscripts relative to the surrounding text. Both of these tags can be nested to produce multiple levels of subscripting and superscripting.

- **\<u\>** displays the enclosed text with an underline. Especially in cases where text color has been specified using the text= attribute of the \<body\> tag or the color= attribute of the \<font\> tag (see below), you should be careful with the use of underlined text, as it may suggest to the user that the underlined text is a hyperlink. Clicking on an underlined but nonhyperlinked phrase, of course, will do nothing at all.

- **\<dfn\>** marks the enclosed text as the "defining instance" of a word or phrase. This is usually rendered in italics or some other distinctive style.

- **Font size and color tags** are used for setting or overriding the indicated characteristics of the default font. Note that some more recent browser versions support attributes beyond those listed here, especially for specifying particular typefaces (e.g., Times New Roman, Garamond, Courier New); however, these extensions are not supported under HTML 3.2. The approved tags and their attributes are:

  - **\<basefont\>** defines the font size to be used from this point forward, until encountering another \<basefont\> tag (or being overridden by an embedded HTML tag which alters the size temporarily). This tag has just one attribute, size=, specifying the font size from 1 to 7.

  - **\<font\>** defines an overriding size and/or color for the enclosed text, using the size= and color= attributes, respectively. The size can be either absolute (an integer from 1 through 7) or relative to the current value (e.g., +2, -4). The color specification is as described earlier in this chapter (see especially Table 2-1).

Except for \<basefont\>, all the new HTML 3.2 font formats require both a start tag (e.g., \<sub\>, \<font\>) and a stop tag (\</sub\>, \</font\>).

2

8-bit Characters

Everything covered so far deals with English (i.e., Roman-alphabet) and the 7-bit per character ASCII that is used to make each letter. Because 7-bit ASCII is insufficient for many languages, an alternative is available to display most of the standard Latin-1 characters.

The ampersand (&) character indicates that the characters following it are evaluated as a single entity. The semicolon (;) prevents concatenation of several characters into a single character. For example, Á is written as Á and Ü is written as Ü. A space can also be used to terminate such a string, but the space will be displayed. Therefore, a semicolon must be used if the special character appears within a word.

There is a second method of indicating these characters. The ampersand character starts the string, followed directly by the pound, or number, character (#), and the numerical ASCII value of the character. This method doesn't use the semicolon; instead, the numerical value will always be a value between 128 and 256.

2. **Load** `Chapter2/eightbit.html`.
    This example shows the word Ádios twice.

3. **View the HTML text by pulling down the View menu and selecting Page Source.**
    This example shows the two different methods of displaying 8-bit characters. On the Netscape browser, it looks like the display at the left side of Figure 2-11.

Figure 2-11   Sample of 8-bit Characters

A complete list of characters, their 8-bit ASCII values, and string values can be found in 8-bit ASCII Characters in Appendix A.

This method doesn't meet the needs of users of the Cyrillic, Greek, Hebrew, Chinese, Japanese, Korean, and other alphabets. To display these alphabets, you will need to obtain a special browser capable of handling their non-Roman character forms. Details about these browsers are beyond the scope of book.

Other Special Characters

Since the characters <, >, and & have special meaning in HTML and hence to Web browsers, they are considered to be metacharacters and cannot be displayed directly in the browser window itself. They also cannot be escaped, which in UNIX parlance means that you cannot use a metacharacter to indicate that some other metacharacter should be treated as a regular character instead of its special designation. HTML metacharacters are composed by using the &*string* method discussed above.

Some browsers also implement the 8-bit numerical ASCII rendering of these characters. Mosaic does not do so; however, as mentioned in the Introduction, development of Mosaic has been halted. Furthermore, according to the seventh annual usage survey by Georgia Tech,[1] Mosaic does not even show up as a commonly used browser (except in the form of the little-used version licensed from NCSA by SpyGlass).

One other special character, the nonbreaking space, can also be composed in this manner. The nonbreaking space tells the browser, "Even if this is the end of a line as displayed in the current window size, *do not* wrap the line at this point."

Table 2-3 summarizes special characters.

Table 2-3   Metacharacters

Character	8-bit ASCII	String Name
<	&#060;	&lt;
>	&#062;	&gt;
&	&#038;	&amp;
nonbreaking space	&#032;	

---

1. Results of this survey are tabulated at: http://www.gvu.gatech.edu/user-surveys/survey-1997-04/graphs/use/Browser_You_Expect_to_Use_in_12_Months.html.

4. **Load** `Chapter2/special.html`.
   This page demonstrates what is implemented on your browser and what is not implemented.

5. **View the HTML text by pulling down the View menu and selecting Page Source.**
   This example shows the different methods of displaying special characters.

Lists

People tend to organize things into lists. These may be numbered lists or bulleted lists or even lists of lists. The formatting covered so far is not enough to make lists. Luckily, HTML does provide a special set of formatting tags devoted to making them. Various steps outlined in this section illustrate the use of HTML tags in formatting lists.

Regular Lists

All formatting discussed so far has been via either a single tag, or start and end tags placed around the text to be operated on. Lists have a slightly more complex form. The list itself is defined with start and stop tags. Then each list item within the list's start and stop tags is defined separately. There is no stop tag for each list item; it ends either when the next list item begins, or when the list itself stops. The basic format is shown in HTML Example 2-6.

HTML Example 2-6   List Formatting

`<ul>`	Start by defining the type of list that you want to use.
`<li> first item text`	Indicate that the following text is a list item.
`<li> second item text`	Indicate that the following text is another list item.
`</ul>`	Close the list.

The four types of lists are unordered (also called unnumbered) `<ul>`; ordered `<ol>` (i.e., numbered); menu `<menu>`; and directory `<dir>`. Menu and directory lists have the same appearance as unnumbered lists and can be used interchangeably on most browsers.

1. **Load** `Chapter2/list1.html`.
   This page shows the various types of lists and demonstrates the bullet styles associated with each list type. On Netscape Navigator, this format looks like the display on the left side of Figure 2-12.

- This is the first list item for an unnumbered list.
- This is the second list item for an unnumbered list.
- This is the third list item for an unnumbered list.
- This is the fourth list item for an unnumbered list.

1. This is the first list item for an ordered list.
2. This is the second list item for an ordered list.
3. This is the third list item for an ordered list.
4. This is the fourth list item for an ordered list.

- This is the first list item for an menu list.
- This is the second list item for an menu list.
- This is the third list item for an menu list.
- This is the fourth list item for an menu list.

- This is the first list item for an dir list.
- This is the second list item for an dir list.
- This is the third list item for an dir list.
- This is the fourth list item for an dir list.

- This is the first list item for an unnumbered list.
  - This is the first list item for an dir list nested in a unnumbered list.
  - This is the second list item for an dir list nested in a unnumbered list.
  - This is the third list item for an dir list nested in a unnumbered list.
  - This is the fourth list item for an dir list nested in a unnumbered list.
- This is the second list item for an unnumbered list.
  - This is the first list item for an unnumbered list nested in a unnumbered list.
  - This is the second list item for an unnumbered list nested in a unnumbered list.
  - This is the third list item for an unnumbered list nested in a unnumbered list.
  - This is the fourth list item for an unnumbered list nested in a unnumbered list.
- This is the third list item for an unnumbered list.
  1. This is the first list item for an ordered list nested in a unnumbered list.
  2. This is the second list item for an ordered list nested in a unnumbered list.
  3. This is the third list item for an ordered list nested in a unnumbered list.
  4. This is the fourth list item for an ordered list nested in a unnumbered list.
- This is the fourth list item for an unnumbered list.
  - This is the first list item for an menu list nested in a unnumbered list.
  - This is the second list item for an menu list nested in a unnumbered list.
  - This is the third list item for an menu list nested in a unnumbered list.
  - This is the fourth list item for an menu list nested in a unnumbered list.

1. This is the first list item for an ordered list.
  - This is the first list item for an dir list nested in a ordered list.
  - This is the second list item for an dir list nested in a ordered list.
  - This is the third list item for an dir list nested in a ordered list.
  - This is the fourth list item for an dir list nested in a ordered list.
2. This is the second list item for an ordered list.
  - This is the first list item for an unnumbered list nested in a ordered list.
  - This is the second list item for an unnumbered list nested in a ordered list.
  - This is the third list item for an unnumbered list nested in a ordered list.

Figure 2-12   List Samples

2. **Load** `Chapter2/list2.html`.

   The list items are nested within one another in this example. Note that when unnumbered, menu, and directory lists are nested, a different bullet character is used for each level. Ordered lists merely start over from 1 every time (unless you override this default numbering using the new HTML 3.2 attributes—see below). On Netscape, this format looks like the display on the right side of Figure 2-12.

3. **Load** `Chapter2/list3.html`.

   Different characters are used as the bullet symbol for the first three nested layers. Starting with the fourth layer, the bullets keep the same shape. On Netscape, this format looks like the display on the left side of Figure 2-13.

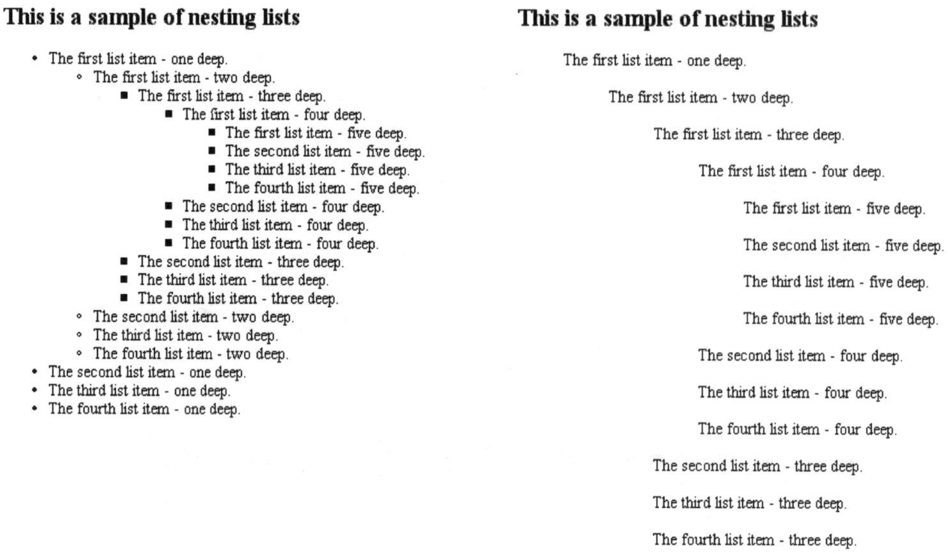

≡ 2

This is a sample of nesting lists

- The first list item - one deep.
  - The first list item - two deep.
    - The first list item - three deep.
      - The first list item - four deep.
        - The first list item - five deep.
        - The second list item - five deep.
        - The third list item - five deep.
        - The fourth list item - five deep.
      - The second list item - four deep.
      - The third list item - four deep.
      - The fourth list item - four deep.
    - The second list item - three deep.
    - The third list item - three deep.
    - The fourth list item - three deep.
  - The second list item - two deep.
  - The third list item - two deep.
  - The fourth list item - two deep.
- The second list item - one deep.
- The third list item - one deep.
- The fourth list item - one deep.

This is a sample of nesting lists

The first list item - one deep.

The first list item - two deep.

The first list item - three deep.

The first list item - four deep.

The first list item - five deep.

The second list item - five deep.

The third list item - five deep.

The fourth list item - five deep.

The second list item - four deep.

The third list item - four deep.

The fourth list item - four deep.

The second list item - three deep.

The third list item - three deep.

The fourth list item - three deep.

Figure 2-13   Nested Lists

4. **Load** `Chapter2/list4.html`.
   Using list start and end tags without using the list item tags provides indenting without having a defined bullet character. This technique allows nesting of indents. On Netscape, this format looks like the display on the right side of Figure 2-13

5. **View the HTML text by pulling down the View menu and selecting Page Source.**
   Notice that the tag `<li>` doesn't appear anywhere.

New in HTML 3.2: The new HTML specification defines a number of new attributes for controlling the formatting or appearance of items in both unordered and ordered list tags:

- Within unordered lists, the `<li>` tag has a single new attribute, `type=`. This attribute defines the type of bullet to display alongside the list item's text. Allowable values for this attribute are `disc` (a small filled circle), `circle` (a small hollow circle), and `square`. Note that if you so chose, you could assign a different bullet type to each item in a list (although this wouldn't be logical). Also note that not all browsers will handle bullets in succeeding nested lists intelligently, so you may have to change their bullet types as well if you want different nested levels bulleted differently.

2 ≣

- Within ordered lists, there are new attributes for both the `<ol>` and the `<li>` tags. You can control the type and starting number of items in ordered lists. The new `type=` attribute can take the values 1 (the numeral "1"), for the usual Arabic numerals; a, for lowercase letters; A, for uppercase letters; i, for lowercase Roman numerals; and I, for uppercase Roman numerals. You can use the `type=` attribute in both the `<ol>` and the `<li>` tags; if you use it in both, the entry in the `<li>` tag overrides the numbering style for that list item and for subsequent items in the same list. (Again, this seems to be of limited usefulness.)

  - The new `start=` attribute is followed by an integer and designates the starting number for the items in the list. This attribute applies to the `<ol>` tag only. You use an integer regardless of the ordered list type (Arabic numbers, letters, or Roman numerals), so, for example, to start an ordered list of items with the letter "j" (the tenth letter), you'd use the code `<ol type=a start=10>`.

  - The new `value=` attribute is used to assign a particular number to a given list item (that is, it applies to the `<li>` tag only). This causes subsequent list items to be numbered from the new value on and therefore overrides whatever was entered (or defaulted) as the `start=` attribute of the parent `<ol>` tag. As with the `start=` attribute, the value you can assign here must be an integer.

Description Lists

HTML also has a special kind of list called a *description list*. This list is usually used for a glossary or list of items and associated descriptions. It follows the same formatting conventions as the other list types, in this case with start `<DL>` and end `</DL>` tags. However, it has two different list items inside the list: a data term `<DT>` and a data description `<DD>`.

A sample of a description list is shown in HTML Example 2-7.

HTML Example 2-7   Description List Sample

`<DL>`	Start by defining the type of list that you want to use.
`<DT> Book`	Indicate that the following text is a data term.
`<DD> Tree-killer copy of on-line documentation`	Indicate that the following text is a data description.
`</DL>`	Close the list.

6. **Load** `Chapter2/dlist1.html`.

A description list indents the data description, while leaving the data term at the left margin, as seen in Figure 2-14.

This is a data term
    This is a data description.
Book - This is a data term
    Tree-killer copy of a document. - This is a data description.

Figure 2-14   Sample Description List

7. **Load** `Chapter2/dlist2.html`.

By use of multiple description-list start tags, data terms can be indented and data descriptions can be indented even farther. Description-list components can be used to provide additional indenting capabilities above and beyond the `<blockquote>` and `<pre>` paragraph formatting methods noted previously.

8. **Load** `Chapter2/dlist3.html`.

A new paragraph can be started and indented as long as the last tag was a `<DD>`, as seen in Figure 2-15.

This is a data term
    This is a data description.

    I would like to continue the data description with a new paragraph that is still indented.

Figure 2-15   Variation in a Description List

For the curious, it may be of interest that the "bookmarks" file automatically maintained by the Netscape Navigator browser is an extended description list. (Note: By all means, examine the structure of your bookmarks file with a text editor. Under no circumstances should you *change* the file's contents, however, as this can result in serious damage to it when you again run Netscape.)

Summary

In this chapter you learned:

- What tags are and how to use them.
- How to add the tags that provide the underlying structure to an HTML document.
- Tags for formatting paragraphs of text.
- Tags for formatting individual characters.
- How to create 8-bit and special characters.
- How to make lists.
- When the document is not defined as HTML with the appropriate tag, the default font is a fixed-width font.

You have just learned the basics for creating an individual document, including tags and attributes defined by the new HTML 3.2 specification. In the next chapter you learn how to tie individual documents together to make hypertext.

Looking Forward

The next version of the HTML specification, HTML 4.0, will probably enhance a number of the tags discussed in this chapter.

Particularly, it is likely that with the continued market dominance of GUI-based browsers, tags will be added and enhanced (with new or changed attributes) in ways that enhance the physical appearance of the page, as opposed to its logical or structural appearance. These changes will primarily affect the `<basefont>`, `<font>`, and related tags at the character-formatting level, and the `<div>` tag at the document-formatting level.

2

Tags Used in This Chapter

Name and Description	Start Tag	Stop Tag
Document Formatting		
HTML document type directive	`<!doctype>`	
HTML document indicator	`<html>`	`</html>`
Document head	`<head>`	`</head>`
Document body*	`<body>`	`</body>`
Document section/division*	`<div>`	`</div>`
Owner/contact	`<address>`	`</address>`
Headings*	`<h1>...<h6>`	`</h1>...</h6>`
Title	`<title>`	`</title>`
Comment	`<!-- -->`	
Character Formatting		
emphasized	`<em>`	`</em>`
variable	`<var>`	`</var>`
citation	`<cite>`	`</cite>`
italics	`<i>`	`</i>`
strong	`<strong>`	`</strong>`
bold	`<b>`	`</b>`
code	`<code>`	`</code>`
sample	`<samp>`	`</samp>`
keyboard entry	`<kbd>`	`</kbd>`
teletype	`<tt>`	`</tt>`
keyword	`<key>`	`</key>`
dfn*	`<dfn>`	`</dfn>`
strike-through*	`<strike>`	`</strike>`
document base font*	`<basefont>`	
font size/color*	`<font>`	`</font>`
enlarge font*	`<big>`	`</big>`

reduce font*	`<small>`	`</small>`
subscript*	`<sub>`	`</sub>`
superscript*	`<super>`	`</super>`
underline*	`<u>`	`</u>`

Paragraph Formatting

blockquote	`<blockquote>`	`</blockquote>`
paragraph*	`<p>`	
line break*	` `	
horizontal rule (horizontal line)*	`<hr>`	
preformatted text	`<pre>`	`</pre>`

List Formatting

list item*	`<li>`	
unnumbered list*	`<ul>`	`</ul>`
ordered list*	`<ol>`	`</ol>`
menu list	`<menu>`	`</menu>`
dir list	`<dir>`	`</dir>`
description list	`<dl>`	`</dl>`
data term	`<dt>`	
data description	`<dd>`	

*Items flagged with an asterisk are new/changed under HTML 3.2.

2

HTML for Fun and Profit

Hypertext — Linking Documents 3

The documents created in the previous chapter stand by themselves. The Web, however, is a *hypertext* document system, linking pertinent data from different documents. If you want to know more about what is being said before continuing to the next topic in a document, you can select a link shown in highlighted text and read about it.

This chapter describes how to create such links, both between documents and within documents.

Note – Most of what you need to know in order to construct hyperlinked documents is general in nature and "correct" regardless of specific environmental issues like your operating system and server type. In some cases, though, you may need to work closely with your server administrator in order to configure your site correctly. (Of course, you may need to configure it yourself if you have site-administration responsibility.) These cases are *server-specific* — what works under a Windows 95/NT server may not work under a UNIX server, or vice versa, or the steps to make it work will vary from platform to platform. In this chapter we will focus on general principles and techniques, noting server-specific information when it is necessary for illustration of some key point. Full server configuration details are beyond the scope of this book; if in doubt, check with your server's vendor for technical details.

Elements of Hypertext

It would be nice to be able to tie together related information—for example, a document that discusses apple growing and a second document that shows what fruits grow best across the state of Colorado. Hypertext is the medium that made this joining of information, called a *link*, common. In HTML this link is made by placing an *anchor* tag around the referenced text; the anchor refers the user's browser to the other document.

Since the WWW works across multiple platforms, the naming convention for doing so needed to be universally recognized. The *Universal Resource Locator*, or *URL*, naming scheme was proposed to create a standard naming convention for documents on the Web. URLs are the method by which links are named in the WWW.

Universal Resource Locator (URL)

URL components are shown in Figure 3-1 and described below. The terms "required" and "optional" in this list refer to *absolute* URLs. *Relative* URLs, on the other hand, allow you to omit many of the so-called "required" components. Relative URLs are discussed later in this chapter.

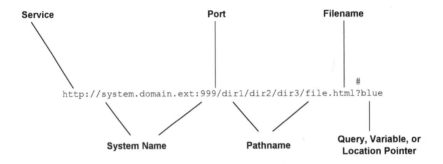

Figure 3-1   URL Components

- **Service type** — *A required part of a URL.* (Current versions of both the Netscape Navigator and Internet Explorer browsers have made this optional *when entered via the browser.* This doesn't get the HTML author off the hook though—you still need to include it in a hypertext anchor tag.) The service tells the client browser how to contact the server for the requested data. For most of the examples here, *HyperText Transfer Protocol* or http is used. The WWW can handle several other services—including gopher, wais, ftp, news, and telnet—and can be extended to handle new ones.

- **System name** — *A required part of a URL.* The system is the fully qualified domain name of the server of the data being requested. Partially qualified domain names should be used only for documents that won't leave your domain. It is always good practice to use fully qualified domain names.

- **Port** — *An optional part of a URL.* Ports are the network socket addresses for specific protocols. By default, http connects at port 80. In some cases, the default port is not used by the server. This may be for several different reasons: The server may be a proxy server; or a nonstandard port is used to discourage robots and crackers from polling the system; or some other service is already using that port. This number comes after the : and before the first / of the directory name. If the port is omitted, so is the colon that precedes it. You need to provide this part of a URL only when the server doesn't communicate on the default port for that service.

- **Directory path** — *A required part of a URL.* Once connected to the system in question, a path to the file must be specified. It is important to note here that the directory path listed in the URL may not exactly match the path to the file on the system itself. There are several ways to shorten the pathnames, including aliasing. Each level of the directory tree is delimited by a /. The directory is also separated from the filename with a /.

- **Filename** — *An optional part of a URL.* The filename is the data file itself. The server can be configured so that if a filename isn't specified, a default file or directory listing will be returned. Normally the default file for any path is `index.html` or `index.htm`; if neither of those files is found, a listing of the specified directory's contents is displayed instead.

- **Search components, variables, or location pointer**— *An optional part of a URL.* If the URL is a request to search a database, the query can be embedded in the URL. This is the text after the ? in a URL. In the case of forms, the URL can return the information collected from a form in this area. If a # appears, the text which follows it is the name of a particular *location* within the file identified by the other URL components.

Note – A special type of URL, used in `mailto` links, does not follow this general format. Using mailto is covered later in this chapter.

Adding Links

Links between documents and points within documents are created by placing anchors in the text. These anchors are of two types: reference anchors and named anchors. The reference anchor points to the destination of that hypertext link. The named anchor defines a name or place marker for a specific place in a document.

Many—probably most—hypertext references are links to the start of other pages, not to specific points on the same (or another) page. In this case, the named anchor isn't required. Named anchors are used primarily when the hypertext link points to a specific portion of a document instead of pointing to the document as a whole.

Reference Anchors

The concepts of start and end tags were discussed in the previous chapter, as was the notion of a tag attribute.

The anchor tag `<a>` has the `href=` or *hypertext reference* attribute added to it. An example of an appropriate anchor tag is:

```
<a href="http://system/dir/file.html/">Some Text</a>
```

The value of the `href=` attribute is the location (that is, the URL) of the document that will be displayed when the user clicks on the phrase `Some Text`. The phrase enclosed within the start and stop tags (including spaces) will appear highlighted in some way in the browser window—typically in blue underscored text until the link has been visited and then in purple underscored text. (This default highlighting in a GUI browser can be overridden by user preference and/or by use of the `link=`, `alink=`, and `vlink=` attributes of the `<body>` tag, as described in the previous chapter.)

1. **Load** `Chapter3/apples.html`.
   This document contains a link in the section Growing Apples. In the browser, the anchored text is displayed in a different color with a line underneath it.

2. **Pull down the View menu and select Page Source.**
   Another window is opened in which the HTML source for that document is displayed. There is an anchor tag around the text `Growing Apples in Colorado`.

3. **Return to the main browser window. Click on the** `Growing Apples in Colorado` **link.**
   The name on the document URL name line of the browser now indicates that the file `colorado-fruits.html` is being displayed.

4. **Click on the Back button at the bottom of the browser to return to the** `Apples` **document.**
   Notice that the anchored text has changed colors, indicating that this link has already been traversed.

Named Anchors

An anchor doesn't have to be a pointer to other data. It can be a place mark for other data to point to. For example, the `Growing Apples` document points to `Fruit Growing Areas of Colorado`. But it isn't fair to make someone who wants to know about apples scroll through the entire document, including all the information about peaches and pears, so an anchor can be created that marks the start of the apple-growing information. This anchor is named by using the name= attribute with the `<a>` tag. An example is:

```
<a NAME="apple">Apple Growing Areas</a>
```

Notice that this anchor, unlike the one above, has no `href=` attribute. This anchor isn't pointing to anything else; it is being pointed to.

To reference this specific point within the document, the reference anchor uses a # sign to indicate the named pointer within the document. For example, the reference anchor looks like:

```
<a href="colorado-fruits.html#apple">are grown in Co.</a>
```

In the case of a long document, pointers should be made to other sections of the same document to save scrolling through large bodies of data.

Note – In this example, note that the URL includes the filename and the location pointer but omits the service, system name, and path. This is known as a *relative URL*—the location of the named document is specified *relative to* the location of the linking document. This procedure is discussed in detail in the section Using Addressing Relative to Files below.

A relative reference anchor looks like

```
<a href="#apples">apples</a>
```

In this case, since the document name is the same, the only part of the `href=` that changes is the pointer to the name. The # is prepended to indicate a named reference in which everything before the # is the same as the linking document.

Addressing Variations

As outlined at the start of this chapter, URLs are more or less complete strings of `service://system/dir/file`, which is quite a bit to have to enter and reenter as you build your hyperlinked documents. It is also inconvenient to have the entire URL hardcoded into a document or set of documents when the documents are moved to a new location on the same server or when the data are moved to another server. Therefore, you can specify *relative* or *partial URLs*.

Remember that the browser does not send a partial URL when it requests data. The browser takes a predetermined URL base and appends the relative URL listed in the `href=` attribute to that base. The initial character following the `href=` determines how much of the current document's URL is parsed to obtain the base URL for the new document.

The URL base can also be modified by the use of the <BASE> tag and by directory aliasing by the server. This process can be very confusing, so step slowly through the details below.

Using Addressing Relative to Files

Absolute addressing uses absolutely everything—all of the required URL components as listed at the start of this chapter plus whatever optional components are necessary to retrieve the linked document. Relative addressing uses the difference between the location of the current document or reference point and the desired destination.

Each of the required parts of a URL has a unique delimiter character. To create a relative URL, start the relative URL with the desired delimiter character. The current URL is used to obtain the rest of the information. Everything to the left of that delimiter character in the current URL is kept. Everything to the right of that delimiter character is replaced by the new relative URL. For example, if the full URL is `http://www.finesse.com/Examples/toomuch.html`, use:

- A `:` to indicate that the service stays the same and everything else changes. For example, `://www.sun.com/` loads the server www.sun.com with the same service, `http`.

- A `/` to indicate that the service and the server stay the same but the entire pathname changes. For example, `/Chapters/Chapter1.html` loads `Chapter1.html` from the directory `Chapters` on the server `www.finesse.com` rather than the directory `Examples`.

- No delimiting character to indicate that only the filename changes. For example, `notenough.html` would load a document by that name located in the same directory as `http://www.finesse.com/Examples/toomuch.html`.

- A `#` to indicate that the service, server, path, and filename stay the same, but the place within the document changes. For example, `#halfway` searches for the named anchor `halfway` somewhere in the middle of the file and displays that part of the document.

Since a pathname is treated as a single unit, the method for using a partial path in a URL is the same as using a relative path on a UNIX or MS-DOS system (using a . to refer to the current directory, .. to refer to the parent, and so on). A relative path can be specified using the directory of the current document as a starting point instead of a fixed portion of the URL. For example, `../Sibling/justright.html` points the browser to the parent of the current document's directory (the ..), then down to the `Sibling` subdirectory of the parent, and then to the `justright.html` document itself.

Note – For security and other administrative reasons, some servers may be configured to disallow the use of relative pathnames as described in the preceding paragraph, at least under some circumstances. For example, if a server is configured for use by three different websites, each of these three may be established in a subdirectory of some root directory to which only the server administrator should have access. Obviously, in a case like this, allowing a user (or an HTML document) to point to anything in the parent directory (..) would not be a wise practice.

Files in Relative Directories

1. Load the `Chapter3/rel.html` **document.**
   If you are loading the document through a server, notice that the full URL is listed in
   the Document URL line at the top of the browser. If you have loaded it as a local file,
   notice that the URL displayed at the top of the browser is `file:///`*{path to specified*
   directory}/`Chapter3/rel.html`.

2. Use View Page Source to view the HTML specified in the document.
   It looks like the code in Code Example 3-1.

Code Example 3-1   Relative Path Example

```
<html> <head>


<title> Relative Paths Exercise

</title>

</head>


<body>
<a href="file1.html"> filename only </a>


<p><a href="../file1.html"> file in parent </a>


<p><a href="down/file2.html"> file in subdirectory</a>


<p><a href="file2.html"> second filename only</a>

<address> me

</address>

</body>

</html>
```

3. **Return to the main browser window. Select the link,** `filename only`, **which in the source is a filename without anything around it.**
   In this case, the browser removed the filename from the URL in the browser's URL field and appended the new filename to this base URL. Loading this document was successful because the requested document was in the same directory.

4. **Click on Back to return to the original page.**

5. **Select the item** `file in parent` **which is a filename one directory up from the current file.**
   In this case, the browser removed the filename from the URL in the Document URL window and appended the new pathname, including the ../ to this base URL. Loading this document was successful because the requested document was in the directory above the current one.

6. **Click on Back to return to the original page.**

7. **Select the item** `file in subdirectory`, **which is a filename in the directory below the current file.**
   In this case, the browser removed the filename from the URL in the Document URL window and appended the new subdirectory and filename to this base URL. Loading this document was successful because the requested document was in the directory below the current.

8. **Click on Back to return to the original page.**

9. **Select the item** `second filename only`, **which is a filename without any path information preceding it.**
   In this case, the browser removed the filename from the URL in the Document URL window and appended the new filename to this base URL. Loading this document was not successful because the requested document was in the directory below—not in the current directory.

To reiterate, partial URLs can be followed if they look like standard UNIX or DOS path specifications. Use only the filename and place the files in the same directory or in directories relative to the current working directory.

Virtual Hosts and the Document Root

Most HTML authors and webmasters do not operate their own servers, except perhaps for development and testing purposes. (And that's the reason, of course, that we've provided server software on the CD-ROM which accompanies this book.) Rather, they place their publicly accessible production documents and other files on a computer operated by an Internet service provider (ISP). The ISP, functioning as the *web hosting service*, instructs the webmaster how to address his or her pages, typically something like this on UNIX-based servers (as most, but not all, of them are):

`http://www.`*providername*`.com/~`*username*`/`*filename*`.html`

First, note the tilde (~) character. This convention originated in the UNIX environment's C shell as a method of accessing a user's home directory. The home directory itself is determined from the password information maintained on the server, such as `/etc/passwd`. The httpd daemon examines this resource to locate the exact physical directory, which may or may not be the same as the username itself. (That is, if the username is `simpson`, there may or may not actually be a directory on the server called `simpson`.)

This is one illustration of the ways in which the *virtual name* of a directory is mapped onto its *physical location*. (Precisely how this mapping occurs varies from server to server.) At a higher level of abstraction is the concept of a *virtual host*.

In the list of URL components at the beginning of this chapter was a particularly important one, the system name. Corporations and individuals with the technological and financial resources to do so run their own servers. The names for these servers (known as the "domain names") are registered with a central organization whose function is to ensure that no two systems on the Internet have the same system name. (As of this writing, there is only one organization, called the InterNIC, which does this "officially." Various proposals are in the works to decentralize this authority.) As confusing as the Internet is to some newcomers, imagine the chaos if there were more than one `www.sun.com` or `www.netscape.com`, for example.

Smaller organizations, even without their own physical servers, can also acquire their own unique domain names. Their web hosting provider establishes them as a *virtual host*; the true physical location of their documents is mapped by the web hosting provider, working with the InterNIC, to a "virtual location"—the domain name.

This enables an important concept, that of the *document root*, to be universal, regardless of the specific server software or whether the domain name itself represents an actual server or is merely hosted. The document root (the "starting point" for your website), together with relative addressing and directory aliasing and mapping, makes it possible for you and your website's users to ignore the server's true directory structure and reference document locations as if you had a simple server all to yourself.

Using the <BASE> Tag for Relative Links

Usually a document is not published alone in a hypertext environment. The related documents tend to stay in the same directory or general area (real or virtual). The base of a set of documents can be defined with the tag <BASE>. The <BASE> tag was originally designed to supply a base URL when the HTML document was taken out of context, such as when a document is e-mailed to someone.

However, since indiscriminate use of the <BASE> tag causes problems, limit its use. If <BASE> is defined, then, when the document is mailed, that value is retained instead of the actual base of the document. Defining <BASE> also causes the browser to list the value of <BASE> instead of the actual URL of the document in the hotlist and Document URL field of the browser. Thus, when a document is reloaded, the document will not be reloaded, but the <BASE> value is loaded instead. Use the <BASE> tag only when the documents will be routinely taken out of context.

Secondary Directories

One of the worst habits for a personal computer user to get into is to dump all files, programs, and so on into a single directory. This creates numerous problems:

- It becomes almost impossible to find anything, especially given the cryptic names of many computer-based resources.

- It becomes *literally* impossible to have more than one file of the same name on the computer.

- If the physical computer is used by more than one person, they all have access to the same resources, and they can't "hide" anything from one another. The embarrassing early draft of Sam's novel is as easily viewed by Sara as is the final manuscript.

These problems are duplicated—indeed, worsened—on websites. You can, if you choose, dump all your documents and other files into a single directory. But it becomes much easier for you to organize your site and to control user access to various portions of it if you've planned ahead by using various server-specific features to do so.

For example, the Apache server and others employ a simple text file called .htaccess to control which users can get access to which directories. This control can take the form of username and password prompts, in the case of a site which wants to provide access by all users to general information but requires that a user register in order to get access to special features. (This can be critical in the case of forbidding general user access to a testing directory, or in preventing hackers from accessing anything at all except what they can get to through your "front door.")

For this reason (and many others) it is essential to *know your server.* If you are not the server administrator, you may not need to know for example how the logical-to-physical mapping is performed. But as the HTML author or webmaster, you can construct the best website only if you are familiar with as many of your server's features as possible—not least of all, how to establish and control access to secondary directories beyond the document root itself.

Special Case: The `mailto` Link

You have probably seen Web documents containing hyperlinks which do not point to other documents but instead invoke the browser's e-mail function.

This is simple to accomplish: The `href=` attribute to the `<a>` tag is given a value of `mailto:`*address@domain.* (Of course, the given e-mail address must be a valid one.) It should be obvious that this form of `href` is not a standard URL.

As an example, within the `<address>` block of your HTML document template you might add a hypertext link as follows:

```
<address>
This page maintained by:
    <a href="mailto:webmaster@nonprofit.org>John E. Simpson</a>
</address>
```

The phrase `John E. Simpson` would appear underlined (like any other hypertext link) within the address block. When a user clicks on that link, the browser's mail function is fired up, and the indicated e-mail address is automatically entered in the mail client's To: field.

Note that all browsers do not include an e-mail feature. Always provide alternative means of contacting someone referenced in a `mailto:` link, unless you are reasonably certain that this will not be a problem for the user.

Summary

Partial URLs are a boon to the developer of a complete set of documents. By use of these URL methods, documents do not require significant changes when moved. You can determine when to use each method, based on how the documents are to be maintained.

In this chapter you learned:

* When documents might be moved from one directory to another, the method of using relative pathnames is the most effective. Since full pathnames aren't listed in the document, changes to the pathname aren't needed. This is one effective method for

mirroring data on multiple servers and for setting up a development and testing environment on a local machine to mimic the production machine's own directory structure.

- When documents are to be fixed to a formal directory structure, use the method of using pathnames relative to the root and aliases. This method compensates for the need to move documents to a new disk or path as the size of the document structure grows, by changing only the alias mapping for that directory structure. This is the other effective method for mirroring data on multiple servers.

- Symbolic links are a method of mimicking the behavior desired above. They work only for UNIX systems, and they exact a small overhead per request in following the symbolic link. Use symbolic links for moving document directories on-the-fly, when the daemon can't be reloaded, or for testing. Long-term use of symbolic links is not recommended.

- The <BASE> tag was originally designed to supply a base URL when the HTML document was taken out of context, such as when a document is e-mailed to someone. If a <BASE> is defined, it causes problems with standard browsing. Use the <BASE> tag only when the documents will be routinely taken out of context.

- A mailto: link can be provided for users with e-mail-enabled browsers as a contact method.

Tags Used in This Chapter

Tag	Attribute	Description
<A>		Anchors hyperlinks.
	HREF	Points to destination of link.
	NAME	Defines a named anchor so that a link can point to a place in a document, not just to the document itself.

Multimedia—Going Beyond Text   4 ≣

Most Internet tools are limited to one type of medium. In the case of netnews, gopher, IRC, and basic mail, this medium is text. A few tools, like the Internet Talk Radio, use sound or video as their medium. The deciding characteristic of all of these applications is that they can cope with only one medium.

Using multiple media, or multimedia, in a web document has become virtually a requirement. Web pages aren't considered complete without at least one image. However, it is important to keep the audience in mind when developing multimedia documents. Support for many specialized types of media viewers and browser plug-ins has been ported to most platforms, but there still are some platform-specific media formats. If the audience that you intend to reach is the Internet itself, use the standard formats outlined below.

Other audience characteristics to take into consideration when developing multimedia web pages include quantity, size, and page layout.

Multimedia

E-mail has been the catalyst for a whole new world of information transmission. In the late 1980s and early 1990s many e-mail systems enabled two new options. The first option was to let the user send full 8-bit data instead of 7-bit ASCII by automatically converting the 8-bit data to and from a 7-bit version (encoding and decoding it, respectively). The second new feature was the ability to attach a file to an e-mail message. Since these files could now carry 8-bit converted data, a kind of sneaker net evolved where networking was still limited. The files could be dragged from the e-mail message to a folder and used without additional processing.

The next step in this evolution was the incorporation or binding of tools to the e-mail readers that were specifically designed for viewing or playing the attached files. This allowed the files to be viewed directly within the e-mail system, removing the steps of dragging to a folder, starting the application, and loading the file.

It wasn't enough to be in touch with all of the other CCMail™ users or Internet-type mail users. People needed to communicate with everyone, and the e-mail vendors and on-line services like CompuServe provided gateways from one type of mail to another. This method was fine for text, but unsatisfactory for handling the attached data files. There weren't many common data formats in the beginning. Microsoft Windows used BMPs for images and WAVs for sound. SunOS and eventually Solaris 2.x used PostScript® or Sun Raster™ files for images and AU (audio) files for sound. The technology was ready for standards, and the MIME (Multipurpose Internet Mail Extensions) standard was developed to meet that need.

Note – Throughout this discussion, you will note the rather common occurrence of trademark and copyright symbols. Multimedia applications are largely the result of vendors' successes at marketing their proprietary formats, rather than (with some exceptions) the work of non-commercial industrywide groups such as the W3C. Also note that many of these proprietary multimedia formats require either special viewers or plug-ins for the user's browser, or special software on the server which delivers the media to the user, or both. As always, *know your server*—and take into consideration the possible impact on your users of formats which are not yet widely supported on all platforms before deciding to plunge headlong into the bright new world of multimedia.

MIME Formats

When configuring servers, MIME formats are associated with specific filename extensions. The browsers associate the filename extensions to MIME types and the MIME types to specific viewers. Among the more popular are:

- **GIF**™ — The Graphics Interchange Format© popularized in the late 1980s as a result of its widespread use on CompuServe. (The GIF format was actually developed at Unisys, which has caused various ugly legal battles in recent years.) This bitmapped format came into being because people wanted to exchange images between different platforms. This format is now used on almost every platform that supports graphical applications. GIF format is the standard image type for WWW browsers; its one drawback is that it is limited to 256 colors.

  An extended standard called GIF89a was developed to add functionality for specific applications. One notable use of this extended standard in web pages is the use of transparent backgrounds. Images can be made to "float" by making the background color the same as the background of the browser. However, browsers don't always come with the plain gray background, and the user can override the choice of background color. Therefore, designating a specific color *in the image* as transparent compensates for the user's specific configuration.

- **JPEG** — Another bitmap format with compression that was designed and named after the Joint Photographic Experts Group. JPEG has some advantages over GIF, among them that it supports millions of colors (vs. GIF's 256) and is much more highly compressible (and therefore takes up less space, and downloads faster, than a GIF image with similar detail). It is also the basis for the most common moving image format, MPEG. All GUI browsers offer support for in-line JPEG images.

- **TIFF** — The Tagged Image File Format designed by Microsoft and Aldus for use with scanners and desktop publishing programs. Most external viewers support this format (although browsers themselves still do not).

- **Other Image Formats** — Several other image formats that are usually platform specific or not widely supported by browsers. (One of these, the PNG format, holds special promise as a replacement for the aging GIF standard. It is not yet directly supported by most browsers, though.) Unless you know that your audience will be limited to a specific platform or will be equipped with the required plug-ins, limit your graphics images to the above formats.

- **PostScript** — A document display language that originated from the need to display and print high-quality documents. Almost all platforms can print PostScript, but there are some holes in the ability to display PostScript.

- **PDF** — The Portable Document Format used for Adobe® Acrobat™ documents. Acrobat uses hypertext links within a document in a way similar to that in HTML. Since version 2.0, Acrobat products have also supported links *between* documents. A chief advantage of the PDF format is that, unlike basic HTML, it is indeed WYSIWYG. Furthermore, Acrobat viewers are available for most platforms. However, while popular, it still requires the use of an external viewer, the Acrobat Reader, rather than a plug-in which appears within the browser window; also not to be ignored is that PDF files can be huge.

- **MPEG** — An animated video standard format based on the JPEG methods. Like JPEG, the format received its name from the group that defined the standard, Motion Picture Experts Group. This is the most common movie format for the WWW, primarily because viewers exist for all platforms.

- **AVI** — The movie format native to Microsoft Windows (all versions).

- **QuickTime** — Developed by Apple Computer, this video standard is felt to have many advantages over the MPEG and AVI formats. Players are available on many platforms, and support for QuickTime has begun to be incorporated directly into browsers. However, there are not as many QuickTime resources available as there are for the other video standards.

- **Basic Sound** — A sound that evolved on UNIX systems. There is a sound player for almost every platform. When in doubt of the audience, use this format.

- **WAV** — The native sound-file format for Microsoft Windows (all versions).

- **MIDI** — This popular electronic-music format is supported by a wide variety of browsers and platforms. Unlike most WAV and basic sound files, MIDI files are digitally synthesized directly from a computer rather than recorded. The results can be pleasing or horrific, depending on the skill of the creator.

- **RealAudio** — A *streaming* audio format (arguably the most popular). One difficulty in using many of the common audio formats is that the sound files can be large and hence take a long time to download over common modem connections. *Streaming* audio, however, begins to play as soon as a minimal portion of the file downloads; while that portion is playing, the next is downloading, and so on. Streaming audio files are not appreciably smaller than their other more common counterparts, but their streaming nature makes them more suitable for "immediate" playback.

- **VRML** — In one respect, the Virtual Reality Modeling Language (developed initially by Silicon Graphics) is not a true "multimedium" type. Files in this format are, like HTML files, composed of straight 7-bit ASCII text. However, at the viewing end these files are perceived as multimedia because the browser displays an apparently three-dimensional window in which the user can fly around, walk, rotate, and so on. Rather elaborate "virtual worlds" can be constructed, with buildings, rooms, even furnishings, and objects can be hyperlinked to other objects or to HTML documents. Most GUI browsers include built-in support for VRML, and there are a number of external viewers available as well.

Adding Multimedia Links

In your HTML document, a link to an external multimedia file doesn't look much different from a text link. The important thing to remember is to name the referenced file properly. The file should have an extension that declares what type of file it is. For example, if it is a GIF or GIF89a type of file, the name would be *filename*.gif. Older Microsoft Windows servers can serve only files with a three-character extension. Other platforms (including all flavors of UNIX and Windows 95/NT 4.0) don't have this restriction. Table 4-1 lists common filename extensions for standard MIME types and the abbreviations for three-character extensions where needed.

Table 4-1   Filename Extensions for MIME Type

MIME Type	Standard Extensions	3-Character/DOS Extensions
Image/GIF (and GIF89a)	.gif	
Image/JPEG	.jpeg	.jpg .jpe
Image/TIFF	.tiff	.tif
Text/HTML	.html	.htm

Table 4-1   Filename Extensions for MIME Type (Continued)

PostScript	`.eps .ps`	
Adobe Acrobat (PDF)	`.pdf`	
Video/MPEG	`.mpeg`	`.mpg .mpe`
Video/AVI	`.avi`	
Video/QuickTime movie	`.mov`	
Sound/AU (Basic)	`.au .snd`	
Sound/WAV	`.wav`	
Sound/MIDI	`.mid .midi`	`.mid`
Sound/RealAudio	`.ra .ram`	
VRML	`.vrml`	`.vrm`

The link itself is a standard anchor with reference. An example is:

```
<a href="http://system/dir/file.gif/"> Some Image </a>
```

or:

```
<a href="http://system/dir/file.mpeg/"> Some Movie </a>
```

1. **Load** `Chapter4/image1.html`.
   This document contains a link to a picture.

2. **Pull down the View menu and select Page Source.**
   Notice that the only difference between a text link and the image link is the extension at the end of the name.

3. **Click on the link** Some Image.
   The image is "downloaded." If your browser alone is not capable of viewing that type, an external viewer is started to display it (or you will be prompted for the name of the viewer, if none was previously specified).

In-line Images

Some of the external images, sounds, and movies that you add to your documents require an external viewer, such as Adobe Acrobat Reader for PDF files. GIF and JPEG images, as well as some other basic multimedia types, can also be incorporated into the web page itself. By carefully embedding images and other media directly in the text, your web pages can be made to resemble real books, magazines, and documents.

Design Considerations

Some people feel that a document is not complete without a picture or two. Since a large percentage of the users do have image-capable browsers, this expectation isn't unreasonable. However, it is important to consider the audience when designing a web page. Clients with a slow connection, such as SLIP or PPP at 14.4kbps, don't like to download large images because they take more time to load than the text itself.

For this reason, browsers allow the user to delay image loading until it is convenient for them. Additionally, the browser will also supply a generic image if there is a problem with the image (such as an incorrect filename, or a file which no longer exists at the specified URL). The images shown in Figure 4-1 serve as placeholders for images like this.

Figure 4-1   Common Filler Images

Not all users are aware of the delay image-loading feature, and the filler images don't really add anything to a web page. (Indeed, they can mar or completely obliterate the usefulness of an otherwise well-designed page.) If your audience isn't likely to load the images or if it will take more than a few seconds to load the images, keep them to a minimum or omit them entirely. One rule of thumb—although nothing is iron-clad—is that if a document, including its in-line images, is over 30 Kbytes in size, users will grow impatient. We will discuss some workarounds for the increased download times of image-heavy pages in the section Image Efficiencies.

The standard horizontal rules and bullets used in lists are pretty boring. Customized horizontal rules and colored bullets can be used to spruce up a page. By "customized" in this case we're not referring to the new attributes of the `<hr>` and unordered list item tags discussed in the previous chapter; we mean the practice of using tiny in-line images (readily available at many web sites, and easily created using common paint programs) in place of these page makeup elements. However, when the images are delayed, the page layout can change. A custom "horizontal rule image" may stretch across the page, whereas the filler image (as in Figure 4-1) will never do so. If the average user is going to delay image loading, your beautifully customized page will not have the same impact.

An example of this philosophy is the id Software home page. id's clientele tend to be users of their popular game software, with high-powered computers and sometimes even high-speed network connections. Thus, their home page has quite a few images, as shown in Figure 4-2.

Figure 4-2   id Home Page

If the audience were primarily users with slow connections and delay image loading enabled, then the same image would look like Figure 4-3.

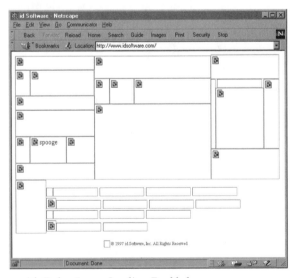

Figure 4-3   id Home Page with Delay Image Loading Enabled

Remember: *The audience is the primary consideration when designing a page!*

4

Adding an In-line Image

An in-line image is placed on a page with the <IMG> tag. The SRC=*href* attribute is required. As with the text anchor <A> tag, the value of *href* can be either an absolute or a relative URL. An example of this is:

```
<IMG SRC="http://{system}/Chapter4/earth.gif">
```

1. **Load** Chapter4/iimage1.html.

2. **View the HTML source with View Page Source.**
   The page here has only one item, the in-line image. Notice that when the image doesn't fill the line, text following the image is placed next to it.

3. **Load** Chapter4/iimage2.html.
   Notice that different alignment is specified for each image and notice how the text is laid out.

Images will be laid out side by side if there is space to accommodate them. To force an image to start below the previous one, start a new paragraph with the <P> tag.

Aligning an Image

In the previous example, the image took up only about half of the screen horizontally. Text showed up to the right of the image. The text started at the bottom of the image. The alignment of the first line of text can be changed by adding the align= attribute with one of three options: top, middle, or bottom. An example of this is:

```
<IMG ALIGN=top SRC="http://{system}/Chapter4/earth.gif">
```

The one problem with using alignments other than bottom is that only the first line of text is affected. All text after the first line appears under the image.

New in HTML 3.2: The new HTML specification adds two new values to the align= attribute, left and right. These are used to flow text around the specified image. If you align the image to the left margin, text flows around it to the right; if aligned to the right margin, text flows around the image along its left side.

Add the following step to the preceding ones:

4. **Load** Chapter4/iimage4.html.
   Notice that the text starts where the alignment is specified for each image, but the second line of text always starts at the bottom of the image.

New in HTML 3.2: There are some additional image-positioning attributes available with the new version. The first two, hspace=*pixels* and vspace=*pixels*, cause the specified amount of empty space (an integer, represented by *pixels*) to surround the image on the sides and at the top and bottom. You can use either or both of these attributes (or neither, of course).

The new `border=`*pixels* attribute forces a border of the specified thickness to be rendered around the image.

Finally, under HTML 3.2 (as discussed briefly in the previous chapter), remember that the line-break tag `<br>` has a new attribute, `clear=`. Although this is not strictly speaking an image-related element, it can be used to establish the vertical placement of text relative to an image. Specifying `<br clear=left>` at the start of a line of text says, in effect, "Start this line only when the left margin is free of other elements (including images)"; `<br clear=right>` does the same thing relative to the right margin.

5. **Load** `Chapter4/iimage5.html` **for examples of the use of these new attributes.** Note especially the relationship between text flow and image placement.

Alternatives to Images

A few text-based browsers, for example, Lynx, cannot display the image. An attribute to the `<img>` tag, `alt=`*imagelabel*, accommodates these systems. The `alt=` attribute defines a text string to be put in place of the image for text-only browsers. Also, some graphical browsers use the `alt=` value instead of displaying a generic image for delayed or suppressed image loading. (Current-generation browsers even display the `alt` text in "tool tip" form when the user places the mouse cursor over the image.) In this case, if the new HTML 3.2 `border=` attribute is also specified with a thickness greater than 0, the alternate text appears within a border.

An example of the use of this attribute is:

```
<IMG ALT="Earth" SRC="http://{system}/Chapter4/earth.gif">
```

This `alt=` attribute tells the browser to display the word "Earth" where the image would normally appear. Note that the value of *imagelabel* must be surrounded by quotation marks when it contains spaces or other special characters; the quotation marks are optional otherwise.

Another alternative (admittedly more labor intensive to maintain) is to create two sets of documents: one set with images and one without. Then, on the home page, you can offer the user the option of browsing with or without images. If you offer the choice of running without images, don't make references to pages with images. The user-specified preference should be respected.

Image Efficiencies

This section assumes that you have decided to include images on your page but are still concerned (rightly or wrongly, depending on the images' total size) that the page will take too long to download and display over a modem connection. The objective in most cases is to get *something* on the user's screen, even if it's not *everything*, as quickly as possible. (This objective obviously doesn't apply in the case of web documents whose entire contents consist of images—not a recommended practice, although this doesn't stop many designers from following it anyway.) It also assumes that you have already struck a balance in the images between appearance (resolution and color depth) and file size—that you can't reduce the image file sizes themselves without introducing undesirable degradation in the images' appearance.

There are two general approaches to solving this problem: manipulating the image itself and/or using HTML to control the image's display.

When using GIF and/or JPEG images that you have some creative control over, one fairly simple thing to do is to create the images so that they will be rendered by the browser in a blurry sort of preview first. The terms for this kind of image are *interlaced GIFs* and *progressive JPEGs*; most good image-manipulation software, including the commercial Adobe PhotoShop and the shareware PaintShop Pro, are able to create GIFs and JPEGs of this type.

Although the technology behind and behavior of interlaced GIFs and progressive JPEGs are not identical, the general effect when viewed is the same: The browser paints a bit of the image at a time rather than waiting until the entire image has been downloaded. (This is similar in approach to that of "streaming" multimedia, such as RealAudio.) Be aware that interlaced/progressive images are slightly larger in size than their normal counterparts.

Aside from direct image manipulation, you can also speed things up a bit through the use of HTML. It is not part of the official HTML 3.2 specification, but most GUI browsers accept an optional `lowsrc=`*lowresimage* attribute of the `<img>` tag. The value of *lowresimage* is the URL of a low-resolution form of the final image as defined in the `src=` tag. Because the low resolution image *is* low-resolution, it will be smaller and hence download faster.

New in HTML 3.2: You can now take "official" advantage of a couple of `<img>` attributes that have been unofficially supported by GUI browsers for some time: `height=`*pixels* and `width=`*pixels*. These attributes, obviously, specify the height and width of the image to be displayed. The advantage in terms of display efficiency is that the browser can allocate that much space for the image and display any surrounding text at once, positioned and flowing around the image's space; the user can proceed to read the text while the images are being "filled in." If image loading is delayed or suppressed by the user, the empty box placeholders will be shown in the specified dimensions.

(You can also use the new `height=` and `width=` attributes to *scale* the image to a size different than it actually is. For example, if the original image is 200 pixels high by 400 pixels wide, you can specify `height=100 width=200` to display it at half the normal size. Scaling is *not* an official HTML 3.2 use of these new attributes, however. There's a good reason: If the 200x400 image is 150 Kb in size, that much data must still be downloaded, regardless of the final display size.)

Finally, you can take advantage of the browser's caching behavior. As noted elsewhere in this book, browsers save downloaded pages locally, including images as well as text, to the user's hard drive. This reduces the need to redownload the pages' contents when the user revisits them, especially when using the Back and Forward buttons. Reading large quantities of data from a local drive is enormously quicker than downloading them over a modem connection.

The simplest way to take advantage of caching is by careful planning: by reusing images on later pages that are placed on your home page. For example, don't create a new, slightly different company logo to be displayed at the top left of every page—use the *same* logo everywhere.

A somewhat more exotic use of caching is to *preload* images on pages that are otherwise image-light, setting the images' `height=` and `width=` attributes both to 1. While the user is reading the text on such a page, the image loading—and caching—is taking place in the background. When the images are finally needed for a given page, they're already in the user's cache and display much faster. Use this technique with care, however: It merely hides but does not eliminate the image downloading. If the user jumps from the preloading page to another before the image caching has completed, you may not have saved him anything after all.

6. **Load** `Chapter4/iimage6.html`. **It and the pages it links to demonstrate the use of some of these efficiency tips.**

Creating Transparent Backgrounds

By use of the transparent color definition used in GIF89a files, an image can appear to float above the web page. Transparent images are used in web pages in the same manner as regular in-line images. The only difference is that the image needs to be processed so that it has a transparent color.

GIF images use a colormap or list of color values to manage the colors in an image. GIF images have a section in the header that identifies the number of colors in the colormap, and then goes on to list the RGB values for each color. For example, if the palette on which image was based had 256 colors, the header would have a table of 256 RGB values, even if the image itself used only 12 unique colors. Different programs use different methodologies for determining which colormap entry should be used for the transparent color. The `giftrans` utility (for UNIX , MS-DOS, and a DOS window in one of the Windows environments) can either take an index number in the colormap table and transform it to the transparent color or change a specific RGB value.

Note – By using `giftrans` in the examples, we don't mean to suggest that it's the only, let alone the best, utility for this purpose. Adobe PhotoShop and PaintShop Pro both let you specify the transparent color for an image simply by clicking on an area of the image that is painted in the desired color. However, `giftrans` has the advantage of being available across platforms (in both C sources and executable versions), and is a good teaching tool.

In `giftrans`, a specific color is created on the screen by specification of a value for the amount of red in that color, the amount of green, and the amount of blue. For example, there is no red in black, so the red value is 0. The same applies to green and blue. Therefore, the RGB value is #000. The # sign indicates that the value is in hexadecimal, not decimal, notation.

Look at `Chapter4/neat.gif`, either by loading it in your browser or by viewing it with a paint program. This is a fractal whose black background is a good candidate for conversion to a transparent background. However, the color black is not isolated to one cell of the colormap; it exists in 17 different colormap slots. Therefore, a program that changes the background by specific color would be a better solution than changing the colormap slot by slot.

Setting Transparent Background by Color

A transparent color is defined with `giftrans` by defining the RGB value of the color in the `-t` option, using # to specify the color definition. The `-o` option specifies a new output filename so that you don't write over your work in progress. It is a good idea to avoid writing over your work files. An example of using giftrans is:

```
giftrans -t #000 -o new.gif neat.gif
```

Setting Transparent Background by Colormap Cell

A transparent cell is defined with `giftrans` by defining the cell number of the color in the `-t` option. Note that in this case `giftrans` knows the `-t` refers to a cell number rather than a specific color because its value is not preceded by a #. An example of this is:

```
giftrans -t 0 -o new2.gif neat.gif
```

Listing the Colormap of an Image

A list of the current color values can be obtained by using the `-l` (the letter "el," not the number 1) option of `giftrans`.

```
giftrans -l new.gif
```

Adding Links to Images to Simulate Buttons

An in-line image can be anchored just like text. Then, when the user clicks on the image, a new web page is brought up, giving the appearance of having buttons. An example of this is:

```
<a href="new.html"><img src="small_new.gif"></a>
```

When the user clicks on this image, the document new.html opens.

By default, the hyperlinking image is surrounded by a one- or two-pixel border. The color of the border is determined in the same way as the color of any other hyperlink.

New in HTML 3.2: You can control the size of the border here, as with any other image, by using the new border=*pixels* attribute of the <img> tag.

Some webmasters prefer, for design reasons, to set their image borders to 0; this can be especially useful for nonrectangular graphics with a transparent background. The decision to do so for hyperlinking images must be balanced against the user's expectations that hyperlinks will be rendered in a different color than surrounding elements. It is true that the mouse pointer changes shape over a hyperlinking image as it does over hypertext. On the other hand, many users will not even think to position their mouse pointer over an image that is not obviously rendered as a hyperlink. Also, if you suppress the colored border altogether, users will not know if they've already followed this link.

Imagemaps

A favorite design element for many webmasters is the use of clickable *imagemaps* in place of text-based menus for navigating around a site. An imagemap is a standard image file divided up into hyperlinked "hot spots." When users click on one area of the imagemap, they are taken to one document; when they click on another area, a different document is brought up; and so on.

Server-Side Imagemaps

The first form of imagemaps that could be rendered in HTML were server-based. An image is designated as a server-side imagemap by using the ismap attribute (no value, hence no = sign) of the <img> tag. You bracket the <img> tag with an anchor tag <a>, as for any other hyperlinking image; but the value of the anchor's href= attribute is the URL not of an HTML document but of a special text file, the *map* file. For example:

```
<a href="menubar.map"><img src="menubar.gif" ismap></a>
```

The exact format of the map file varies from server to server. In general, each record of the file defines a separate hot spot, giving its shape and coordinates within the image, and the URL of a document which should be fetched and displayed when the user clicks within the designated area of the image.

For example, if the server is NCSA based, a map file might look like this:

```
rect home.html 1,1 25,25
poly sales.html 26,1 50,25 26,26
default deadspot.html
```

This tells the server:

- If the user clicks within the rectangle bounded by x,y coordinates 1,1 and 25, 25, display the document at URL `home.html`.

- If the user clicks within the triangular area (note the three pairs of x,y coordinates), display the document at URL `sales.html`.

- If the user clicks anywhere else on the image, display the document at URL `deadspot.html` (presumably a generic "Sorry—you've clicked on a portion of the image with no meaning" page).

Determining the exact coordinates of the different hot spots can be an involved task. Various GUI-based "imagemap editors" have been developed to simplify this task; you simply draw the hot spots over the surface of the image, and the image map editor generates a map file in the desired server format. The newer generation of GUI HTML editors also contain imagemap editors to perform this task automatically.

New in HTML 3.2: Client-Side Imagemaps

There are some problems with the use of server-side imagemaps. First, you must know the format of the map file appropriate to your server. Second, and less obvious, is a matter of efficiency: It puts additional load on the server, which not only must do its usual work of serving up web pages but must also coordinate the mapping of hot spots (as defined in the map file) with user actions that take place in the browser interface.

Netscape Communications developed an unofficial standard for solving these problems which was adopted more or less wholesale in HTML 3.2: the use of *client-side* imagemaps. (The term "client" here refers, of course, to activity that takes place at the user's end of the web transaction.)

To specify a client-side imagemap, your HTML needs three additions:

- The new `usemap=`*mapname* attribute of the `<img>` tag. No anchor tag is used.

- The new `<map>` tag, which assigns a name to the map and acts as a container for the various `<area>` tags (defined next). Multiple client-side imagemaps can be incorporated into a single HTML document by defining them in multiple `<map>` blocks. The `<map>` tag requires a stop tag `</map>` to close the block.

- `<area>` tags, which define the image's hot spots in much the same way as the older server-side map files did. No stop tag is needed.

Here's the client-side version of the server-side HTML shown above:

```
<img src="menubar.gif" usemap="#menubar">
<map name="menubar">
<area shape=rect href="home.html" coords="1,1,25,25">
<area shape=poly href="sales.html" coords="26,1,50,25,26,26">
<area shape=default href="deadspot.html">
</map>
```

As you can see, the value of the `usemap=` attribute points to the location, within the same HTML document, of a named map block. (Note the # sign to designate the block name in the value of the `usemap=` attribute.) The various `shape=`, `href=`, and `coords=` attributes of the `<area>` tag perform functions analogous to those fields in the server-side imagemap's map file.

The `shape=` attribute can take the value `rect` (for a rectangle; requires two pairs of *x,y* coordinates); `poly` (for a polygon; requires *n* pairs of *x,y* coordinates, where *n* equals the number of vertices in the polygon); `circle` (requires one pair of *x,y* coordinates, which locates the center of the circle, and a radius in pixels); or `default` (to define an area other not covered by any other `<area>` tags; no coordinates required). Note that the coordinate pairs are not separated by a space, as in the NCSA server-side example, but by a comma, and that the quotation marks are necessary because of the imbedded commas in the coordinates string.

In place of the `href=` attribute for any `<area>` tag, you can use the simple `nohref` tag (no = sign). This defines a "hole" in the imagemap—that is, an area which when clicked will result in no action at all. This is *not* the same thing as using the `shape=default` attribute.

Also included in the HTML 3.2 version of client-side imagemaps is an `alt`=*label* attribute of the `<area>` tag. This functions similarly to the same attribute of the `<img>` tag itself, except that with it you define different text labels for different areas of the image.

Bells and Whistles

Trying to keep abreast of all the multimedia options available to HTML authors sometimes seems an exercise in frustration as much as an exercise in creativity. In this chapter we've concentrated on the use of images, but we encourage you to explore all dimensions of multimedia in your own work. (Always remember the webmaster's twin credos: "Content is king," and "The audience is the primary consideration.")

Because they are popular and (in one case) demonstrate yet again the importance of knowing your server, we will conclude this chapter with information on two additional features: animated GIF images, and using RealAudio sounds on your web site.

Animated GIFs

This is not really a feature of HTML (for fun or for profit), and furthermore its mis- or overuse can drive many users crazy. (When the battery in a smoke detector starts to run down, the detector beeps intermittently, repeatedly, until you're driven to replace it. Animated GIFs can be like graphic equivalents of this audio nuisance, with the caveat that there's no way to shut the things off without completely suppressing *all* images.) Nonetheless it's undeniably an attention-getter and is interesting from a technical standpoint.

In addition to the ability to make a color transparent, the GIF89a format established the ability to define an animated image. Internally, this is actually a *series* of GIFs stacked one after the other, separated by timing information that sets the duration of each succeeding image's display. Also included is a flag which indicates that the sequence of images is not to recycle at all, or is to recycle *n* times, or is to recycle indefinitely. Schematically, such an image's innards might look like this:

```
display image1.gif
pause for 2 seconds
display image2.gif
pause for 5 seconds
display image3.gif
pause for 1 second
repeat 5 times
```

The overall effect is similar to flicking through a deck of cards adorned with incrementally different images (although if you want, the images can be completely unrelated).

Most conventional paint programs cannot create animated GIFs. They *can* create the component GIFs that are to be stacked up, of course. So the usual approach is to create the component images in a paint program and then concatenate them one after the other (together with timing and recycling information) using a special utility program (see Appendix B for pointers to some of these utilities).

One arguably praiseworthy use of animated GIFs is that they can function in a manner similar to that of the `lowsrc=` attribute of the `<img>` tag supported by most GUI browsers and described above in the section Image Efficiencies; with that attribute, however, you're limited to just a single low-resolution "placeholder" for the final image. Using an animated GIF you can render a whole *series* of successively higher-resolution images, providing more of a fade-in effect. (In this case, of course, you should not specify a recycle value at all: The objective is to get the final image displayed and then stop.)

Aesthetic drawbacks aside, a major drawback of animated GIFs is that they can become huge. A GIF 10 Kb in size, which loads comparatively quickly, will bloat to over 70 Kb if converted to an animated GIF made up of seven iterations. For this reason alone, approach the use of animated GIFs with caution.

RealAudio Files

Note – Actually implementing the procedures described in this section assumes that your server is configured with the RealAudio server component. It may be of interest even if that component is not available, however.

Current-generation browsers come with built-in support for these streaming audio files, and for users of older browsers the RealAudio vendor, RealNetworks, provides a free "player" add-on that can be downloaded from their website. (That is also where you can obtain software for *creating* files in the RealAudio format.) The player handles not only standard RealAudio files but also those in the RealVideo streaming-video format recently introduced by RealNetworks.

Most in-line multimedia is specified within an HTML document the same way a standard in-line image is specified: with an anchor tag whose `href=` attribute points to the desired multimedia file. When the user clicks on the hyperlink, the file is transferred to his or her browser and the correct viewer/plug-in automatically starts up. Most multimedia files can be handled by the http protocol just as if they were plain old text or HTML documents in that for any activation of a given hyperlink, the content is retrieved *once* from the server and delivered *once* to the end user. Assuming a file with the standard RealAudio extension, for example, you might code this as its anchor:

```
<a href="/realaudiofiles/broadcast.ra">Broadcast Plays Here!</a>
```

This won't work with streaming media, however: The connection between the client and the server has to be maintained (or repeatedly reopened), allowing the file to be transferred a chunk at a time, until it has been received completely. If you actually use the above anchor, the file will download and play—but it won't stream; it will be downloaded in its entirety before playing begins.

4

RealNetworks has devised a work-around for this obstacle. In place of the .ra filename in the anchor, use a .ram filename. This special file (the extension stands for RealAudio Metafile) is a simple text file on your server which contains pointers to one or more true .ra files. These pointers look like standard URLs except that the service type portion of the URL has pnm:// instead of http://. Here's what a RealAudio metafile might look like:

```
pnm://{server}/www.mysite.com/realaudiofiles.broadcast1.ra
pnm://{server}/www.mysite.com/realaudiofiles.broadcast2.ra
```

This .ram file type is intercepted by the RealAudio server component (rather than being passed downstream to the user's browser); the server reads the .ram file and feeds to the user (in streaming form) the .ra files to which it refers, one after the other (if it refers to more than one). Thus the delivery of the .ra files is controlled not by the server's regular httpd daemon, but by a special server-installed program provided by RealNetworks.

Headaches: Browser-Specific Multimedia

A side effect of all the press and market attention the Web has received in the last couple of years is that the browser vendors, notably Microsoft and Netscape, are locked in a can-you-top-this battle for the support of new media.

The good news is that competition drives innovation. The bad news is that innovation frequently requires divergent "standards." A full examination of all the media types supported by different browsers is much beyond the scope of a general reference such as *HTML for Fun and Profit,* but you should be aware of how trying to incorporate references to these new formats into your web pages can complicate your life as a webmaster.

Possibly the best example of this is how to play a background sound when a user loads a page. For whatever reason, the Netscape browser understands the <embed> tag, while Microsoft's Internet Explorer recognizes <bgsound>. (Both of these tags take an href= attribute to point the browser to the correct sound file.) If you want your page to be accessible to users of either of these two major browsers, you have to do some complicated nesting of tags (or construct a small JavaScript program to do it for you—see Chapter 11 for information about JavaScript).

One draft element of the HTML 3.2 specification that didn't make it into the final version was a new <object> tag. This was intended as a replacement for the <img> tag, and also a simple expansion of the older tag's role in order to include new media. Again, maybe we'll get this simplification in HTML 4.0.

Summary

In this chapter, you learned about:

- MIME types — Several file formats can be used on multiple platforms to make web pages truly multimedia.

- Adding multimedia links — The only difference between links to other text and links to pictures, sounds, and images is that the pictures, sounds, and images will be downloaded and displayed on external viewers.

- Adding in-line images — GIF images can be incorporated into the document itself.

- Creating transparent backgrounds — Images can appear to float on the web page by changing a color in the colormap to be transparent.

New Tags Used in This Chapter

Tag	Attribute	Description and Notes
`<IMG>`		Incorporates images in a document.
	`SRC`	The href for the image.
	`ALIGN`	Text can be aligned to start at the top, middle, or bottom of the side of an image.
	`ALT`	A name that can be displayed on browsers that don't have image capabilities.

≡ 4

HTML for Fun and Profit

Tables   5 ≡

Most of the HTML elements covered in the last few chapters had been around long enough to be officially included in the HTML 2.0 specifications. Tables, surprisingly, are a new feature formalized only in HTML 3.2—surprisingly, because tables were the one area of formatting needed to make HTML a true publishing medium.

This chapter covers the basics of making tables. Several proposed but not yet implemented items are also discussed.

Plan Ahead!

The document markup we've discussed so far has not required a great deal of advance planning. Tables, too, can be simple to code in HTML. Now, however, you will be faced with some of the messy issues that come into play when attempting to force quasi-WYSIWYG document elements into the non-WYSIWYG world of HTML—unless you plan carefully.

Let's talk about simple tables first. They might be said to have these characteristics:

• They can be represented as a straightforward grid of rows and columns.

• All cells in a given row or column are the same width and the same height.

Such tables are easily rendered with HTML. Often, however, you will find yourself needing to set up tables with complex structures: Some column headings, for example, may be considered "major headings," broken down into multiple columns or subcategories of data. An actuarial table might require a Gender heading, with two subheadings for Male and Female, and within each of those subheadings there may be further data breakdowns according to age group—all this before any actual data are displayed. More complex table layouts such as this can be difficult to visualize in HTML, and even harder to debug.

For these reasons, it's always a good idea to sketch out a schematic of all but the most rudimentary tables. You don't need to spend a fortune on graph paper and rulers; just a pencil and a pad of those yellow self-adhesive notes will do. Lay out the overall grid, and the grids within grids, and enter sample text in both the headings and the individual data cells. Affix the sticky-note to the frame of your monitor. Then and only then, turn to HTML.

Note that many current-generation HTML editors, as discussed in Chapter 14, include table wizards and similar devices which simplify the coding task. To our knowledge none of these tools will plan the table for you, though—and many of them do not help at all if your table falls outside the straightforward row-and-column model.

Table Components

Only a few tags are necessary to make up simple tables.

- Tables are defined with the <TABLE> and </TABLE> tags.

- The tables are subdivided into rows with the table row <TR> tag. In some cases, the closing </TR> tag is used as well, but the most common use is the <TR> tag by itself.

- Each row in a table is made up of cells of data. A cell is defined by the table data <TD> and </TD> tags.

The markup for a basic table is shown in HTML Example 5-1. Notice that the first table row is *implied*; you can therefore omit the <tr> tag that would normally start this row.

HTML Example 5-1   Table Markup Tags

```
<TABLE>

<td> a Column</td>

<td> another Column </td>

<td> yet another Column </td>

<tr>

<td> a Column in a new Row </td>

<td> another Column in a new Row </td>

<td> yet another Column in a new Row </td>

</table>
```

Figure 5-1 shows the basic table as rendered by the Netscape browser.

Table Example #1

a Column	another Column	yet another Column
a Column in a new Row	another Column in a new Row	yet another Column in a new Row

Figure 5-1   Basic Table—table1.html

Table Borders

In the table shown above, no lines separate the cells. In this case, there is plenty of space on a page, so the columns are well defined. In cases where it is important to visually segregate the rows and columns of data, the BORDER= attribute can be added to the <TABLE> tag to add a border around each cell. The value of the attribute is an integer representing the border width in pixels. Specifying a border of 0 is identical to not specifying a border at all—that is, it produces results similar to those of Figure 5-1. Unlike most attributes that we've discussed so far, you can use just the border attribute alone, omitting the = sign and the value; in this case browsers render the table the same as if you specified border=1. However, the HTML 3.2 specification does not mention this behavior; if you want a one-pixel border you should code your tag that way. The full tag looks like HTML Example 5-2.

HTML Example 5-2   Border Tag

```
<TABLE BORDER=1>
```

Figure 5-2 shows the result.

Table Example #2

a Column	another Column	yet another Column
a Column in a new Row	another Column in a new Row	yet another Column in a new Row

Figure 5-2   Table with Borders—table2.html

Note – Complex tables can sometimes be difficult to debug if their cells are borderless. If a complicated nest of rows and columns isn't behaving as you expected, try setting the border= attribute to a value greater than 0 before proceeding.

Table Headings

Headings within basic HTML body text were created to provide a different font for section breaks. This method has continued with the creation of table heading cells, <TH> and </TH>. Table heading cells act the same as table data cells in every other way. Table headings will be rendered in a different font, typically boldface, than that for regular table cell data. You *can* create table headings by bracketing each of the desired cells in a normal row or column with the bold <b> or emphasis <em> tags, but this adds unnecessary complexity to the structure of most tables. HTML Example 5-3 is an example of using the table heading tag.

HTML Example 5-3   Table Heading Tag

```
<table border=1>

<th> a Column Heading </th>

<th> another Column Heading </th>

<th> yet another Column Heading </th>

<tr>

<td> a Column </td>

<td> another Column </td>

<td> yet another Column </td>

</table>
```

Figure 5-3 shows the result.

Table Example #3

a Column Heading	another Column Heading	yet another Column Heading
a Column	another Column	yet another Column

Figure 5-3   Table Heading Example—table3.html

Spanning Columns

In the tables examined so far, each row has the same number of cells and thus the same number of columns. In the browser, this displays as a simple grid. Sometimes you need to create a table with a more elaborate structure, in which some cells (normal or heading) are wider than others. The COLSPAN=*columns* attribute changes the number of columns that a cell covers or spans. This attribute can be used with both the <TD> and <TH> tags. An example of this is shown in HTML Example 5-4.

HTML Example 5-4   Cell Column-Spanning Attribute

```
<table border=1>

<th> a One-Column Heading </th>

<th> another One-Column Heading </th>

<th colspan=2> a Two-Column Heading </th>

<tr>

<td> a Column </td>

<td> another Column </td>

<td> yet another Column </td>

<td> yet another Column </td>

</table>
```

In this case, the heading has two single-wide cells and a double-wide cell (COLSPAN=2), for a total of four cells wide. The next line down has four single-wide cells, also for a width of four cells. Figure 5-4 shows the resulting table.

Table Example #4

a One-Column Heading	another One-Column Heading	a Two-Column Heading	
a Column	another Column	yet another Column	yet another Column

Figure 5-4   Spanning Columns—table4.html

Spanning Rows

Just as a cell can be more than one column wide, it can also be more than one row high. The ROWSPAN=*rows* attribute to <TD> and <TH> tags accomplishes this. HTML Example 5-5 is an example.

HTML Example 5-5   Cell Row-Spanning Attribute

```
<table border=1>
<th rowspan=2> a Double-High Main Heading </th>
<th colspan=2> a two-Column Main Heading </th>
<tr>
<th> a normal (Sub-)Heading </th>
<th> yet another normal (Sub-)Heading </th>
<tr>
<td> a Cell </td>
<td> another Cell </td>
<td> yet another Cell </td>
</table>
```

In this case, the first (heading) column is two rows high; the second (heading) column is one row high but two columns wide. Then a new row is started. The new row starts in the second column, as shown in Figure 5-5.

Table Example #5

a Double-High Main Heading	a two-Column Main Heading	
	a normal (Sub-)Heading	yet another normal (Sub-)Heading
a Cell	another Cell	yet another Cell

Figure 5-5   Spanning Rows—table5.html

Counting Rows and Columns

It may seem unusual to count rows and columns, as was done in the two previous examples, but at this stage, it is necessary. A browser counts the number of cells in each row and column; the largest number that it finds in each direction determines the dimensions of the entire table. Remember when you count your rows and columns to count each rowspan= and colspan= cell not as a single cell, but as multiples. If there is an additional cell on one row, like the <TD> line noted in bold in HTML Example 5-6, the entire table could be distorted. This effect is especially noticeable (and ugly) in tables for which a border is specified.

HTML Example 5-6   Uneven Columns and Rows

```
<table border=1>

<th rowspan=2> a Heading </th>

<th> another Heading </th>

<th> yet another Heading </th>

<tr>

<th> another Heading </th>

<th> yet another Heading </th>

<tr>

<td> a Cell </td>

<td> another Cell </td>

<td> yet another Cell </td>

<tr>

<td> a dangling Cell </td>

</table>
```

Since the data row has one more cell than the heading rows, the table looks like that shown in Figure 5-6.

Table Example #6

a Heading	another Heading	yet another Heading	
	another Heading	yet another Heading	
a Cell	another Cell	yet another Cell	a dangling Cell

Figure 5-6   Sample of Unequal Columns—table6.html

Notice one additional thing in Example 5-6. The table has a stray <TR> tag at the end, also noted in bold. On some browsers, this tag creates an additional blank row. For consistency, do not finish a table with a <TR> tag.

Other Table Features

In the examples above, we've concentrated on the basic tags and attributes required in building tables. There are some other HTML elements to be aware of in order to fine-tune your tables' appearance.

Word Wrapping

There has been very little text in each cell in the previous examples. With more text, how the words wrap within their cells can become an issue. HTML Example 5-7 demonstrates how a browser does column layout when it must wrap the words.

HTML Example 5-7   Long Lines in a Table

```
<h1> Table Example #7 </h1>


<table border=1>
<td> This is a long set of table data to show how to make a page
that has 3 columns of text. </td>
<td> This cell has very little data. </td>
<td> This cell will be longer than either the first or second
It will show that the 3 columns will end up
being the same height and have different widths. </td>
</table>
```

Figure 5-7 shows examples of word wrapping. As you can see, the browser attempts to even out the height of each row and then apportions the cell widths according to the relative amount of text in each cell. Result: The columns are not the same width.

Table Example #7

This is a long set of table data to show how to make a page that has 3 columns of text.	This cell has very little data.	This cell will be longer than either the first or second It will show that the 3 columns will end up being the same height and have different widths.

Figure 5-7   Examples of Word Wrapping—table8.html

You can, of course, ensure that each column is exactly the same width by putting exactly the same text in each cell. This is usually not practical for any real table. A better method is to use the HTML 3.2 attribute width=*value* to the <td> tag. *Value* can be specified as either an absolute number of pixels, or as a percentage relative to the entire table width. Note that using the percentage option is not formally supported in the HTML 3.2 specification, although major browsers recognize it and treat it correctly.

Note – The width of the table itself can also be controlled with a width=*value* attribute. If the table width is specified as a percentage (as in width=75%), it is a percentage of the width of the browser's display window. As with the cell width, the table width expressed as a percentage is not formally endorsed under HTML 3.2.

A number of design issues come into play when altering the widths of tables and/or their constituent cells. These design issues are discussed at greater length in Chapter 13.

If you decide to use the width= attribute of the <td> tag, you don't have to specify the width of all cells in the row. Any cells with unspecified widths will be adjusted according to the browser's default behavior. For example, if the browser display is 400 pixels wide, a two-column row in which the first column has a width of 50 pixels will force the second column to be 350 pixels wide. If the first column is designated as 25 percent of the table's width, the second column will take up the remaining 75 percent.

What happens if by design or accidentally you specify two different widths for different cells in the same column? Other browsers may differ, but both the Netscape and Microsoft products force all cells in a column to the widest width specified in any of the column's cells. Under current HTML behavior, *there is no way to make the width of a column vary from one cell to another.*

Suppose you don't want the text to wrap at all? In HTML Example 5-8, the NOWRAP attribute is used in <TD> tags to force the columns to be as wide as necessary to display the cells' text without wrapping to subsequent lines.

HTML Example 5-8   Controlling Line Breaks with NOWRAP

```
<h1> Table Example #8 </h1>


<table border>
<td nowrap> This is a long set of table data to show how to make a
page
that has 3 columns of text like a newspaper. </td>
<td nowrap> This column has very little data here. </td>
<td> This column will be longer than either the first or second
It will show that the 3 columns will end up
being the same height and have different widths. </td>
</table>
```

This creates a table that looks like the one shown in Figure 5-8. Note the scroll bars added to the browser's window, since the table no longer fits within the display area. The result in this case is unattractive, but there may be cases in which you need to force this behavior.

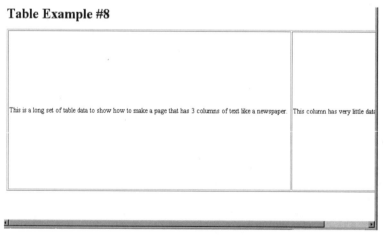

Table Example #8

This is a long set of table data to show how to make a page that has 3 columns of text like a newspaper. | This column has very little data

Figure 5-8   The *NOWRAP Option*

Remember that if you want to control where the words wrap, even in a NOWRAP cell, you can use the <BR> tag to force a new line where desired.

Formatting Data in Cells

All the text in the examples above is left-justified by default. Alignment can be modified cell by cell with the ALIGN=*value* attribute to the <TD> and <TH> tags. *Value* can be LEFT, RIGHT, or CENTER, as in Code Example 5-9.

HTML Example 5-9   Justifying the Text in Cells

```
<table border>

<td align="center"> This is a long set of table data to show how to make

a page that has 3 columns of text like a newspaper. </td>

<td align="right"> This column has very little data here. </td>

<td> This column will be longer than either the first or second

It will show that the 3 columns will end up

being the same height and have different widths. </td>

</table>
```

Figure 5-9 shows the result.

Table Example #9

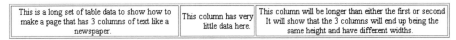

| This is a long set of table data to show how to make a page that has 3 columns of text like a newspaper. | This column has very little data here. | This column will be longer than either the first or second It will show that the 3 columns will end up being the same height and have different widths. |

Figure 5-9   Justified Text

Note – One of the most confusing issues surrounding the formatting of data in table cells has to do with the <font> tag. It may seem "obvious" that if a <font> tag encloses a table, the cells within that table will be rendered in the font specified. This is not true, however, because tables are considered to be separate elements embedded within but more or less independent of the document itself. Even using a <basefont> tag doesn't seem to help. If you need to control the font used within a table, you must use a <font></font> container *within* the individual <td></td> containers. This seems like an oversight in the HTML spec, but there may be some good reason for it.

Captions

Ideally, tables should have captions to label them. The <CAPTION> tag serves this purpose; it takes an optional align= attribute, which can have a value of either top or bottom to force the caption to that position relative to the table itself (above or below, respectively). Default in both the Netscape and Microsoft browsers is to place the caption centered at the top. The Microsoft browser also supports left and right values for the align= attribute, but this is not included in the formal HTML 3.2 specification; there is also no way to specify both bottom and either left or right values.

Miscellaneous Table-Formatting Techniques

The HTML 3.2 specification comes with a variety of other options for controlling the appearance of the table as a whole and of the individual cells. Here's a rundown of these other options:

Other Attributes for the <TABLE> Tag

- **align=** defines how the table is aligned, with allowable values left, right, and center. It defaults to left, unless there's a <div> or <p> tag which modifies the general alignment and includes the table in its scope. If you do not also specify a width for the table as a whole, this alignment will have no effect (that is, the table will run from the left to the right margin). If the specified table width is smaller than the browser display window, however, specifying the table's alignment as either left or right will flow the text around the other side (just as the align= attribute did for in-line images in the previous chapter).

- **cellspacing=** tells the browser how much space to render between adjacent cells, in pixels. By default, the cell spacing is a few pixels (the exact amount varies by browser). Note that although this seems similar to adjusting the border size, the results as rendered can be quite different; also, this is the only way to adjust the cell spacing when you want an invisible border (with no border attribute at all, or border=0).

- **cellpadding=** specifies the space in pixels that is to be rendered *within* each cell, from the edge of the cell to the enclosed text. As with the cell spacing, the default cell padding is a pixel or two.

Other Attributes for the <TR> Tag

- **align=** takes a value of left, right, or center. This specifies the *default* alignment for cells within that row. The alignment of individual cells can be overridden within the individual <td> or <th> tag (see below). If you don't specify the alignment attribute here, browsers will assume the default alignment to be the same as the alignment of the table itself.

- **valign=** defines the default *vertical* alignment for cells within that row, with a value of top, middle, or bottom. The alignment of individual cells can be overridden within the individual <td> or <th> tag (see below). If you don't specify the vertical alignment attribute here, browsers will assume the default alignment to be middle.

Other Attributes for the <TD> and <TH> Tags

As mentioned above, individual cells within a table row can override the default formatting of the row by adding the align= and/or valign= attributes to their corresponding <td> or <th> tags. In addition, the height of the cells in the row can be defined with the optional height=value attribute, where value is an integer, in pixels. (Microsoft Internet Explorer accepts a percentage value for the height= attribute, as well, but this is not supported by either the HTML 3.2 specification or the Netscape Navigator browser.)

Summary

In this chapter, you learned:

- How to make a table.

- How to make different sized rows and columns.

- How to format the text within the cells.

5

Tags Used in This Chapter

Tag	Attribute	Description and Notes
<TABLE>		Defines the table.
	BORDER	Adds borders to separate rows and columns in tables.
	ALIGN	Defines the overall alignment of the table itself within the browser window. Also affects text flow.
	CELLSPAC-ING	Sets the amount of space between adjacent cells, in pixels
	CELLPAD-DING	Sets the amount of space within cells, in pixels, measured from the edge of the cell to the edge of the closest text.
	WIDTH	Specifies the width of the table as a whole, either in absolute pixels or as a percentage of the browser display's width.
<TR>		Marks the end/start of a table row.
	ALIGN	Specifies the default horizontal alignment for cells in that row.
	VALIGN	Specifies the default vertical alignment for cells in that tow.
<TD>		Encloses a cell of table data.
	COLSPAN	Modifies the number of columns a cell will span.
	ROWSPAN	Modifies the number of rows a cell will span.
	ALIGN	Defines the horizontal text alignment within a cell.
	NOWRAP	Declares that the cell text cannot be broken up to wrap from one line to the next.
	HEIGHT	Specifies the height of a cell.
	VALIGN	Defines the vertical text alignment within a cell.
	WIDTH	Specifies the width of a cell.
<TH>		Encloses a cell of a table heading.
	COLSPAN	Modifies the number of columns a cell will span.
	ROWSPAN	Modifies the number of rows a cell will span.
	ALIGN	Defines the horizontal text alignment within a cell.

HTML for Fun and Profit

	NOWRAP	Declares that the cell text cannot be broken up to wrap from one line to the next.
	HEIGHT	Specifies the height of a cell.
	VALIGN	Defines the vertical text alignment within a cell
	WIDTH	Specifies the width of a cell.
<CAPTION>		Creates a title for the table, outside of the table.
	ALIGN	Specifies the placement (top or bottom) of the caption, relative to the table.

≣ *5*

Frames   6 ☰

Frames are a relatively recent addition to HTML formatting. This chapter provides examples and exercises to illustrate how they work. To make these frame examples function correctly, you will need a frames-capable browser such as Netscape 2.x, Internet Explorer 3.0, or better, although a server is not necessary. You will need a simple text editor. (The HTML source code can of course be examined with your browser's View Page Source feature in place of the text editor.)

What Are Frames?

Frames are like separate panes of a browser window that can be operated independently. You can make each pane of the window fit your own design, so that you can control where in the display your data appear. You can use one frame, for instance, to display a table of contents in one pane of your browser window, and another frame to display the documents which are activated by the hyperlinks in the table of contents.

As with tables (discussed in Chapter 5), your work with framed documents will go much more smoothly if you plan ahead of time. Sketch out the general arrangement of panes within the window, subject to these constraints:

- Like tables, frames are (sometimes nested) *grids*. For instance, you cannot (at least for now) devise a framed window such that a pane occupies only one quadrant of the window. When you look at a framed window, there must be at least one "dividing line" which extends all the way across the window, either left to right, or up and down.

- In a framed window, the entire display area must be framed; you can't, say, subdivide a window into a framed left half and a nonframed right half. This is explained further below.

Frame Components

Frames are constructed with container tags, like others used in HTML documents. A regular HTML document uses HTML tags to identify the start and end of the document, and a title to announce the topic. A frame document does the same.

Before proceeding, you should understand the difference between a *master document* (also called the frameset) and its component *framed documents*. A master document includes minimal HTML as it has been discussed so far in this book; its only real purpose is to provide a title for the display window, and to define the size and arrangement of the individual panes. It can also include <meta> tags that are to apply to the overall frame. Each pane within the window is a framed document—these are constructed using the full array of HTML tools you have learned so far (except, of course, for the title).

As an example, think of the daily listings of television programs commonly printed in newspapers and entertainment magazines. The "master document" in this case would be the grid as a whole, probably with a title across the top such as Listings for Sunday, January 4, 1998. Arrayed down through the listing would be a series of rows, one for each broadcast or cable channel. (Note that each of these rows stretches the width of the "display.") And within each row is a series of rectangles, whose width varies depending on the duration of the programs in each rectangle. Each row is a "framed document," consisting of a single column (if there is only one program for the entire time span covered in the particular grid) or of several. Each column in a multicolumn row is itself a framed document—and all these subframes can also be defined by HTML code in the master.

Within the master, the overall frame declaration begins and ends with <FRAMESET> tags, creating a container for the frames within. The ROWS and COLS attributes to the <FRAMESET> tag establish the dimensions of the individual containers. Rows describe the horizontal dimension, columns describe the vertical, as in a table. Basic markup for a frame—a master document subdivided vertically into two columns—is shown highlighted in HTML Example 6-1.

HTML Example 6-1   Frame Tags with Column Definitions—frex01.html

```
<html> <head>
<title>Frames Example #1 </title>
</head>
<FRAMESET COLS="100, *">
<frame src="frdata01.html">
<frame src="frdata02.html">
</FRAMESET>
</html>
```

If we wanted, we could substitute ROWS for COLS to create a window subdivided horizontally. Again, note that there is little markup here, except for the frame definition itself.

Creating Frames

In HTML Example 6-1, <FRAMESET=COLS="100,*"> makes two columns, side by side. The value 100, separated by a comma, followed by an asterisk, indicates that the frameset will consist of one column 100 pixels wide, and a second column using the rest of the available space. If you use absolute pixel values in both columns, the results are unpredictable, because the size of the browser window itself cannot be predicted.

1. **Load** Chapter6/frex01.html.

2. **View the HTML source with View Page Source.**
   Notice that within the frameset container the start of each single frame is marked by a <FRAME> tag. Since this is not a container, it has no end tag. The line:

   ```
   <frame src="frdata01.html>
   ```

   indicates the <FRAME> tag's SRC attribute—the source of the file (in this case fradata01.html) which will occupy the declared space.

Figure 6-1 shows the result of frex01.html as rendered by Netscape.

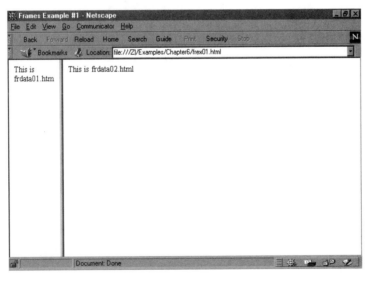

Figure 6-1   Two-Column Frame Format

Note – <FRAMESET> and <FRAME> tags do not go in the head of the document, nor do they go in the body. <BODY> tags must be placed in each framed document, but not in the master.

Changing Frame Column Sizes

In the previous example, columns were created with the COLS=100, * attribute to specify pixel widths. Columns can also be created in proportions of the display window, however many pixels wide it is at a given moment, using percentages, such as COLS=30%, 70%. If the sum of all percentage values within a frameset exceeds 100, proportions will be scaled.

HTML Example 6-2 shows the code for creating two columns using percentages to scale the size of the panes in the window, rather than absolute pixel widths.

HTML Example 6-2   Adjusted Two Column Frame—frex02.html

```
<html> <head>
<title>Frames Example #1 </title>
</head>
<FRAMESET COLS="30%, 70%">
<frame src="frdata01.html">
<frame src="frdata02.html">
</FRAMESET>
</html>
```

Figure 6-2 shows the result.

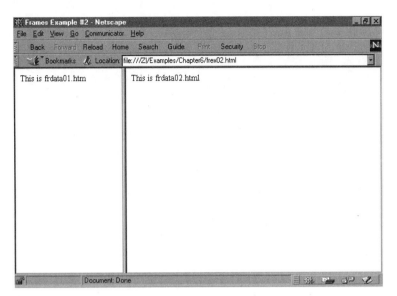

Figure 6-2   Frame Column Sizing with Percentages

Creating Horizontal Frames

Just as vertical columns can be defined in percentages, so can rows. HTML Example 6-3 uses the `<ROWS=30%,70%>` to make horizontal window panes sized proportionately to the overall height of the frameset. If desired, row heights can also be specified in pixels, like column widths.

HTML Example 6-3   *Frame Rows—frex03.html*

```
<html> <head>
<title>Frames Example #1 </title>
</head>
<FRAMESET ROWS="30%, 70%">
<frame src="frdata01.html">
<frame src="frdata02.html">
</FRAMESET>
</html>
```

Notice how vertical and horizontal adjustments scale in the result, shown in Figure 6-3.

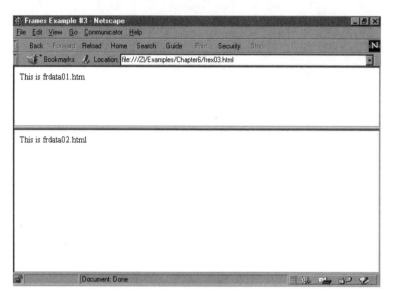

Figure 6-3   Vertical Frames Using Percentage

Creating a Compound Frame

When rows and columns are combined in the same frameset container, they can be expressed together as in HTML Example 6-4. In this example, a 2 x 2 grid is defined. The columns are sized absolutely (in pixels), the rows as a proportion of the window height.

Each window pane in the grid requires its own frame source file, identified separately: Since there are four cells in this 2 x 2 grid, there are four <frame> tags with corresponding src= attributes.

HTML Example 6-4   Markup for Compound Frame—frex04.htm

```
<html> <head>
<title>Frames Example #1 </title>
</head>
<FRAMESET COLS="200,*" ROWS="10%, 90%">
<frame src="frdata01.html">
<frame src="frdata02.html">
<frame src="frdata03.html">
<frame src="frdata04.html">
</FRAMESET>
</html>
```

1. **Load** `Chapter6/frex04.html`.

2. **View the HTML source with View Page Source.**

Figure 6-4 shows the order in which the source files are displayed. Notice also that when the size of the file exceeds window space, scrollbars automatically appear.

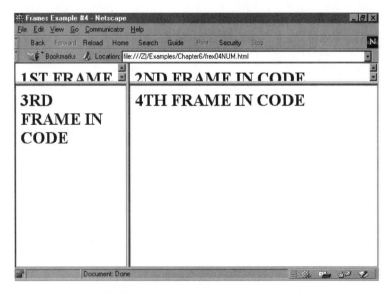

Figure 6-4   Ordering of Source Files for a Compound Frame—frex04.html

Figure 6-5 shows the result of the code in HTML Example 6-4.

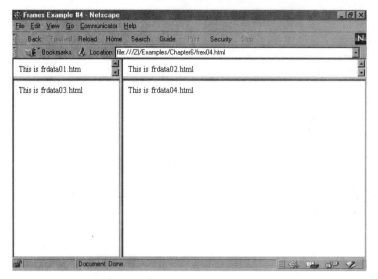

Figure 6-5   Compound Frame Using Horizontal and Vertical Windows

Creating the Nested Frame

To create a more complex window, a subframe can be nested inside a larger space. HTML Example 6-5 creates three rows, the middle row consisting of two nested frames. Here the code `<FRAMESET ROWS="100,*,100">` produces two equal fixed-pixel rows (one at the top, the other at the bottom), with the middle row filling the remaining space.

Two columns are declared in the nested frameset:

```
<FRAMESET COLS="30%,70%">
```

Two closing tags are required, one for each `FRAMESET` (the outer and the inner).

1. **Load** `Chapter6/frex05.html`.

2. **View the HTML source with View Page Source.**

HTML Example 6-5   Markup for Nested Frame—frex05.html

```
<html> <head>
<title>Frames Example #1 </title>
</head>
<FRAMESET ROWS="100, *, 100">
<frame src="frdata02.html">
<FRAMESET COLS="30%, 70%">
        <frame src="frdata01.html">
        <frame src="frdata04.html">
</FRAMESET>
<frame src="frdata03.html">
</FRAMESET>
</html>
```

Notice the order of the code lines in the markup identifying the source files and compare them to Figure 6-6 describing the way they appear in the window.

Note – In this HTML example, notice that we have indented the nested frame definitions. This is not required and has no effect on how the browser interprets or displays the code. However, it is a good device to use when you start nesting framesets in order to keep from getting "lost."

The browser fills the rows with source files in the order in which they are declared, filling from left to right. The contents of the middle row are established by the nested <FRAMESET> container, which itself defines two framed documents in the lines:

```
<frame src="frdata01.html">
<frame src="frdata04.html">
```

Since the text overflows the leftmost column in this row, a horizontal scrollbar appears to let the user move the hidden text into view.

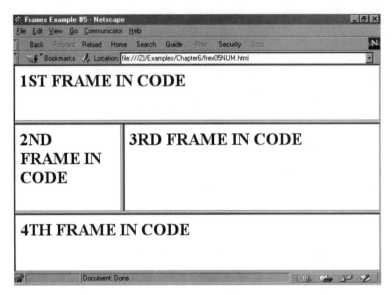

Figure 6-6   Ordering of Source Files in Sample Nested Frame

Figure 6-6 identifies where each of the files in the following code example appear on the display. Figure 6-7 shows the result.

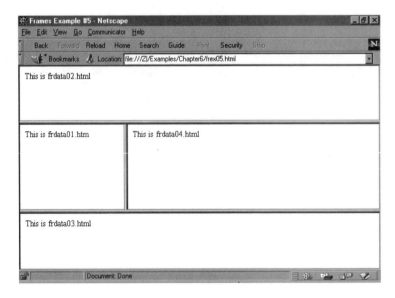

Figure 6-7   Compound Nested Frame

Creating a Named Frame

In Chapter 3 we saw an example of a named anchor in an HTML document. This example used <A NAME="apple">Apple Growing Areas</A> to take the viewer to a specific place in a document. Similarly, we can name a frame—allowing the named frame to act as a *target* in which other frames may display their contents.

A named frame looks like:

```
<frame src="frdata05.html" NAME="nav">

<frame src="frdata04.html" NAME="content">
```

In this case the name nav has been assigned to the file frdata05.html, and the name content to the file frdata04.html.

The HTML code in HTML Example 6-6 shows the use of named files in the markup.

HTML Example 6-6   Markup for Named Frame—frex06.html

```
<html> <head>
<title>Frames Example #1 </title>
</head>
<FRAMESET COLS="100, *">
<frame src="frdata05.html" NAME="nav">
<frame src="frdata04.html" NAME="content">
</FRAMESET>
</html>
```

Having named the frames, look at the source for frdata05.html. (For convenience, it is shown below in HTML Example 6-7.)

1. Load Chapter6/frdata05.html.

2. View the HTML source with View Page Source.

HTML Example 6-7   Markup for Target Frame—frdata05.html

```
<html> <head>
<title>Navigation Sample Page </title>
</head>
<body>
<A HREF="frdata06.html" TARGET="content">This</A>
will load content in the content window.
<P>
</body>
</html>
```

Adding the TARGET= attribute to the anchor tag tells the browser, "When the user clicks on this hyperlink, open the new document *in the frame named herein.*" Since we previously (in frex06.html, the master document for the window as a whole) named frdata04.html as content, the line

```
<A HREF="frdata06.html" TARGET="content">This</A>
```

gives a target frame where frdata06.html should be loaded.

Note – In this example, the master document initialized the frame named content to frdata04.html. When the user clicks on the hyperlink in frdata05.html, the latter's contents replace frdata04.html with the new document. In order to return to the frame's previous contents, the user must use the browser's "Back in Frame" feature rather than the simple Back button. This can lead to a certain amount of confusion. (We trust you are not among the confused, however.)

Figure 6-8 shows the way the named files are loaded, with navbar loaded into the first column, and content loaded into the second. A hyperlinked keyword in the first column activates the loading of another file into the content frame.

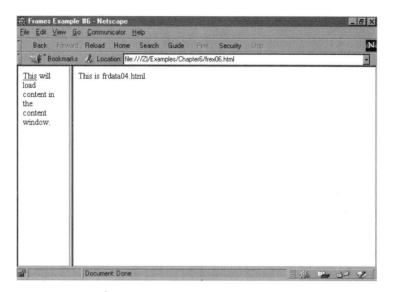

Figure 6-8   Named Frames

The TARGET attribute can also be used with <FORM>, <BASE>, and <AREA> tags. <FORM> is used when a form is to be displayed in a target window, <BASE> when most links are targeted in the same window, and <AREA> when a shaped area of an imagemap forces the load of the linked document into a target window.

Special Frames

Special frames introduce special ways of using the TARGET attribute. Most TARGET names must begin with an alphabetic character. The exceptions, sometimes called "magic" names, are _blank, _self, _parent, and _top.

The attribute _blank replaces the entire visible window with a new window. _self loads into the pane from which the anchor was clicked (the originating window). _parent loads into the immediate FRAMESET parent, if any, and defaults to _self if there is none. _top loads into the entire screen and defaults to acting like _self if the document is already at the top. This is useful for breaking out of deep FRAME nesting.

Begin by looking at the frames for named files:

1. **Load** Chapter6/frex07.html.

2. **View the HTML source with View Page Source.**
   The window panes are filled with named frames navbar, content, and glossary identified in HTML Example 6-8.

HTML Example 6-8   Special Frames HTML Tags—frex07.html

```
<html> <head>
<title>Frames Example #1 </title>
</head>
<FRAMESET COLS="100, *">
<frame src="frdata02.html" NAME="nav">
<FRAMESET ROWS="10%, 80%,10%">
      <frame src="frdata03.html" NAME="navbar">
      <frame src="frdata07.html" NAME="content">
      <frame src="frdata02.html" NAME="glossary">
</FRAMESET>
</FRAMESET>
</html>
```

Figure 6-9 shows the order in which the special frames are loaded. The numbers refer to the data files which load into them, based on the code in HTML Example 6-8.

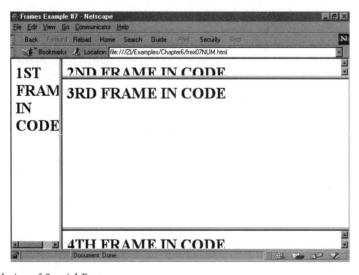

Figure 6-9   Ordering of Special Frames

The content frame named in the above example, containing frdata07.html, is shown below in HTML Example 6-9. This content frame defines four targeted windows: _blank, _self, _parent, and _top, activated by four occurrences of the anchor word >This<.

HTML Example 6-9   Special Frames Tags—frdata07.html

```
<html> <head>
<title>Navigation Sample Page </title>
</head>
<body>
<UL>
<LI><A HREF="frdata06.html" TARGET="_blank">This</A>
will load content in a new window.
<LI><A HREF="frdata06.html" TARGET="_self">This</A>
will load content in the same window.
<LI><A HREF="frdata06.html" TARGET="_parent">This</A>
will load content in the parent window.
<LI><A HREF="frdata06.html" TARGET="_top">This</A>
will load content in the topmost window.
</UL>
<P>
</body>
</html>
```

The result is shown in Figure 6-10.

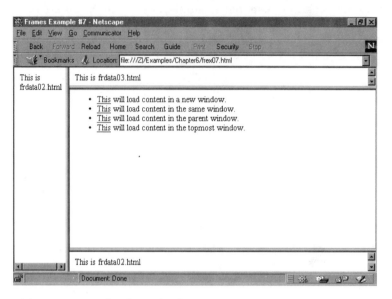

Figure 6-10   Special Frames Example—frex07.html

What About No-Frame Clients?

Some browsers cannot display frames. To accommodate them, put messages in
<NOFRAME> tags. Notice the <NOFRAME> tags are used at the end of the regular frame
tags *in the master document*, not the individual framed documents.

Note – Since the only route to the individual frames is through the master, a frames-
impaired browser can't get to them this way. It is therefore a good idea to provide an
alternate route to your site's content for such users—perhaps with a more conventional
table of contents or index document. In fact, you can even include within the
<NOFRAMES> container the entire HTML to display such a conventional "menu," rather
than a simple message as in the below example. Such a message can frustrate the no-
frames user.

Frames-aware browsers ignore the contents of the <NOFRAMES> container.

HTML Example 6-10 shows the NOFRAMES tag at work with the previous example so that
it can be displayed on a no-frames browser.

HTML Example 6-10   No-Frames Tags—frex08.html

```
<html> <head>
<title>Frames Example #1 </title>
</head>
<FRAMESET COLS="100, *">
<frame src="frdata02.html" NAME="nav">
<FRAMESET ROWS="10%, 80%,10%">
        <frame src="frdata03.html" NAME="navbar">
        <frame src="frdata07.html" NAME="content">
        <frame src="frdata02.html" NAME="glossary">
</FRAMESET>
</FRAMESET>
<NOFRAMES>
This will be displayed on a non-frames browser.
</NOFRAMES>
</html>
```

Scrolling

There are occasions when you may want to limit scrolling of a frame's contents. (For example, if you place a company logo in a banner frame across the top of the window.) Normally scrolling automatically occurs if the text to be displayed exceeds the window or frame size chosen. By preventing scrolling, you can force the window to confine the image.

Note – Do not force "no scrolling" for text frames as this may truncate text, particularly if the user resizes text.

HTML Example 6-11 shows the same three rows in the nested frameset as in the previous example, with "no scrolling" assigned to the top frame. The SCROLLING="yes" attribute in the middle frame's definition need not have been specified, since the default is to allow scrolling.

HTML Example 6-11   No-Scrolling Tags—frex09.html

```
<html> <head>
<title>Frames Example #1 </title>
</head>
<FRAMESET COLS="100, *">
<frame src="frdata02.html" NAME="nav">
<FRAMESET ROWS="10%, 80%,10%">
      <frame src="frdata03.html" NAME="navbar" SCROLLING="no">
      <frame src="frdata07.html" NAME="content" SCROLLING="yes">
      <frame src="frdata02.html" NAME="glossary">
</FRAMESET>
</FRAMESET>
<NOFRAMES>
This will be displayed on an non-frames browser.
</NOFRAMES>
</html>
```

Figure 6-11 shows the result. Note that the top row in the right column no longer has a scrollbar.

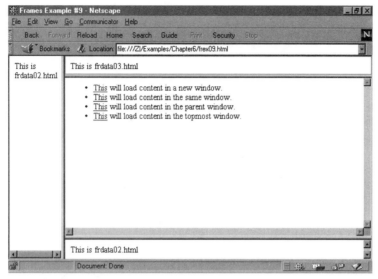

Figure 6-11   No-Scrolling Example—frex09.html

Establishing Margins

For greater control over where text appears within a pane, you can create margins using the attributes `MARGINWIDTH` and `MARGINHEIGHT`. In HTML Example 6-12, the `MARGINHEIGHT="30"` attribute forces the top margin of the `content` frame to drop by the designated number of pixels. The `MARGINWIDTH="20"` attribute shifts the contents of the frame that many pixels to the right.

HTML Example 6-12   Margin Tags—frex10.html

```
<html> <head>
<title>Frames Example #1 </title>
</head>
<FRAMESET COLS="100, *">
<FRAME SRC="frdata02.html" NAME="nav">
<FRAMESET ROWS="10%, 80%,10%">
      <FRAME SRC="frdata03.html" NAME="navbar">
      <FRAME SRC="frdata07.html" NAME="content" MARGINHEIGHT="30"
```

HTML Example 6-12   Margin Tags—frex10.html

```
              MARGINWIDTH="20">

          <FRAME SRC="frdata02.html" NAME="glossary">

</FRAMESET>

</FRAMESET>

<NOFRAMES>

This will be displayed on an non-frames browser.

</NOFRAMES>

</html>
```

Figure 6-12 shows the result.

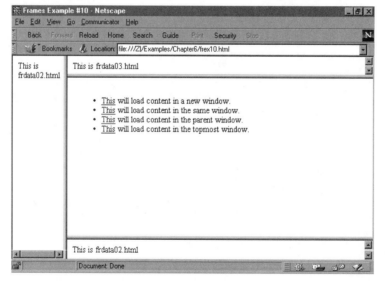

Figure 6-12   Frame Margin Example—frex10.html

Design Concerns

In working within frames, a few simple guidelines help your work appear more visually attractive.

- Don't make frames too small. If scrolling is on, users will probably have to scroll more often than not to see the frames' contents; if off, the frames' contents may never be entirely visible.

- Don't use too many frames. This creates a jigsaw-type effect—perhaps useful if your intention is to complicate your user's view of your pages, but not generally an effective way to structure information.

- Allow reasonable gutters around images so scrollbars don't occur.

- Ideally, only the main content window should scroll.

Summary

In this chapter, you learned:

- How to create a frame.

- How to arrange frames using different dimensions.

- How to make sure a file appears in the frame where you want it, by using named frames as targets.

- How to accommodate a "no-frames" browser.

6

Tags Used in This Chapter

Tag	Attribute	Description
`<FRAMESET>`		Encloses the individual frame definitions (requires a `</FRAMESET>` stop tag)
	`ROWS=`	Defines the number of rows in the frameset
	`COLS=`	Defines the number of columns in the frameset
`<FRAME>`		Defines the start of a new window (frame) within a frameset
	`SRC=`	Defines the source file to be loaded into the window
	`NAME=`	Names the window (frame)
	`MARGINHEIGHT=`	Defines the vertical margin around the window
	`MARGINWIDTH=`	Defines the horizontal margin around the window
	`SCROLLING=`	Defines whether scrolling should be employed
`<A>`		
	`TARGET=`	Identifies the specific window into which the HREF document will be loaded

Using the Common Gateway Interface (CGI) 7 ≡

Displaying Web information on a user's client, like a browser, is a good start. However, it is even better to be able to *customize* the information sent to the client—better still, to *receive* information from it. Web servers can execute scripts and programs using data that a client sends and then pass the results of these programs and scripts back to the client. External processing on the Web has been standardized with the Common Gateway Interface (CGI).

This chapter discusses basic CGI principles and then demonstrates an elementary CGI application, creating clickable server-side imagemaps. Later chapters will look at more advanced CGI techniques, including the use of forms to gather and process user-provided data.

Note – CGI programming is a *server-side* technology. That is, the client program (the browser) knows nothing about how to process CGI program code; this code is run by the server, which takes various actions (for example, formatting an HTML page which *can* be viewed by the browser) depending on conditions spelled out in the code. For this reason, unlike with earlier examples in this book, in order to develop and test CGI applications you will have to use a Web server as well as a browser. If you do not have an account with an Internet service provider (ISP) which lets you run CGI programs, you will have to use a Web server program running on your local computer.

The CD-ROM accompanying this book comes with two server programs: Apache (for UNIX-based computers) and O'Reilly Associates WebSite 2.0 (for Windows 95/NT-based computers). Examples in this chapter use the WebSite Server; the appearance of your own screens and other implementation details may vary slightly.

Also note that in order to give control to the server rather than your browser, all URLs in this chapter must be entered starting with http://{servername}—you cannot simply open the HTML files as in earlier examples. The latter lets the browser interface directly with the code, bypassing the server, and your CGI programs will not work.

7

Ultrabasics: What's a "Program"?

Note – If you are already familiar with programming principles, by all means skip this section and proceed directly to Where's the Gateway?, below.

In its simplest form, a program is just a sequence of commands that instruct a computer to behave in various ways. A UNIX shell program or an MS-DOS batch file fit into this category: One line instructs the computer to perform action A, the next to perform B, the next to perform C, and so on. You run the program simply by typing the filename.

More elaborate programs add other concepts to that of simple sequence. These concepts include:

- Conditional processing: If condition 1 is true, perform step A; otherwise, step B.

- Repetition: Perform step A *n* times. Perform step B until condition 1 is true.

- Branching: If condition 1 is true, branch to section B of the program.

- Subroutines: Run another program at this point; when that program is complete, return to this point in the main program and continue on.

Programs are written in *languages*—words, punctuation marks, and other ASCII codes, entered into a text file by the programmer according to some standardized syntax which the computer (or another programmer!) understands, but which a user of the program does not need to understand in order to run it. Some languages are *interpreted*. This means that the code in which they're written is read and processed by a utility program (the interpreter) in the same form as entered by the programmer. Interpreted programs are commonly referred to as *scripts*. Simple examples of script languages include both the UNIX shell and MS-DOS batch language.

Another kind of program goes through an intermediate step: The code entered by the programmer is first passed to a special utility program on the computer, called a *compiler*. The compiler reads the code and translates it from its human-readable form into more efficient *machine code,* a (usually lengthy) series of bits not intended, as the saying goes, for human consumption. You compile a program once, and from then on its executable form can be run directly on the same kind of machine that it was created on. Examples of compiled languages include Fortran, C, and C++.

Whether to use an interpreted or a compiled language for CGI programming is a matter of trade-offs:

- Interpreted languages generally have simpler syntax and are therefore easier to write and debug. Furthermore, because interpreters are less dependent than compilers on platform specifics, scripts are generally more portable from one platform to another.

There are two downsides: performance and (possibly) security. Running a script always adds the overhead required by the interpreter to that required by the true purpose of the script. And because a script is in readable ASCII format, it may be unsuitable for some purposes in which you want the processing never to be visible, such as a program which generates passwords.

- Compiled languages, on the other hand, are generally powerful and tend to have correspondingly elaborate (even mysterious) syntax. They come with complete libraries of subroutines to perform standard tasks, such as financial and mathematical operations, that would be tedious and error-prone to develop yourself. Debugging a compiled program, especially a complicated one, can be tedious. The best you can do is include enough error-handling processing so that an error that occurs will point you to the section of the readable ASCII code where it happened; then you change the code, re-compile the program, and try again. The primary advantage of compiled code is performance—the compiled program is directly executable on the target machine, without requiring the compiler's intervention every time it's run.

We will cover a number of basic programming constructs in this book, but *HTML for Fun and Profit* can't begin to cover all the ins and outs of programming. If you're interested in details beyond the scope of this book, you should obtain reference materials specific to the language you want to learn.

Note – HTML is a formatting language, not a programming language. It is possible, using new technologies such as JavaScript, to embed true programs within HTML code; however, to speak of "HTML programming" is to misuse the *English* language.

Where's the Gateway?

Obviously, the *Common* in Common Gateway Interface refers to the fact that its behavior is standardized; *Interface* is likewise easy to understand. But what about *Gateway*—what is it a gateway from, and what is it a gateway to?

Simply put, a CGI program acts as a gateway between program output and input. The "output" in that sentence refers typically to data from a document displayed in a Web browser, which are passed as input to the CGI program; the program processes these data, and as its own output creates a different document. Aside from visible raw data fed from a web page, input to a CGI program can also be in the form of variables passed to the CGI program, but hidden from the user. Similarly, the program's output can be straight text or HTML dynamically generated by the CGI program, as well as data from other input sources, such as a database kept on the server. You might say that the gateway transforms the output of a user action to the CGI program's input, and that the CGI program itself transforms its input into a new, customized output stream.

This notion of output transformed into input and back again will be familiar to aficionados of the UNIX operating system, where it is integral from the simplest command lines on up through the most complex C and C++ programs. In UNIX, the standard source of input is called *stdin* (pronounced "standard-in") and of output, *stdout*. When you use a pipe (the | character), for example, you're passing the standard output from one program as standard input to the other.

Normally, the UNIX shell's `pr` command is used to print a file to the terminal; used by itself on the command line, it will simply wait patiently as you key data into it. When you conclude the keyboard entry with an end-of-file character, everything you just typed is displayed on the terminal. What you type at the keyboard is the UNIX default for *stdin*. What's displayed on the terminal is *stdout*. But with a pipe character you can connect the `stdout` of one command to the `stdin` of another, as in this example (not particularly useful for any purpose other than illustrating the pipe concept, by the way):

```
ls | pr > filelist.txt
```

In this case, the `ls` command (which normally displays the contents of a directory) passes its *stdout* to the pipe, which transforms *stdout* to *stdin* for processing by the `pr` command. (The output from the `pr` command in this example is not displayed but copied into a text file with the > character. This is another, more subtle form of transformation.)

(DOS users can also use pipes in some cases. The DOS command type `filename.txt |`
`more` passes the output of the `type` command to the `more` command, which displays the contents of `filename.txt` one screen at a time.)

The pipe acts as a rudimentary gateway between the output of one program and the input to another. In this sense, a CGI program is just a complex pipe. The Common Gateway Interface is the environment (like the UNIX or DOS shell) in which the CGI program runs.

Figure 7-1 depicts this process in graphic form.

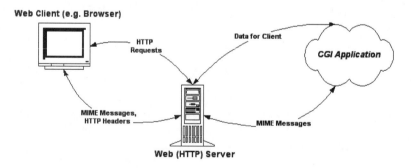

Figure 7-1   Overview of the Common Gateway Interface

Directory Assistance

Aside from the general notions of *stdout*, *stdin*, and the transformation of one into the other using program code, it will also be helpful at this point if you understand some things about the typical directory structure that CGI programs operate in.

First, of course, on your server there will be a document root directory (as discussed in Chapter 3). Here (or in a set of subdirectories) is where your normal HTML documents, images, and so on reside.

Next, you should set aside at least one subdirectory for storing your programs (whether interpreted or compiled). This directory must be readable by any users who will be running the programs, and the programs themselves (especially if compiled) need to be executable. Commonly this directory is referred to as *cgi-bin*, whether or not that is the actual name of the directory. (Often that *is* its name, though; one very common sign that a CGI program is in control of the content displayed in your browser is when the browser's URL field contains cgi-bin as part of its path.)

Finally, if using an interpreted language for your CGI programs, you need to have some place on the server where the interpreter resides. This directory needs to be readable by all users, and the interpreter must be executable. (Whether it is on the user's path is immaterial, since the script informs the server where to look.)

CGI Basics

Perl

In this book, we will be using the language Perl for our CGI examples. Perl is an acronym for "Practical Extraction and Reporting Language." It is an interpreted language which has attained widespread popularity as a CGI tool. Most web servers come with a Perl interpreter. (The accompanying CD-ROM includes Perl interpreters for both the UNIX and the Windows 95/NT platforms.)

The "extraction" in Perl's full name refers to its powerful abilities to extract meaningful data from a stream of input characters. The "reporting" reflects the language's capability as a formatter of output. Put those two classes of behavior together and (it should be obvious) Perl is an excellent tool for transforming a given program output into different input (and vice versa).

7

Note – You don't need any high-wattage software to create Perl scripts: a simple text editor, such as Windows NotePad or UNIX vi, is all that's necessary. The extension for Perl script files is usually .pl (for example, getdate.pl). Remember to store your scripts in a directory of their own. We will use the directory /cgi-bin/ in our examples throughout this chapter; substitute your own executable directory as needed..

Perl "Reporting"

Let's first take a look at the "reporting" that Perl does. If you've used report writers from other languages or from database applications, you probably think of a report as a hard-copy document, more often than not data represented in rows and columns, with reportwide and/or page headings, footings, and the like.

With typical CGI programs, output is directed not to a printer and not (at least directly) to the user's screen, but to the user's browser. And what does a browser understand? Right: HTML code and plain text. For this reason, by far the most common use of CGI programs—Perl in particular—is the generation of HTML. Rather than remaining static in a file, though, CGI-generated HTML is dynamic, created on-the-fly depending on the logic coded in the CGI program itself.

The HTML you've coded so far in this book generally starts with an <html> tag. There's an "invisible" piece of information normally provided to the browser by the server, though, and your CGI program must supply this unseen information itself (since it, and not the httpd, is in control of the process at this point). The information normally provided by the server is the *content type*. This content type is related to the MIME types discussed in Chapter 4; it tells the browser, in effect, "You're about to receive a stream of data of type X."

In Perl, a content type of straight ASCII text is announced to the browser with a line that looks like this:

```
print "Content-type: text/plain \n\n";
```

What's going on here?

- print is the Perl command that creates a line of text to be sent to standard output. It's followed by the actual text to be sent to standard output, surrounded by quotation marks. Because the word print is not within the quotation marks, it is processed by the Perl interpreter but is not itself passed to the browser.

- Content-type: says to the browser, "Here is the MIME type of the forthcoming data."

- text/plain is the standard way of specifying a MIME type of ASCII text.

- \n is a newline character; it has same the effect as if you had pressed the Enter key on your keyboard. Two newline characters equate to "hit the Enter key twice"—that is, they insert a blank line at that point. (One newline terminates the present line; the second inserts the actual blank line.) This blank line is necessary to separate the content-type definition from the actual text that is to follow. If you omit these newlines, your CGI program will generate an error message.

- Finally, the closing ; is the standard way of terminating a Perl command. It says to the interpreter, "That's all for that command"—and (like `print`) it does not get passed to the browser. *Every Perl command is terminated by a semicolon.*

At this point the browser isn't actually displaying anything—it's waiting for the stream of input text that the content-type definition has just warned it to expect. (In fact, if you were to stop entering commands in your CGI program at this point and execute it, the Netscape browser will display an error message, "Document contains no data.") The remainder of a simple Perl script will consist of nothing more than a sequence of further print statements, each followed by some plain text or HTML code (in quotes) and terminated by a semicolon. The program itself terminates when the interpreter reaches end-of-file in the script, and at that point the generated page is displayed in its entirety on the user's display.

Note – How does a server know that the message it has just received from the user's browser is a request to run a program, rather than to return a document directly? Simple. When the server parses the URL it has received and determines that the URL is in the executable directory, the URL is not used to retrieve and serve a new document but instead is passed to the CGI for execution.

In the examples below, substitute the correct path to your own Perl files for the cgi-bin path. Also remember to substitute the name of your own server in place of *{server}*.

A Basic CGI Script

1. **In your browser's URL field, load:** `http://{server}/cgi-bin/hello.pl`.
   A simple "Hello world!" message is returned in a fixed-width font. You can use View Page Source to examine the output generated by the `hello.pl` program.

2. **Examine the file** `/cgi-bin/hello.pl` **with a text editor (or with** `more` **if operating in the UNIX environment).**
   When executed, this displays the text following the `print` command. No output device is mentioned. When the destination (the output device or file) is not defined, the results of the script are passed directly back to the `httpd` and forwarded to the requesting client.

   Note that the message is displayed in the browser in a fixed-width font because the content-type of this program's output is specified as text/plain.

3. **Load** `http://{server}/cgi-bin/hellonone.pl` **in your browser.**
   Instead of the message printed by the above script, an error message is received.

4. **Examine the file** `/cgi-bin/datenone.pl` **with a text editor or with** `more`.
The only difference between the `hellonone.pl` and the `hello.pl` scripts is the following line, found in the `hello.pl` script:

```
print "Content-type: text/plain \n\n";
```

It is important to return the `Content-type` line before the actual data. The server has problems with data when it doesn't know how to return those data to the client.

Perl Extraction

In many ways, Perl's extraction features—the ways in which a Perl script can extract and process data passed to it—are much more powerful than how it formats its output. In this respect, Perl follows in the footsteps of many other programming tools that started out in UNIX—sed, grep, awk, and the like.

This chapter will not cover any of Perl's input-processing features (although the `textcgi.pl` script used in some of the examples demonstrates some elementary features). We will examine these capabilities in greater detail in Chapter 10. Remember, though, that Perl (and other CGI technologies) are not restricted to handling data passed in from forms; that is merely their most common use.

Perl Variables

In any program, some information is constant from one execution to the next. Numbers are a good example of this—2 always "means" the same thing—as are strings of text such as "Mary had a little lamb. Its name was John, you know."

If programs were able to process only constant data, they would be of little practical use (they would always produce the same result). For this reason, a feature common to all programming languages is the ability to manipulate *variables*.

In general, a variable is a string of characters that is not a constant and is not a word reserved for use by the programming language in question. (When the Perl interpreter sees the word `print`, for example, it knows to perform the action associated with that command.) The exact names of the variables are determined by the programmer.

In Perl, simple variables (referred to as *scalars* for reasons not particularly important for our purposes here) are named with a character string starting with a dollar sign $. (The names of arrays, discussed below, begin with an "at sign," @.) So although `print` is recognized as a reserved word by the Perl interpreter, `$print` is assumed to be a variable name (albeit not a particularly descriptive one). The first character after the $ must be a letter, and the remainder (if any) of the variable's name can be any combination of letters, digits, or the underscore character (_). A valid variable name, for example, might be `$Good_Stuff_1`. (Certain "built-in" variables consist of just the `$` and another special character, such as `$]`, which returns the Perl interpreter's version.)

Unlike some other languages, Perl makes no determination of the type of a variable (integer, string, floating point, or what have you) based on the name. The type of a variable is simply determined by the type of its contents. Look at this code fragment:

```
$x = 268;
$x = "The Heart of the Matter";
```

Here the variable `$x` is first assigned an integer value, and then a string.

Also unlike some other languages, Perl variable names *are* case sensitive. `$goodstuff` and `$GoodStuff` refer to two different variables.

CGI Environment Variables

A standard component of almost all programming languages is the use of *environment variables*. These are variables that do not need to be set explicitly by a program—the environment (the CGI, in this case) "knows about" them implicitly. The CGI implementation provides several preconfigured variables which vary slightly from server to server. Refer to Table 7-1 at the end of this chapter for a list of environment variables that apply to various platforms.

5. **Load:** `http://{server}/cgi-bin/testcgi.pl` **in your browser.**
   This file displays in the browser window all the environment variables from Table 7-1 and their current values. If the value of a given variable is blank, it is either not a supported environment variable on your platform or has no meaning in the present context.

   If you view the `testcgi.pl` script in a text editor or with `more`, note that environment variables are referred to with slightly different syntax than standard scalar variable names. Environment variables are kept in a special type of variable, called an array (discussed further below). You refer to individual elements within this array of variables, called $ENV, by referencing the corresponding names, enclosed in "curly braces" {} and double quotes (e.g., `$ENV{"CONTENT_LENGTH"}`).

Path Usage

The path of the `cgi-bin` script is important. (The script itself need not necessarily be in the root of the cgi-bin directory, however.)

The URL that calls a CGI script or program may be longer than the path to the script itself. This additional path information is stored in the PATH_INFO variable and can be used by the script.

For example, in the URL

```
http://{server}/cgi-bin/directory/script.pl/additional/
```

- http://{server}/cgi-bin indicates that the remainder of the path is an executable program. The presence of the executable cgi-bin directory anywhere in the path is sufficient to make this determination.

- directory is examined to see if it is a script or program to run. Since it is neither, it is examined to see if it is a directory, which it is. The CGI looks for a script in the directory directory.

- script.pl is then examined to see if it is a script or program to run. Since it is a script, everything after script.pl, namely additional, is placed into the PATH_INFO environment variable, and script.pl is executed (receiving PATH_INFO as well as other environment variables).

6. **Load:** http://{server}/cgi-bin/testing/testcgi.pl.
   Notice that scripts can be executed anywhere within the directory structure that has been defined as executable—in this case, in the testing subdirectory of the normal cgi-bin directory. Thus, scripts can be organized into subdirectories by general function, user type, and so on, in order to make the scripts easier to work with.

7. **Load:** http://{server}/cgi-bin/testcgi.pl/testing.
   In this case, the script is found at the top level of the cgi-bin tree. The path information after the script name is still retained (testing) but assigned to the PATH_INFO variable. This information can be used to call HTML files for customization before returning them to the client.

Passing External Variables, or Arguments

As explained in Chapter 3, variable information can be appended to the end of the URL following a question mark. This information will be passed into the CGI script to use or ignore, as the programmer has provided for. Although the term "variable" is sometimes used for data passed in this manner, more commonly such data items are referred to as *arguments*.

In Perl programming, as in C and other languages with their roots in the UNIX operating system, the arguments passed to the program are captured in a special variable called argv (short for "argument value"). This is actually not a single value, but an *array* of values, which makes it possible to process more than one argument. Individual values are identified as *elements* of the argv array. The number of elements in the argv array is stored in another special variable, called argc ("argument count").

Note – Newcomers to programming languages that originated in UNIX are sometimes familiar with the notion of arrays but confused by the way in which these languages refer to individual elements. You might think that the first element of an array is element #1. However, Perl (and others) refer to the first element as #0, because it is *offset* zero elements from the start of the array. The value of argc follows this convention: If there is one argument passed to the program, then argc will be 0; if 2, then argc is 1; and so on. Although this seems to fly in the face of logic, it actually simplifies the processing of argv, which typically occurs in a loop from the "0th" (that is, the first) element to the one corresponding to argc.

The following steps use the same testcgi.pl script used above. However, by appending a question mark and some other text to the name of the script, additional information is passed into the script. Direct your attention in these three steps to the lines in the browser's display labeled "ARGV element(s) passed:" and "QUERY_STRING =".

8. **Load:** http://{server}/cgi-bin/testcgi.pl?testing.
   In this case, the word testing becomes a command-line argument to the script. This information appears in both the ARGV data and in the variable QUERY_STRING. The question mark (?) in a URL originally indicated that the text after the ? constituted a query. Use of the question mark has since been expanded for use by any CGI script.

9. **Load:** http://{server}/cgi-bin/testcgi.pl?testing+test1.
   In this case, the QUERY_STRING variable is identical to the input after the question mark (testing+test1). However, note that this is treated in ARGV as two arguments, each on its own line. The plus (+) character between individual components of a query string enables them easily to be parsed into separate variables.

10.**Load:** http://{server}/cgi-bin/testcgi.pl?testing%2btest1.
   In this case, there is only one argument shown in ARGV, and it includes the *literal* + sign, as opposed to the + used to break the string up into multiple arguments as in the previous step. When you need to pass a special character such as the plus sign itself into the script, use a percent sign (%) followed by the ASCII equivalent of the special character. Here, the value 2b is the ASCII equivalent of a +, which forces the plus sign to be included in the ARGV list.

Note – Additional parsing items of note are covered in the section Basic CGI Input and Output in Chapter 9, where they are used.

HTML Output from CGI Programs

In the above examples, the output of the Perl program was displayed in the browser window in a fixed font such as Courier. This is the default for browsers when displaying a content type of `text/plain` (or when displaying a file whose extension is `.txt`, which is mapped onto that content type.) Additionally, none of the typical "look and feel" of a GUI browser display is available with plain text CGI output.

To render a page using HTML code, start by replacing the `Content-type: text/plain` line with one specifying `Content-type: text/html`. Also, use the line break `<br>` and paragraph break `<p>` tags in place of newline characters (*except* the newlines at the end of the content-type definition). Remember that these tags (as well as any other HTML tags you want to use) must appear within the quotation marks.

Note – The newline character \n may continue to be useful as you develop CGI programs. Inserting it within the generated HTML code causes the code itself to be broken up across lines; if you do not use the newline, the HTML code when viewed in the browser's View Source window will simply appear on one enormous line (depending on how text is wrapped).

---

11. **Load** `http://{server}/cgi-bin/testcgi2.pl` **in your browser.**
    The contents of this display are identical to those of the earlier examples, except that they have been formatted with more of a "Web look." The browser's title bar displays some information, sections of the display are broken up with headings and horizontal rules, and individual elements are displayed as bulleted lists.

12. **Examine the** `testcgi2.pl` **file with a text editor or with more.**
    As you can see, the contents of this file are very similar to those of `testcgi.pl` used in earlier examples, with HTML codes used to format the resulting "document." Also note the content-type definition at the start of the file, which specifies `text/html` instead of `text/plain`. (If the content-type were left unchanged, the browser would display the resulting page contents in the same way that your browser's View Page Source does: as a string of HTML code.)

    Any Perl program can create a document on-the-fly in this way, using any HTML code at all within the quotation marks which follow the `print` commands. (Remember that `print` "prints" to standard output, which by default is the browser window and not a real printer.)

As a rule, especially for pages that will have complicated formatting such as tables, you will find it easiest to follow these steps in creating a Perl script to generate an HTML-formatted document:

- Create the HTML code first, using whatever HTML editor or other tool you normally use, and save the results in a file of type .htm or .html. Remember to include the <html>, <head>, and <body> containers as well as the page contents themselves.

- Use placeholders such as "USER'S NAME HERE" for any information which will vary when the program itself runs.

- Load the document in your browser to be certain the appearance is as desired. If not, modify the HTML markup and other document contents until the look is right.

- Once the HTML has been debugged, rename the HTML file with a .pl extension and move it (if it's not already there) to the cgi-bin directory.

- Edit the file and insert the content-type definition at the top. Be sure to specify a type of text/html.

- Using the global search-and-replace feature of your HTML editor or other text editing utility, insert print " (including the opening quotation mark) at the start of each line of the file. Also append "; (the closing quotation mark and the semicolon) at the end of each line. (If you want the document's source HTML to be formatted line by line instead of on a single line, also insert a newline \n before the closing quotation mark.)

Note – Perl optionally uses a special syntax (borrowed from the UNIX shell) referred to as the "here document" (think "print this stuff right *here*") which can greatly simplify the generation of HTML in CGI programs. Instead of using multiple print statements as described above, follow a structure something like the following:

> print <<*marker*;
> *{straight HTML code}*
> *marker*

You can use any string you want for *marker*; if you put such a block of code in a Perl script which generates the document's head, for example, you might begin the block with print <<HEAD and end it with HEAD. Printing begins at the line following the print <<*marker*; command and continues down to the line immediately before *marker* (on a line by itself, with no surrounding whitespace). The HTML code embedded between the two occurrences of *marker* does not need end-of-line semicolons or any other "Perlisms," making the conversion from working HTML to working Perl much simpler.

- Confirm that the Perl program is formatting the page correctly by loading it in the browser (using a server, of course—not just by opening it as a file). Make any necessary changes to the embedded HTML code before proceeding.

- Replace the "placeholders," if any, with variable names or other data.

- Finally, add any "pure CGI" code (such as loops for processing the `argv` array, file handling, and so on). From this point on you should not need to change any embedded HTML, only CGI program logic.

Making Server-Side Clickable Images

In Chapter 4, we discussed how to make both server- and client-side imagemaps. As mentioned in that chapter, the latter form of imagemaps (new in HTML 3.2) has a number of advantages over the older server-side imagemaps. However, building server-side imagemaps remains a useful way of understanding CGI processing.

Server-side imagemaps can be implemented with CGI scripts. A clickable image is created by defining regions such as squares, circles, and other polygons around within the image. The coordinates of each region are then associated with a URL in a configuration file specific to the image; together, the image and the configuration file constitute a server-side imagemap. In the HTML code for a page with a server-side imagemap, the `usemap=` attribute to the `<img>` tag tells the server where to find the region definitions—the value of the tag is the URL of the imagemap configuration file.

Note – In the following examples, use `http://{server}/Chapter8/getpoints.html` to determine the boundary values for your image regions. It is currently set up to use a default image. If you want, modify it with the name of a different image of your own choosing and use it to obtain coordinates for areas other than those in the examples. This `getpoints.html` page returns an `x,y` pair for each spot that you click on. Then, click on the Back button to return to the image to get values for the next point.

Steps in Making a Clickable Image

- Get a GIF image. The image must be in GIF format.

- Define the coordinates of the desired clickable areas.

  Follow the steps below to identify the coordinates of each region on an imagemap.

1. **Load** `http://{server}/Chapter8/getpoints.html`.
   For our example we will use the image `/Chapter6/web16.gif`. This image is loaded by the `getpoints.html` file.

   The first region to define is a rectangular (approximately square, in this case) region around the dollar sign.

2. **Click on the upper-left corner of the square with the dollar sign in it.**
   The x and y coordinates of the point that you selected are displayed on the screen. Results: Example 7-1 shows an example.

Results Example 7-1 Coordinates for the Square Region

```
Query Results

You submitted the following name/value pairs:


X=456

y=87
```

The numbers that you get may be slightly different from the ones shown here. You are selecting a specific pixel in the image. On some screens you may not be precisely at the same spot.

3. **Record these numbers and then click on the Back button.**
   You still need to select one more point to define the square region—the diagonally opposite (bottom-right) corner.

4. **Click on the lower-right corner of the square with the dollar sign in it.**
   A square can be described by two points, upper left and lower right or upper right and lower left.

5. **Record these numbers and then click on the Back button.**
   You have the coordinates for the square.

   Now define a circular area in the image. A circle is defined by two points as well: the center point and a point anywhere along the edge of the circle.

6. **Click on the center of the circle.**
   The x and y coordinates of the point that you selected are displayed on the screen.

7. **Record these numbers and then click on the Back button.**
   You need to select one more point to define the circular region.

8. **Click on a point anywhere on the edge of the circle.**
   Record these coordinates as well.

   Next, you will define a polygon—in this case a simple triangle. A polygon is a shape with n points (that is, pairs of x,y coordinates) defining the edges. For example, a triangle is a polygon with three points defining the edges.

9. **Click on one of the triangle's vertices.**
   Record these numbers and then click on the Back button.

   You need to select two more points to define the triangle region.

10.Click on a second point on the triangle.
Record these numbers and then click on the Back button.

11.Click on a third point on the triangle.
Record these numbers.

You should now have recorded the necessary information to build a configuration file defining a square (rectangle), a circle, and a triangle.

- Make the imagemap configuration file with a text editor.

The imagemap file will contain one line for each area that is to be active. It will also contain a definition for default, so that the program won't fail if the user clicks outside of all defined regions. If the regions overlap, then the one that is defined first in the imagemap file is returned. Code Example 7-2 illustrates this.

Code Example 7-2   Imagemap Specification

```
# Comments are indicated with a # sign
default     http://{system}/imagedefault.html
rectangle   http://{system}/imagesquare.html      456,87 510,54
circle      http://{system}/imagecircle.html       222,46 261,18
polygon     http://{system}/imagetriangle.html     420,2233,8233,18
```

- **If on a UNIX server, make or add to the** `imagemap.conf` **file, using a text editor.** This file goes in different directories depending on each UNIX server. Specify the full pathname to the imagemap file, not to the `httpd` modified path. As with the imagemap file, use # to comment out text.

- Create the HTML documents that are referred to in the imagemap file.

- Create the HTML document that calls the imagemap program.
To define an image as a client-side imagemap, create the image with the <IMG SRC=*path*> definition and surrounded with an anchor, just as when you converted an image to a button in Chapter 4. There are two differences between creating that button and creating a clickable image.

- The anchor tag has an additional attribute, called ISMAP.

- The URL in the anchor points to the imagemap *program* for UNIX servers, and to the imagemap file itself for the Windows NT server.

A UNIX example looks like Code Example 7-3.

Code Example 7-3   Creating a Clickable Image in UNIX Systems

```
<a href="http://{system}/cgi-bin/imagemap/demo">
<img src="http://Chapter8/web16.gif ismap">
</a>
```

In UNIX, as shown above, the anchor should be a link to the imagemap program with the name of the imagemap configuration file after the imagemap command, so that it will be stored in the PATH_INFO environment variable.

A Windows NT server example looks like Code Example 7-4.

Code Example 7-4   Creating a Clickable Image in Windows NT Systems

```
<a href="http://{system}/demo.map" ISMAP>
<img src="http://Chapter6/web16.gif">
</a>
```

On a Windows NT system, the anchor references the imagemap configuration file itself. The call to the imagemap program is not used.

Summary

In this chapter you learned:

- It is important to return a definition of the data that are coming back. Many browsers experience errors when the Content-Type isn't defined.

- Perl is an excellent tool for CGI scripting because of its inherent capabilities to process output from user/browser display interactions and to convert its own output (via simple print statements) into further input to the browser, in the form of HTML.

Environment Variables

Table 7-1   Environment Variables under CGI

Variable Name	Description
AUTH_TYPE	Protocol-dependent authentication method used to validate the user (if running the script requires authentication, of course).
CONTENT_LENGTH	Length of the content (provided by the client, not calculated or otherwise determined by the server).
CONTENT_TYPE	When a query has other information attached to it (e.g., data passed from a POST operation), this shows that information's content type.
DOCUMENT_ROOT	The value of DocRoot for this server.
GATEWAY_INTERFACE	Version number of the CGI specification that is server complies with.
HTTP_ACCEPT	Content (MIME) types this server can process.
HTTP_REFERER	URL that issued the particular request (the "link-from" document).
HTTP_USER_AGENT	Browser name and version number (use with care—there are nearly 1000 valid values).
PATH	Path(s) for CGI executables on this server.
PATH_INFO	The "extra information" following the actual path to and name of the particular CGI script as represented in the URL.
PATH_TRANSLATED	PATH_INFO, translated as necessary (including virtual-to-physical file mapping) by the server.
QUERY_STRING	Information following the ? in a URL which executes the particular script. (URL-encoded, e.g., with each space replaced by + and carriage return/line feed combinations represented as %0D%0A.)
REMOTE_ADDR	IP (Internet protocol) address of the host machine from which the particular request originated.
REMOTE_HOST	Name of the host machine from which the particular request originated. May not be available in all cases, and if it's not, it is supposed to be set to REMOTE_ADDR.
REMOTE_IDENT	Dependent on functionality installed on the server, this is the "remote user name" returned from the server.
REMOTE_USER	Authenticated user name (assuming that running the script requires user authentication, of course).
REQUEST_METHOD	The method employed by the particular request, e.g., GET, POST, etc.

Table 7-1   Environment Variables under CGI

SCRIPT_NAME	Virtual path (URI) to the script.
SERVER_NAME	Server's host name; may appear either as a domain name, e.g., servername.domain.com, or as an IP address, e.g., 111.11.111.
SERVER_PORT	Port number to which the particular request has been directed (usually 80 by default).
SERVER_PROTOCOL	Name and version of the protocol associated with the particular request.
SERVER_ROOT	Directory where the server resides.
SERVER_SOFTWARE	Name and version of the server software.

Note: Not all of these environment variables will be available on every server, or for every request. Also note that several additional environment variables are available using Server Includes (see Chapter 8).

HTML for Fun and Profit

Server Includes

Additional files, the contents of CGI and other variables, and volatile information such as the modification date of any local HTML document can all be included in a document returned by the server. This feature is called *server includes* or *server side includes* (commonly referred to as SSI). Most (but not all) current-generation servers, including the Apache and WebSite servers on this book's CD-ROM, support at least some SSI features.

There are a few caveats to the use of server includes, as we explain below. In general, however, if your server (and its sysadmin policies) support their use, you should become familiar with them — they will make the difficult job of changing your site on a regular basis much simpler and less subject to error.

Server-side includes were first introduced with the NCSA httpd server. They have been enhanced since their introduction, particularly with the Apache server project (which was based on the NCSA httpd); the most recent additions to SSI — commonly referred to as extended server side includes, or XSSI — are marked in this chapter as **New in Apache 1.2**. (Not all servers, including those which support the basic SSI commands, will support these recent extensions.)

Note – Like the CGI scripts introduced in Chapter 7 and delved into further in Chapters 9 and 10, the examples in this chapter require that a server be running in order to view the files successfully. For this reason, the examples' instructions here specify that you view the files not simply by opening them, but by using `http://{server}/path_to_document` as the URL.

Configuring for Server Includes

SSI is not necessarily automatically enabled when server software is installed. While the exact steps to enable it vary from server to server, the following two conditions must *always* be met:

- The server must be able to recognize that a file contains (or potentially contains) SSI instructions. Just as with image files (`.gif` or `.jpg`), various multimedia files (`.mid`, `.au`, `.mpg`, and so on), and even plain text (`.txt`) and HTML files (`.htm` and `.html`), the use of SSI is signaled to the server by the use of a filename extension that defines a new MIME type — usually `.shtml`. Most servers also provide a mechanism for specifying that regular HTML files should be scanned for SSI directives; this can be a big convenience for the developer (no need to worry about maintaining a second file type), but can present a performance problem in actual use on an active website. (See the drawbacks listed below for more information on this.)

- Because SSI is a sort of "executable HTML," any directory that is to contain SSI files must be assigned permission as an SSI directory. This is not the same kind of permission that is set through the operating system itself. Rather, one or more control files (plain text files) identify directories specifically as having (or not having) SSI permission. Two kinds of permissions are involved, *include* and *executable*, and a given directory can have one, both, or neither permission.

Downsides of Server-Side Includes

Obviously, we still haven't covered even the basics of what you can do with server includes. Before diving into the fun part, though, you might want to seriously consider three possible but significant drawbacks to using this powerful tool.

No Ability to Use SSI At All

This drawback may or may not apply in your case: Some web hosting services do not allow the use of *any* server include processing. There may be various reasons why they have made this decision, but usually the reasons are one of the other two reasons listed here. (Of course, if you are administering your own web server, you will have to decide the matter for yourself.)

Performance Hits

In order to process a regular HTML file, a server doesn't need to do much work at all (as such things go): It simply delivers the document to the requesting client, which interprets and displays the various text, tags, and attributes.

A server include file, however, contains special instructions to the server. These instructions must be carried out *before* delivering the document to the user's browser. The process of reading an SSI file and performing any specified actions is called *parsing*, and — especially if there are many such actions — can add not only to the server load, but to the response time necessary to deliver the document to the user.

On the other hand, because many SSI files contain only one, two, or a half-dozen such instructions, the performance hit may be scarcely noticeable (though it will always be present).

Note that performance problems can be greatly exacerbated if the server administrator has specified that regular HTML files are to be parsed. Many — perhaps most — HTML files will contain no SSI instructions at all (hence effectively wasting the server's processing on unnecessary parsing). For this reason, requiring *all* HTML files to be parsed is not recommended.

Potential Security Holes

Many web hosting providers allow the use of SSI *include* directives but expressly disallow at least a portion of the possible *execute* directives. This is because one form of the latter enables the SSI file to execute operating system commands, such as deleting files, mailing files, and so on.

A bit more obscure, but not to be overlooked, is that a CGI script run via SSI might inadvertently pass to the server user data which itself invokes SSI to perform otherwise forbidden — or at least unintended — actions (such as mailing a file). This can be worked around by ensuring that all CGI scripts parse the user's input for angle brackets (< and >, which can signify the start/end of an SSI instruction) and either strip them out or replace them with more innocuous characters before actually serving the page. (Of course, if your script does find evidence of such activity, it would also be wise to log the event for further investigation, and perhaps notify the server's sysadmin.)

Basic SSI Syntax

There's no particular magic at work here: SSI instructions are as simple to code as HTML itself. (Naturally, by now we hope that you're finding *that* to be simple.)

An SSI instruction is inserted into the body of an otherwise normal HTML document and follows the pattern of this template:

```
<!--#command attribute="value".  .  .  -->
```

The `<!--` and `-->` should be familiar to you by now; they are the standard opening and closing of an HTML (actually SGML) comment. Because SSI commands are enclosed in comments, if you open the file directly rather than through your server (as explained in the note at the beginning of this chapter), they will have no effect at all on the document displayed — it will appear as if the SSI instruction has been omitted altogether.

The pound-sign (#) character immediately following the opening `<!--` tells the server, "This is not a true comment but an SSI directive; parse it now and perform the requested action before displaying the rest of the document." Because of this special meaning to the server, it is strongly recommended that you avoid using the pound sign within true comments.

The commands, attributes, and values which follow the pound sign are detailed below. The ellipsis (. . .) is not entered literally but is used here to indicate that some commands can take more than one attribute/value pair at a time.

Finally, note that there is a space between the last attribute/value pair and the closing `-->`. This is to ensure that the server does not confuse the instruction itself with the `-->` which terminates it.

> **Note** – Some reports have indicated that you cannot include a "hard carriage return" within an SSI directive. We haven't experienced this ourselves, perhaps because we haven't been using a particular OS/server/version combination, but you should be aware of the possibility when coding your own server-side includes.

Including Other Files

One of the most dreadful tasks to confront a webmaster is updating a line or two of HTML code — especially if it's complex, such as a table — in 40 or 50 different documents. For example, let's say you have developed a menu bar that is displayed across the top of every page, and a standard footer (the name of your site, your address, and so on) for the bottom of every page. A week or two later you need to add another menu selection, and the e-mail address in the footer has changed. In order to ensure consistency across your site, using plain old HTML you now have to edit every single document. Even with a "search and replace across all documents" feature in a current-generation HTML editor, this prospect can daunt the most happy-go-lucky webmaster.

Server `includes` provide a simple solution to this problem: Put the header and footer (in this case) into two files separate from the main documents; where the header and footer would appear in the main documents, add an SSI `include` directive. When the server parses one of the main documents, it grabs the contents of the document to be included at that point and pulls them into the text being returned to the user's browser, just as if they were embedded in the document to begin with. In order to change the menu or the footer, just change the `included` file.

The `include` directive looks like this:

```
<!--#INCLUDE FILE="earth.gif" -->
```

or like this:

```
<!--#INCLUDE VIRTUAL="/Examples/Chapter8/earth.gif" -->
```

The difference between the `FILE` and the `VIRTUAL` attributes is that `FILE` specifies a path relative to the current document; `VIRTUAL`, a path relative to the DocumentRoot of your site. In many cases you can use either (as long as you supply any required path information relative to the base path), but note these restrictions as well:

- The `FILE` attribute's value cannot include `../`, and it can't be an absolute path.

- The `VIRTUAL` attribute's value cannot contain a protocol (`http://`, `ftp://`, etc.), only the path and (optionally) a query string.

Which one you use for your purposes will be a matter of taste and convenience.

Note that wildcards are not expanded in the attribute's value in either case. So you can't, for example, automatically include all files with the same file specification, such as menu*.shtml. To create this type of configuration, you will need either to include all files separately or to execute an external script. (See Executing Programs in Another Way later in this chapter.)

New in Apache 1.2: However, you *can* use variables in the value of either the FILE or the VIRTUAL attribute, and the variables will be replaced with whatever their values are. See the discussion of variable substitution below for details.

In the example which follows, a simple include virtual command causes the contents of one file to be inserted into another at run time.

1. **Load** http://{*server*}/Chapter8/siinc1.shtml.

2. **View the original file with a text editor or with the** more **command.**
   The server include command is displayed in boldface below, in HTML Example 8-1.

   (Also note, by the way, that in this case the file to be included has an .html extension. This is arbitrary; it could have been .txt or .shtml instead. You should try to maintain consistency, however, so that the extension of any file, whether it is intended just to be included or otherwise, truly reflects its contents.)

HTML Example 8-1   Including a File with the Virtual Attribute

```
<html> <head>
<title>   </title>
</head> <body>
<!-- this is a comment -->
This is a server include.<P>
<!--#include virtual="/Examples/Chapter8/include.html" --><P>
<address>

</address>
</body> </html>
```

3. **View the HTML source with View Page Source.**

Notice that the document source displayed by the browser contains only regular text, *without* the server include instruction: The server replaced the server include with the contents of the included file, *before returning the web page.* The resulting code is shown below, in Example 8-2.

HTML Example 8-2   The HTML That the Browser Receives

```
<html> <head>
<title>    </title>
</head> <body>
<!-- this is a comment -->
This is a server include.<P>
<!-- this is a comment -->
This is the included text <P>
<address>


</address>
</body> </html>
```

4. **Load** `http://{server}/Chapter8/siinc2.shtml`.

5. **View the original file with a text editor or** `more`.

The same file was called with a different method, but the result is the same.

Note – You can nest included files. That is, a file to be included may itself contain server include directives.

Including Information *about* Files

When you are surfing on a slow connection, 14.4 kbps, for example, it is really irritating to find that an interesting file turns out to take five minutes to download (*after* you've begun the download) or, sometimes worse, is a year or more out-of-date (which you generally learn only after you've endured that annoying download wait).

If you're responsible for a site which offers files for download, use SSI to place the size of a file and/or its modification date in the document that refers to it, so you can give people an idea of what to expect.

Adding File Sizes

The size of a specified file is listed in a document with the FSIZE element and either the VIRTUAL or the FILE attribute. As with the INCLUDE element, the FILE attribute gives the filename of a file relative to the original document. An example of this is:

```
<!--#FSIZE FILE="earth.gif" -->
```

The VIRTUAL attribute defines a file relative to DocumentRoot. An example of this is:

```
<!--#FSIZE VIRTUAL="/Examples/Chapter8/earth.gif" -->
```

1. **Load** http://{server}/Chapter8/sisize1.shtml.

2. **View the original file with a text editor or with the** more **command.**
   Note that the size display works equally well regardless of the method (FILE or VIRTUAL) for referencing the file.

Changing Size Formats with config

In the examples above, the size is listed in kilobytes. There may be times when you want to change this formatting. The CONFIG element changes the formatting of the information returned from the FSIZE element. The CONFIG element must come before the server include directive to which it applies.

The SIZEFMT attribute defines size formatting. It has two possible values: BYTES, which lists the size of the file in bytes; and ABBREV, which abbreviates the value to either Kbytes or Mbytes, depending on the size of the file. ABBREV is used by default.

```
<!--#CONFIG SIZEFMT="BYTES" -->
```

or:

```
<!--#CONFIG SIZEFMT="ABBREV" -->
```

Note – The above two size formats do not work with the WebSite server. Website uses formatting codes derived from the C programming language's *printf* function—e.g., %d for decimal numbers.

---

1. **Load** http://{server}/Chapter8/sisize2.shtml.

2. **View the original file (shown below, HTML Example 8.3) with a text editor or with** more.

8

HTML Example 8-3   Including and Formatting File Sizes

```
<html> <head>
<title>   </title>
</head> <body>
<!-- this is a comment -->
This is a server include.<P>
<!--#config sizefmt="bytes" -->
The size of include.hmtl is
<!--#fsize file="include.html" --> bytes.<P>
<!--#config sizefmt="abbrev" -->
The size of siinc2.shtml is
<!--#fsize virtual="/Examples/Chapter8/siinc2.shtml" -->.
<address>


</address>
</body> </html>
```

Dating Document Changes

The last modification date of a specified file is listed in a document with the FLASTMOD element and either the VIRTUAL or the FILE attribute. As with the INCLUDE element, the FILE attribute gives the filename of a file relative to the original document. An example of this is:

```
<!--#FLASTMOD FILE="earth.gif" -->
```

The VIRTUAL attribute defines a file relative to DocumentRoot, the same way VIRTUAL is handled in the above two server includes. An example of this is:

```
<!--#FLASTMOD VIRTUAL="/Examples/Chapter8/earth.gif" -->
```

1. **Load** http://{server}/Chapter8/sidate1.shtml.

2. **View the original file with a text editor or with** more.
   The date of the file's most recent modification is returned with both methods.

Changing Date Formats with `config`

In the examples above, the date is displayed in *day-month-year-timeofday* format. There may be times that you want to change this formatting. The CONFIG element changes the formatting of the information returned from the FLASTMOD element. The CONFIG element must come before the server include element whose configuration it should modify.

The TIMEFMT attribute changes date formatting. This format is very customizable; Table 8-1 summarizes the common available options. In general, a percent sign and letter combination, such as %a, is used to indicate the date format.

Some examples are:

```
<!--#CONFIG TIMEFMT="%a %b %e, %Y %l %M %S %p" -->

<!--#CONFIG TIMEFMT="%m/%d/%y %T %Z" -->
```

Table 8-1   Time and Date Formatting with TIMEFMT

To Format This Time Period	Use This Code	To Display	Examples
Year	%y	two-digit year	97
	%Y	four-digit year	1997
Month	%b	abbreviated month name	Dec
	%B	full month name	December
	%m	number of the month	12
Week	%S	Sunday week number (1-53)	52
	%W	Monday week number (1-53)	52
Day	%a	abbreviated day of the week	Wed
	%A	full day of the week	Wednesday
	%w	number of the day of the week	04
	%j	day of the year	365
	%d	day of the month (no leading 0)	9
	%e	day of the month (leading 0)	09
	%D	full date	12/31/97

Table 8-1   Time and Date Formatting with TIMEFMT (continued)

To Format This Time Period	Use This Code	To Display	Examples
Time	%l	hour (1-12 format clock)	11
	%H	hour (1-24 format clock)	23
	%M	minutes	32
	%S	seconds	57
	%Z	time zone	EST
	%p	AM or PM	PM
	%T	full colon-separated time	23:32:57
Full local time	%c	day, date, and time all at once	Wed Dec 31 23:32:57 1997

If you are on a UNIX system, something like the above may be recognizable as the the output of the `man strftime` command.

1. **Load** `http://{server}/Chapter8/sidate2.shtml`.

2. **View the original file (as shown in HTML Example 8-4) with a text editor or with** `more`.
   Notice the date formats used in the server include `config` elements, and how the result is displayed differently.

HTML Example 8-4   Including and Formatting Dates

```
<html> <head>
<title>    </title>
</head> <body>
<!-- this is a comment -->
This is a server include.<P>
<!--#config timefmt="%a %b %H:%M:%S %p %Z" -->
The modification date of include.hmtl (abbreviated weekday,
abbreviated month, time, AM/PM, time zone) was
was <!--#flastmod file="include.html" --><P>
<!--#config timefmt="%A" -->
The modification date of siinc2.shtml (full day of the week) was
```

HTML Example 8-4   Including and Formatting Dates (continued)

```
<!--#flastmod virtual="/Examples/Chapter8/siinc2.shtml"-->
<address>

</address>
</body> </html>
```

Echoing Variables

Server includes can display all the environment variables that CGI programs can, and a few more. These variables can be included in a document with the ECHO element. The only attribute for this element is VAR. An example is:

```
<!--#ECHO VAR="DOCUMENT_NAME" -->
```

1. **Load** `http://{server}/Chapter8/siecho1.shtml`.

2. **View the original file with a text editor or with** more.
   Notice that the variable DOCUMENT_NAME is called here. This is a variable that isn't available in CGI.

3. **Load** `http://{server}/Chapter8/siecho2.shtml`.
   HTML Example 8.5 lists the environment variables that can be used only with server includes.

HTML Example 8-5   Listing Environment Variables Used with Server Includes

```
<html> <head>
<title>   </title>
</head> <body>
<!-- this is a comment -->
This is a server include.<P>
Document Name: <!--#echo var="DOCUMENT_NAME" --><P>
Full Document Name: <!--#echo var="DOCUMENT_URI" --><P>
QueryString: <!--#echo var="QUERY_STRING_UNESCAPED" --><P>
Local Date: <!--#echo var="DATE_LOCAL" --><P>
Date (GMT): <!--#echo var="DATE_GMT" --><P>
Last modified on:<!--#echo var="LAST_MODIFIED" --><P>
```

8

HTML Example 8-5   Listing Environment Variables Used with Server Includes (continued)

```
<address>

</address>
</body> </html>
```

Note that the `LAST_MODIFIED` variable functions the same as if a `flastmod` directive had been inserted, except that it is always the date of the last modification of the current file, not some other file. Also note that date returned is the date of the file containing the server include itself; if you put a `LAST_MODIFIED` variable in a file to be included, such as a common footer, the modification dates will be those of the including files, not of the footer.

A complete list of the environment variables available under CGI appears at the end of Chapter 7.

New in Apache 1.2: With the introduction of Apache version 1.2, your SSI files gain a couple of additional variable-handling features.

First, the `printenv` element (no attributes) will now print out a list of *all* environment variables in one shot; this can simplify debugging a problematic configuration, since you no longer have to construct `echo` directives for every single one.

Probably more importantly, Apache 1.2 has added a `SET` instruction to create your *own* variables which can be echoed and used as attribute values in other server include instructions. The format of the `SET` instruction is:

```
<!--#set varname="value" -->
```

where *varname* is the name of the variable as you will later be using it, and *value* is (obviously) the variable's value. Note that *value* can itself be the name of an environment or other variable as well as a literal string.

Using `SET` at the top of an SSI file, for example, you could set a variable to the time when the server first began parsing the document, and a second variable (placed at the end) to *that* time. Displaying these two times via `ECHO` directives following the second `SET` would give you a sense of how long the server actually took to parse a particularly large document.

Executing Programs in Another Way

Scripts and programs can be run from within an HTML form using the Common Gateway Interface, or via hyperlink (such as with a server-side image map). We discuss how to do this more fully in Chapter 7, Chapter 9, and Chapter 10. However, depending on the permissions set by the server's sysadmin, you can also run programs and CGI scripts by using the server include EXEC element.

One advantage of using server includes for this purpose is that more than one script can be run per page. Also, the programs run passively, without requiring user intervention (such as clicking on an image map or a form's Submit button).

However, you must be aware of one caveat about using server includes for this purpose: Everything that is returned by the program must have HTML formatting tags or it will be displayed as text formatted with <PRE>.

(A further caveat, as we mentioned earlier in this chapter, is that your server sysadmin may have opted not to permit program execution via SSI. And if your server is Microsoft's Internet Information Server, or IIS, you can't run programs at all; as of this writing, only the INCLUDE directives are supported by IIS.)

There are two attributes, CMD and CGI, for the EXEC element.

The CMD attribute executes a program or script anywhere on the system, instead of being limited to specific directories that are configured as executable. An example is:

```
<!--#EXEC CMD="/usr/sbin/ping localhost" -->
```

1. **Load** http://{server}/Chapter8/siexec1.shtml.

2. **View the original file with a text editor or with** more.
   The system load is returned by calling uptime, which isn't in an executable directory tree.

The CGI attribute executes a CGI program or script found within any directory tree defined as executable, and returns the results:

```
<!--#EXEC CGI="/cgi-bin/test-cgi.pl" -->
```

3. **Load** http://{server}/Chapter8/siexec2.shtml.
   Notice that the results returned here are unformatted.

4. **View the original file with a text editor or with** more.
   The Perl script outputs a newline (\n) after each command. However, because the original page is an HTML page, the newlines are treated the same as all whitespace (just as they would be if you'd entered newlines in the original page itself).

5. **Load** `http://{server}/Chapter8/siexec3.shtml`.
This time the script uses a `<br>` instead of `\n` when formatting the document, and the layout appears correct.

6. **View the original file with a text editor or with the** `more` **command.**
Verify that a `<br>` was used instead of a newline.

7. **Load** `http://{server}/Chapter8/siexec4.shtml`.
This is the way to create a directory of items that you want to display and yet keep separate for easy cleanup. (On a Windows-based system, which doesn't use the `cat` command that appears in this example, you could substitute the `type` command for approximately the same results.)

Reporting Errors

If your document fails for any reason to read the included information, you won't get any error messages, but the added text won't be there, either. With SSI, you can notify the user that an SSI error has occurred, although you can't trap what *kind* of error. In cases where users don't have permission to read the additional information, it is better to remain silent about what they cannot see than tell them that they don't have permission. Furthermore, for hackers, the lack of permission is a challenge you may prefer not to issue.

However, there are times when you may want to find out how often an intermittent problem occurs. It is possible to enable error reporting with the `CONFIG` element and the `ERRMSG` attribute. This only reports that an error occurred. It doesn't specify the nature of the error, and you must supply the text of the error message. An example is:

```
<!--#CONFIG ERRMSG="Oops, something didn't happen here" -->
```

1. **Load** `http://{server}/Chapter8/sierr1.shtml`.

2. **View the original file with a text editor or with** `more`.
The system load should be returned by calling `uptime`; however, since there is no such command on the system, the error message is displayed.

New in Apache 1.2: You *could* under Apache 1.2 add some intelligence to your error messages by scattering multiple `SET` directives for the same variable throughout the SSI file, changing the value of the variable at each point to flag that location in the code; then, as the value of the `CONFIG ERRMSG` attribute, include not just some literal text, but also the name of your variable. Then as the value of the variable changed, the `ERRMSG` would itself change dynamically to indicate how far along the parsing had gotten at the time the error occurred.

New in Apache 1.2: Conditional SSI

Although SSI is still a long way from anything like a full-blooded programming language, the proprietors of the Apache project have introduced a bit of finer control over what your server includes can accomplish. This is done via a set of new XSSI "conditional" — flow control — elements that let you take one action if a particular condition is true, and other actions in other cases.

There are four of these elements, which work in tandem with one another: IF, ELIF, ELSE, and ENDIF. Except for ENDIF, the format of these elements is the same:

```
<!--#element condition --> action_to_perform
```

The *action_to_perform* can be plain old HTML or another SSI instruction. For example, consider the case of the following SSI code, which could be placed in a file of its own and included in SSI files via server includes:

```
<!--#if DOCUMENT_NAME="FirstChoice.shtml" -->

    <!--#include file="FirstOKAlternative.shtml" -->

<!--#elif DOCUMENT_NAME="SecondChoice.shtml" -->

    <!--#include file="SecondOKAlternative.shtml" -->

<!--#else -->

    <!--#exec cgi="cgi-bin/logit.pl" -->

    Sorry -- you can't include this document.

<!--#endif -->
```

This code checks to see if the current document name is FirstChoice.shtml, and if it is, includes a particular other file; if it is not, the code (with the ELIF element) checks to see if the current document is SecondChoice.shtml, and if so, includes a *different* file; and if the document is neither FirstChoice.shtml nor SecondChoice.shtml, the code logs the attempt (via the logit.pl Perl script) and informs the user that it is not possible to run this SSI code from within the current document. Instead of DOCUMENT_NAME, of course, you could substitute any variable — allowing conditional inclusion based on the browser with which the user is viewing your page, for example.

Should you decide to use flow-control SSI, the if and endif directives are required. If you decide to use the elif element, we recommend that you include an else to trap the "otherwise" cases.

The conditions specified in the example above are all "=" but there is a good selection of other tests you can perform. The complete list appears in Table 8-2. (Note that the Boolean operators || and && are used to check for *multiple* conditions simultaneously, by joining other conditional tests into single ones. In theory you could therefore nest conditions to an infinite level, although it is unlikely that a test of the theory would endear you to your server's sysadmin.)

Table 8-2   Conditional Operators Available with XSSI

Conditions	The Test Will Be True If
string	*string* is not empty
string1 = *string2*	*string1* and *string2* are equal
string1 ! = *string2*	*string1* and *string2* are *not* equal
string1 < *string2*	*string1* is less than *string2*
string1 <= *string2*	*string1* is less than or equal to *string2*
string1 > *string2*	*string1* is greater than *string2*
string1 >= *string2*	*string1* is greater than or equal to *string2*
! *condition*	*condition* is not true
condition1 && *condition2*	Both *condition1* and *condition2* are true
condition1 | | *condition2*	Either *condition1* or *condition2* is true

Note – At this time, these conditional tests can be performed only against *string* data. If you do not bear this in mind, some of your code can produce quite unexpected results. For example, if you are comparing two dates, the string "01/01/97" is *less* (i.e., earlier) than "02/01/75." To correct this kind of problem, be sure that you have formatted dates and other nonstring data to produce the results you are hoping for.

Summary

In this chapter you learned:

- Pages can be made from including other pages.

- Pages can be customized with information about files.

- Pages can be generated on-the-fly with scripts and programs.

SSI Elements Used in This Chapter

Element	Attribute	Description and Notes
CONFIG		Used in conjunction with the FLASTMOD and FSIZE elements to customize time and date displays. Also used alone to configure error messages.
	ERRMSG	Defines the error message string.
	TIMEFMT	Defines the date and time format returned.
	SIZEFMT	Defines the size format returned.
ECHO		Returns a variable value.
	VAR	Defines the variable to return.
EXEC		Executes a script or program.
	CMD	Defines the name of the program or script to be executed and that the program can be anywhere on the system.
	CGI	Defines the name of the program or script to be executed and that the program can only exist in an area defined as executable.
FLASTMOD		Displays the last modified date of a file.
	FILE	Defines the location of the document, based on the calling document.
	VIRTUAL	Defines the location of the document, based on the DocRoot variable.
FSIZE		Displays the size of a file.
	FILE	Defines the location of the document, based on the calling document.
	VIRTUAL	Defines the location of the document, based on the DocRoot variable.
INCLUDE		Adds the contents of a file to the document returned from the server.
	FILE	Defines the location of the document, based on the calling document
	VIRTUAL	Defines the location of the document, based on the DocRoot variable.
IF		Defines the first (or only) specific condition that must be met in order to perform some action. **(Apache 1.2)**
ELIF		Defines a subsequent condition that must be met in order to perform some action. **(Apache 1.2)**
ELSE		Defines the "otherwise" condition — perform some action if all other conditions in the flow-control block fail. **(Apache 1.2)**

ENDIF	Terminates an SSI flow-control (conditional processing) block. **(Apache 1.2)**
PRINTENV	Prints a list of all environment variables and their values. **(Apache 1.2)**
SET	Sets a variable for use by other SSI directives. **(Apache 1.2)**

Environment Variables

- DOCUMENT_NAME — The name of the file.

- DOCUMENT_URI — The full Universal Resource Indicator. Unfortunately, this variable displays only the full document path, based on the definition of the server's DocRoot variable.

- DATE_LOCAL — The date and time, based on the local system time.

- DATE_GMT — The date and time, based on Greenwich Mean Time.

- LAST_MODIFIED — Returns only the modification date of the web page itself. Use the FLASTMOD attribute of the ECHO element to obtain modification dates for other files.

Creating Forms 9 ≡

One of the best reasons for having the Common Gateway Interface is that two-way communication is possible through the use of HTML. The client can enter information by selecting buttons, pulling down or scrolling through menus, and entering text into data entry boxes. These interactive building blocks can be brought together and defined as a *form*.

This chapter covers how to create forms, including text entry fields, default values, attributes, radio buttons, pull-down menus, and scrolling lists. The main exercise in this chapter is the creation of a survey tool.

Two Perl scripts, `query.pl` and `testcgi.pl`, are used to display the results of the forms that are created. There are quite a few sample HTML files for this chapter. These forms look slightly different when viewed on browsers in the UNIX, Windows, and Macintosh environments. In addition, only sections of these files are reproduced in the text. It is a good idea to load these files and view the source. Chapter 10 discusses how to manipulate the data after they have been gathered.

Form Creation and Submission

Creating a form is a simple process. The most basic form looks like HTML Example 9-1.

HTML Example 9-1   Basic HTML Form Template

```
<html><head>
<title>Form Template </title>
</head><body>

<FORM ACTION="http://localhost/cgi-bin/query.pl" METHOD="POST">
<INPUT TYPE="submit">
</FORM>
```

```
<address>Me</address>
</body></html>
```

The basic form template consists of:

- **Basic HTML formatting** — Forms should have the five basic HTML tags: `<HTML>`, `<HEAD>`, `<TITLE>`, `<BODY>`, and `<ADDRESS>`. Not only is this a good practice, but also some servers cannot handle forms if the document is not declared to be HTML with the `<HTML>` tag.

- **Form declaration** — A form is declared with the `<FORM>` and `</FORM>` tags. Normally the form declaration would be in the body of the document.

- **Action definition** — The `ACTION=` attribute of the `<FORM>` tag lists the URL of the program or script that will process the data collected by the form. The action must be a call to the `http` service, because the CGI interface used to execute the `ACTION` is available only through the `http` service. If anything other than `http` is used as the service portion of the URL, the script is returned to the browser instead of being executed—which is not normally desirable.

- **Form method** — Form data can be passed to the CGI with either the `GET` or the `POST` method (the `method=` attribute of the `<form>` tag). The choice of method determines how the data are passed to the script or program defined by the `ACTION=` attribute. If a form is returned with `GET`, then the data are placed in the `QUERY_STRING` environment variable. If a form is returned with `POST`, then the data are passed via the standard input method for each operating system, usually referred to as `stdin`.

  As you saw in Chapter 7, `QUERY_STRING` is actually a single list of the variable(s) and argument(s) that are collected from the client and passed to the `ACTION` script. Since the length of the string is limited, the length of the `QUERY_STRING` is also limited. Thus, `POST` is the method of choice for large forms.

Note – At one time, `POST` was considered the wave of the future for forms. You should now think of it as the "wave of the present." Although the `GET` method is still available and functional, you should use the `POST` method for all new work.

- **Submission input definition** — The submission is most commonly an `<INPUT>` tag with the `TYPE="submit"` attribute. Forms can also be submitted with clickable images and single, text-box entries, as shown in the sections Clickable Images in Forms and Text Entry Fields, respectively.

Note – When defining attributes, use double quotes, even if there are no spaces in the attribute.

1. **Load** `http://{server}/Chapter9/form1s.html`.
   This form has only one button that will submit the form to the server for processing. This form is the same as the template shown in HTML Example 9-1. The button looks like the example on the left of Figure 9-1.

2. **Submit the query by pressing the** Submit Query **button.**
   The results of this query are as sparse as the form itself. No values are listed under the comment `You submitted the following name/value pairs:`

Me   Me

Figure 9-1   Buttons on Netscape Navigator

3. **Load** `http://{server}/Chapter9/form2s.html`.
   The button is now labeled Push Me, instead of Submit Query. The button looks like the example on the right of Figure 9-1.

4. **View the HTML source with View Page Source.**
   The definition for the button changed from:

        <INPUT TYPE="submit">

   to:

        <INPUT TYPE="submit" VALUE="Push Me">

   The label on the button was changed by addition of the VALUE attribute. Not all forms are for queries, and this is the way to change the Submit button label to accurately prompt the user.

HTML Example 9-1 is used as a template or starting point for most forms created in this chapter.

Clickable Images in Forms

A second method for submitting a form is with a clickable image in place of a button. With a clickable image, the x and y coordinates of where the image was clicked are returned with the other form information. This is how `getpoints.html` delivered the coordinates for constructing the imagemap file in Chapter 7. This method also provides some artistic control over the look of the submission button. On the downside, if users have Delay Image Loading set on their system, they will need to load the image in order to submit the form. This method should be used for submission only when you are certain that images will be loaded all the time.

A clickable image is placed in a form with the `<INPUT>` tag. The `TYPE="image"` and `SRC="href"` attributes are required. `NAME=value` is an optional attribute. The `NAME` attribute adds a variable name to the x and y coordinate data that are returned. This is useful when more than one clickable image is included in a form because it enables you to distinguish which image was clicked. Examples of this are:

```
<INPUT TYPE="image" SRC="http://{server}/Chapter10/earth.gif">
```

or:

```
<INPUT TYPE="image" SRC="earth.gif" NAME="First">
```

1. **Load** `http://{server}/Chapter9/form1i.html`.

2. **View the HTML source with View Page Source.**
   The `<INPUT>` definition here is the same as the first clickable image example above. The form here has only one input, the clickable image.

3. **Click on the image.**
   The results of submitting the form are that the x and y coordinates of where the image was clicked are returned as x={some number} and y={some number}. These numbers are the x and y coordinates of the location on the image where you clicked. This form was used in Chapter 7 in the section Making Clickable Images. Figure 9-2 illustrates the results.

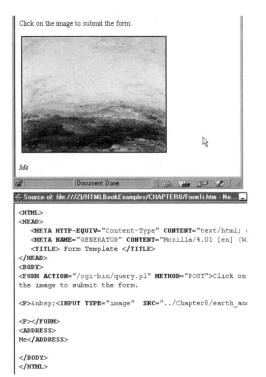

Figure 9-2   Using an Image for Submission, the HTML Behind It, and the Results

4. Load `http://{server}/Chapter9/form2i.html`.

5. View the HTML source with View Page Source.
The `<INPUT>` tag has an additional attribute called `NAME`.

6. Click on the image.
By adding a `NAME` attribute the *x* and *y* coordinates of the image become `name.x` and `name.y`. The x={*some number*} and y={*some number*} shown in the first example now become `testing1.x`={*some number*} and `testing1.y`={*some number*}. Figure 9-3 illustrates this step.

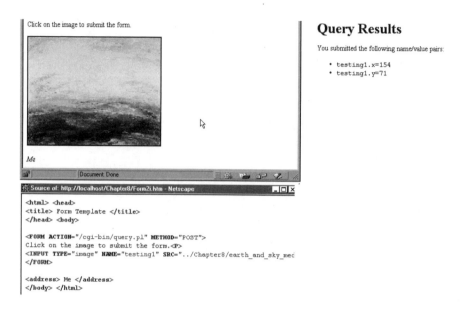

Figure 9-3   Submitting an Image with a Name, the Page HTML, and Results

Buttons

The previous forms were definitely simple. In most cases, however, in order to collect data you must ask questions of your users, not simply have them click on "hot spots." One way to do so is to ask the given question and provide a set of predefined answers, which the user can choose among by clicking on buttons rendered on the screen.

Radio Buttons

Radio buttons are buttons that work together. (The term *radio button* refers to old-style radio push-button tuners. You could select only one button at a time: When you pushed one in, any other that was already in popped out.) Two or more radio buttons are used as a set when the question can have only one response. A typical example of this would be a yes-or-no question. Two buttons would be defined with the same NAME but different VALUE attributes. A single radio button definition looks like

```
<INPUT TYPE="radio" NAME="Question1" VALUE="yes">
```

For radio buttons, the attribute `TYPE="radio"` is used. `NAME=`*string* and
`VALUE=`*definition* are required attributes. `NAME` defines a variable name for the input. Each
piece of data from the form will come back in the form *string=value definition of selected
button*. For instance, if the button in the above definition is selected by the user, the string
returned is `Question1=yes`.

In some cases, data will not be returned.

- If a `NAME` isn't defined for those data, the data will not be returned, regardless of
  whether a button is clicked.

- If the radio button isn't checked, the corresponding data won't be returned. Since only
  one button out of a set can be selected, only one *name=value definition of selected button*
  string will be returned.

1. **Load** `http://{server}/Chapter9/form1b.html`. Compare to the left side of Figure
   9-4.
   On most browsers, the button appears as a circle. The form's Submit button is next to
   the radio button in both cases. Use the View Page Source option to verify that the new
   button line looks like the button definition listed above.

Figure 9-4   Sample Radio Buttons

2. **Load** `http://{server}/Chapter9/form2b.html`.
   Now this form (see right side of Figure 9-4) has a button identified as Of Course. Radio
   buttons are labeled with regular text, outside the button definition itself, instead of
   with the `VALUE` attribute. Use the View Page Source option to verify that the added
   text resembles the following:

   ```
   <INPUT TYPE="radio" NAME="Question1" VALUE="yes"> Of Course <P>
   ```

3. **Click on the** Submit **button.**
   The results of this form are still as blank as the original form. Since the radio button
   wasn't selected, it didn't get a value.

4. **Return to the previous screen by clicking on the browser's Back button.**

5. **Click on the radio button to select it and click on** Submit **again.**
   Since the button was selected, it now has a value and data are returned.

Multiple Radio Buttons

A single radio button can record whether it was selected (the *string=value* is returned) or not (no data are returned). Checkboxes, which are covered in the section Checkboxes, below, can do the same thing. What makes radio buttons unique is this: If a group of radio buttons has the same name, they work together to return only one answer. Single radio buttons are usually used for aesthetics only; for example, some browsers may display radio buttons in a unique diamond shape to distinguish them from checkboxes.

6. Load http://{server}/Chapter9/form3b.html.
This form now has two radio buttons with the same name but different values, as in HTML Example 9-2.

HTML Example 9-2   Multiple Radio Buttons

```
<INPUT TYPE="radio" NAME="Question1" VALUE="yes"> Of Course <P>
<INPUT TYPE="radio" NAME="Question1" VALUE="no"> No Way!!<P>
```

Only one of the buttons can be selected at any given time. Try clicking on one button and then the other and submitting the form. If the Of Course button is selected, then the results will be Question1=yes; if the No Way!! button is selected, then the results will be Question1=no. With radio buttons, only one answer can be returned for each NAME.

7. Load http://{server}/Chapter9/form4b.html.
This form has two questions with two radio buttons each, as in HTML Example 9-3.

HTML Example 9-3   Multiple NAME Values for Radio Buttons

```
Question 1:<P>
<INPUT TYPE="radio" NAME="Question1" VALUE="yes"> Of Course <P>
<INPUT TYPE="radio" NAME="Question1" VALUE="no"> No Way!!<P>
Question 2:<P>
<INPUT TYPE="radio" NAME="Question2" VALUE="yes"> Of Course <P>
<INPUT TYPE="radio" NAME="Question2" VALUE="no"> No Way!!<P>
```

Multiple buttons can be selected, but only one button can be selected for each question. The buttons function as a logical unit, based on the value of the NAME attribute. In this case, one answer is returned from Question 1 and one answer from Question 2. Try various combinations of buttons to familiarize yourself with the way this works.

Checkboxes

Radio buttons are good to use when only one answer is needed. However, the world isn't just black or white; it's black and white and blue and red and green. Checkboxes are the other type of button that can be used in a form. More than one checkbox can be selected at time, and an answer will be returned for every selected checkbox. A checkbox definition looks like the following:

```
<INPUT TYPE="checkbox" NAME="Question3" VALUE="UNIX">
```

For checkboxes, the TYPE="checkbox" attribute is used. NAME and VALUE are required for checkboxes, just as for radio buttons. NAME and VALUE in checkboxes function similarly to radio buttons. If NAME isn't defined for those data, the data won't be returned; if the checkbox isn't checked, data won't be returned, either. The only significant difference is that more than one checkbox can be selected at a time, so NAME can have more than one value returned.

8. **Load** http://{server}/Chapter9/form5b.html.
   The checkbox uses a square instead of a diamond for the button on the UNIX browser only. Use the View Page Source option to verify that the new button line looks like the command listed above.

9. **Load** http://{server}/Chapter9/form6b.html.
   The form has three checkboxes, as shown in HTML Example 9-4, that can all be selected at the same time.

HTML Example 9-4   Checkboxes Example

```
Question 3:<P>
<INPUT TYPE="checkbox" NAME="Question3" VALUE="UNIX"> UNIX<P>
<INPUT TYPE="checkbox" NAME="Question3" VALUE="DOS"> DOS<P>
<INPUT TYPE="checkbox" NAME="Question3" VALUE="WinNT"> WinNT<P>
```

≡ 9

10.Select more than one checkbox and click on Submit.

If all the checkboxes are selected, there are three results for the Question3 variable:

- Question3=UNIX

- Question3=DOS

- Question3=WinNT

Setting Default and Initial Conditions

There may be times when an answer should always be returned. This ensures that such questions will always have answers, which greatly simplifies validation of the user's input. In these cases, a radio button or checkbox can be set to a default value. The attribute CHECKED (no value, hence no =) selects a specific button or checkbox when the form is first displayed. A CHECKED definition looks like the following:

```
<INPUT TYPE="checkbox" NAME="Question3" VALUE="UNIX" CHECKED>

<INPUT TYPE="radio" NAME="Question2" VALUE="Of Course" CHECKED>
```

11.Load http://{server}/Chapter9/form7b.html.

Of Course is automatically selected for Question1, and UNIX is automatically selected for Question3. Use the View Page Source option to verify that the new attributes are the same as in the above example. Figure 9-5 illustrates this step.

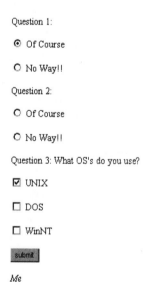

Figure 9-5   Sample Buttons

12. Load `http://{server}/Chapter9/form9b.html`.
The `Question1` radio button definition lines should look like HTML Example 9-5.

HTML Example 9-5   Button Definition Lines

```
<INPUT TYPE="radio" NAME="Question1" VALUE="yes" CHECKED>Of Course <P>
<INPUT TYPE="radio" NAME="Question1" VALUE="no" CHECKED> No Way!!<P>
```

Notice that both buttons for `Question1` are `CHECKED`. Since a radio button can have only one answer, only one button can be selected when the form is displayed. The first occurrence of `CHECKED` is used, and the subsequent occurrences are ignored when the form is initially drawn. However, if the user does explicitly select a button, the corresponding value is always the one returned.

Hiding Variables in Forms

There are times when it is important to record some information that isn't input by the user. This information might be data carried over from a previous form, special user identification or preferences, or a session-tracking number. Displaying this information to the client might be confusing and distract the user from filling in needed information. A hidden variable can hold this information in the form without the user's seeing it.

A hidden variable is incorporated into a form with the `<INPUT>` tag and a `TYPE="hidden"` attribute. The `NAME` and `VALUE` attributes are required. An example of this is:

```
<INPUT TYPE="hidden" NAME="hidden" VALUE="Big Brother">
```

1. **Load** `http://{server}/Chapter9/form1h.html`.
This form appears to have only the submit button, Push Me. There is no visible evidence of any data to be returned from the form.

2. **View the HTML source with View Page Source.**
The source shows the hidden value definition that matches the example above.

3. **Submit the form.**
The results return `hidden=Big Brother`.

4. **Load** `http://{server}/Chapter9/form2h.html`.
Again, this form appears to have only the submit button, Push Me.

9

5. View the HTML source with View Page Source.
The source should be the same as HTML Example 9-6. It shows two hidden inputs. Both inputs have the same NAME but different VALUE definitions.

HTML Example 9-6   Two Hidden Variables with the Same NAME

```
<INPUT TYPE="hidden" NAME="hidden" VALUE="Big Brother">
<INPUT TYPE="hidden" NAME="hidden" VALUE="Big Sister">
```

6. Submit the form.
Both values for the name hidden are returned:

- hidden=Big Brother
- hidden=Big Sister

The hidden variable is like the checkbox in that it can return an arbitrary number of values for a given name.

Text Entry Fields

Answering questions with buttons and checkboxes is very limiting. (To use buttons or checkboxes, you must restrict the user to a predefined list of answers.) Therefore, text is an input type as well. Text entry works well when users are inputting their name, address, or a file to search for. A text box is placed in a form with the <INPUT> tag and a TYPE="text" attribute. Without a NAME for the text, the data will not be returned; thus, the NAME attribute is required. HTML Example 9-7 is an example of this.

HTML Example 9-7   Basic Text Entry Example

```
Full Name
<INPUT TYPE="text" NAME="Question4">
```

1. **Load** `http://{server}/Chapter9/form1t.html`.
   This form has one text box, labeled Full Name, as shown in Figure 9-6.

Full Name [   ]

submit

Me

Figure 9-6   Sample Text Box

2. **View the HTML source with View Page Source.**
   The text definition looks like the example above. Notice that the label Full Name for the text box is in regular HTML text, not part of the `<INPUT>` definition.

3. **Enter a first and last name and submit the form.**
   The result is a string that includes the spaces that were typed in. If `Mary Morris` were typed in, the result would be `Question4=Mary Morris`.

Submitting Forms with a Text Box

The third way to submit a form (aside from an actual Submit button or an image, as described earlier) is to have a form that contains a single text box. When data are entered into the text box and the user presses the Enter key, the form is submitted. *This method is valid only if the form has* only *one text box.* (A further limitation is that the text box cannot be more than one row in height; see below, Changing the Size of the Displayed Text Box, for information about setting a text box's height.)

4. **Load** `http://{server}/Chapter9/form2t.html`.
   There is no Submit button or image shown on this form.

5. **View the HTML source with View Page Source.**
   This form has one text box labeled Name, as in HTML Example 9-8. No Submit button is defined.

HTML Example 9-8   Using a Text Box to Submit a Form

```
<FORM ACTION="/cgi-bin/query.pl" METHOD="POST">
Name
<INPUT TYPE="text" NAME="Question4"><P>
</FORM>
```

6. Enter a name and press Enter to submit the form.

The form is processed, and the text that you entered is returned as `Question4=`*{text typed in}* without a submit button being clicked on.

7. Load `http://`*{server}*`/Chapter9/form3t.html`.

This form has one text box labeled Name and a checkbox labeled Check Me. There is no submit button on this form.

8. View the HTML source with View Page Source.

This form, shown in HTML Example 9-9, doesn't have a submit button..

HTML Example 9-9   Second Example of Using a Text Box to Submit a Form

```
<FORM ACTION="/cgi-bin/query.pl" METHOD="POST">

Name

<INPUT TYPE="text" NAME="Question4"><P>

Check Me

<INPUT TYPE="checkbox" NAME="Question4" VALUE="checked"><P>

</FORM>
```

9. Check the box, enter a name, and press Enter to submit the form.

The form is processed. The results are:

- `Question4=` (the text box was blank)
- `Question4=checked` (the checkbox was checked)

10. Load `http://`*{server}*`/Chapter9/form4t.html`.

This form has two text boxes. Again, there is no submit button on this form.

11. View the HTML source with View Page Source.

This form, shown in HTML Example 9-10, again doesn't have a submit button, but it has more than one text box.

HTML Example 9-10   How NOT to Submit a Form with Text Boxes

```
<FORM ACTION="/cgi-bin/query.pl" METHOD="POST">

Name

<INPUT TYPE="text" NAME="Question4"><P>

Address
```

HTML Example 9-10   How NOT to Submit a Form with Text Boxes

```
<INPUT TYPE="text" NAME="Question5"><P>
</FORM>
```

12.Fill in both fields and press Enter.
This time the form *cannot* be submitted by pressing Enter.

Setting a Default Value for Text

There may be times when a text box should be preset to a default value. The attribute VALUE stores the initial text that is displayed in the text box. An example of this is:

```
<INPUT TYPE="text" NAME="address" VALUE="Some Value">
```

13.Load `http://{server}/Chapter9/form5t.html.`
This form has one text box labeled Name. The text already exists in the text box.

14.View the HTML source with View Page Source.
Figure 9-7 shows how the text definition looks.

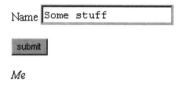

Figure 9-7   Sample Text Box with Default Text

15.Submit the form without any modifications.
The form is processed and `address=Some stuff`, the default value, is returned.

16.Press the Back button to return to the form.

17.Change the text and submit the form.
The form is processed and the result is now `address={text you typed in}`.

Limiting the Length of Text

Databases often have fixed-length fields; additionally, some kinds of data must inherently be no longer than a certain length. (For example, a U.S. postal ZIP code can be no more than 10 characters, including the hyphen.) For these reasons it is a good idea to keep the length of the incoming data within the known size limits. This is accomplished with the MAXLENGTH attribute. An example of this is:

```
<INPUT TYPE="text" NAME="Question4" MAXLENGTH=8>
```

18. Load `http://{server}/Chapter9/form6t.html.`
This form appears to be the same as several previous forms.

19. View the HTML source with View Page Source.
Notice that the MAXLENGTH attribute has been set to 8, as in the example above.

20. Enter the word `snowflake.`
Since `snowflake` has nine characters, the last character cannot be entered here. Most browsers will beep to indicate a problem if the system has that capability. When setting short limits on fields, you can make your forms more user-friendly by displaying a comment to the effect that such fields can accept only *x* number of characters.

Changing the Size of the Displayed Text Box

Keeping data to a specific length is one thing; visually laying out text boxes is another. You cannot control the absolute layout of the screen because the user is free to adjust the characteristics of the browser window. However, if the size of a text box is limited, two text boxes can usually be placed on the same line. By default, a text box is 20 characters wide. Changing the size of the displayed text box is accomplished with the SIZE= attribute. An example of this is:

```
<INPUT TYPE="text" NAME="Question4" SIZE=8>
```

At one time, before the formal ratification of HTML 3.2, SIZE could also be used to create a text box more than one row in height by passing both a line width value and a row height value. An example of this is:

```
<INPUT TYPE="text" NAME="address" SIZE="10,2">
```

21. Load `http://{server}/Chapter9/form7t.html.`
The text box is shorter than previous text boxes were.

22. View the HTML source with View Page Source.
Notice that the SIZE attribute has been set to 8, as in the first example in this section.

23. Load `http://{server}/Chapter9/form8t.html.`
The text box is still only one row high. Text boxes can only be used for single-line input; for multi-line input, see Text Areas, below.

24.Type some text into the text box and press Enter.
As above, in step 12, the form is submitted.

Note – A special value of the `type=` attribute is `password`. This input type is identical (same optional attributes and so on) to the `text` input type, with one important difference: What the user enters in the field is rendered in the browser as a string of asterisks. This secures the entry from curious eyes in the vicinity of the user's browser display but does not encrypt or otherwise secure the data themselves as passed to the CGI: They are received by the CGI program as *clear text*—whatever the user would have seen on the screen in a `text` field is what the CGI receives.

Text Areas

The text entry fields above provide basic multiline capabilities. However, default multiline text can't be placed in those text boxes. Another way of creating text entry fields is to use the tag `<TEXTAREA>`. This tag requires an end tag, `</TEXTAREA>`. The required attribute `NAME` labels the data. An example is:

```
<TEXTAREA NAME="Text1"> </TEXTAREA>
```

(Important: Note that `TEXTAREA` is *not* a `type=` attribute of the `<input>` tag, but a tag in its own right.)

1. **Load** `http://{server}/Chapter9/form1a.html`.
   This form resembles the basic text boxes explored above. It is only one row in height and 20 characters wide. The difference here is that the field has scrollbars even in its most basic definition, as shown in Figure 9-8.

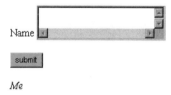

Figure 9-8   Sample Text Area

2. **Type some text into the text area and press Enter.**
   The cursor advances to the next line. Text areas cannot be used to submit forms.

3. Type a second line of text and submit the form.
Note that where the Enter key was pressed, the text shows %0D%0A. This special notation (% followed by a hexadecimal value) is used to pars special characters such as newlines, tabs, and so on, to the CGI. the %0D is an ASCII carriage return, and %0A is a newline.

Sizing a Text Area

The <TEXTAREA> tag uses the attributes ROWS and COLS to define the displayed size. An example of this is:

```
<TEXTAREA ROWS=3 COLS=25 NAME="Text2"> Default text </TEXTAREA>
```

4. Load http://{server}/Chapter9/form2a.html.
The text area is now three rows in height.

5. View the HTML source with View Page Source.
Notice that the ROWS and COLS attributes have been defined as in the example above.

Setting Default Text in a Text Area

Instead of using the VALUE attribute, the default text is placed between the start and end tags. All whitespace between the <TEXTAREA> tags is significant. The two examples in HTML Example 9-11 are not the same. In Example 1, there is a space before and after Default Text. In Example 2, there is a carriage return before and after Default Text. These definitions produce different form displays and returned results.

HTML Example 9-11   Defining the Default Text in a Text Area

Example 1

```
<TEXTAREA NAME="Text2"> Default text </TEXTAREA>
```

Example 2

```
<TEXTAREA NAME="Text2">
Default text
</TEXTAREA>
```

6. Load http://{server}/Chapter9/form3a.html.
The text area has a default value of Start here. This value starts on the second line of the text area. (See Figure 9-9.)

Figure 9-9   Sample Text Area with Default Text

7. View the HTML source with View Page Source.
The text `Start here` begins on the line below the `<TEXTAREA>` tag. Carriage returns are significant characters within `<TEXTAREA>` tags.

8. Submit the form.
Where the blank lines were in the text area, the text shows `%0A`. The results of submitting the form without any changes yields `Question5=%0AStart here %0A`.

9. Load `http://{server}/Chapter9/form4a.html`.
The text area has two lines of default text. The second line has two spaces in front of the text `Text here`.

10. View the HTML source with View Page Source.
The text `Text here` has two spaces at the beginning of the line. Spaces are also significant characters within `<TEXTAREA>` tags.

11. Submit the form.
Where the spaces were in the text area, the text shows spaces as well. The results of submitting the form without any changes yields `Question5=%0D%0A Text here %0AMore Text %0D%0A`.

Pull-Down Menus and Scrolling Lists

Although users shouldn't always have to type in the answers, displaying every option as a button consumes valuable space in the browser window. Pull-down menus and scrolling lists resolve this conflict. The HTML behind a scrolling list resembles a regular list, as shown in Chapter 2, in the section Lists, in that the tags `<SELECT>` and `</SELECT>` mark the start and end of the list and each list item is indicated by an `<OPTION>` tag. The required attribute `NAME` labels the data. The returned data are the text after the option selected. HTML Example 9-12 shows an example.

HTML Example 9-12   Pull-Down Menu Tags

```
<SELECT NAME="Menu-Question6">
<OPTION> Option Text 1
<OPTION> Option Text 2
</SELECT>
```

A pull-down menu is actually a special case of a scrolling list. It can be created only when only one list item at a time is displayed or selectable. (For those familiar with Microsoft user-interface programming, a scrolling list is analogous to a list box; a pull-down menu is like a combo box.)

1. **Load** `http://{server}/Chapter9/form1o.html`.
   This form is a basic pull-down menu. Only one item is displayed. Clicking on the drop-down arrow or push button (depending on the browser) at the end of the item displays all of the items. Figure 9-10 illustrates a sample menu item.

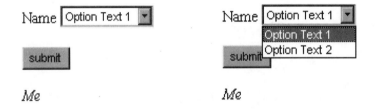

Figure 9-10   Sample Menu Item as Displayed (on left) and Expanded (on right)

2. **View the HTML source with View Page Source.**
   Compare this document with the next example. The `<SELECT>` definition in this example resembles the example above.

3. **Submit the form.**
   The text of the selected pull-down item becomes the returned value for this list. If Option Text 2 is selected, the result is `Menu-Question6=Option Text 2`.

Displaying Two Items at Once

It isn't aesthetically pleasing to display all 10 items on a list, thus filling up the screen with one question or prompt, but there are times when more than one item should be displayed. Displaying multiple items is accomplished by adding the SIZE=*x* attribute to the <SELECT> tag, where *x* is the number of items to display. By displaying more than one item, the pull-down menu becomes a scrolling list.

An example of adding the attribute is:

```
<SELECT NAME="Menu-Question6" SIZE="2">
```

4. **Load** http://{*server*}/Chapter9/form2o.html.
   This form is now a scrolling list with two items displayed, as shown in Figure 9-11.

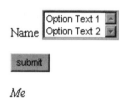

Figure 9-11 Sample Scrolling List

5. **View the HTML source with View Page Source.**
   The only HTML change between the previous form and this one is the SIZE=2 attribute added to the <SELECT> tag. This one modification alone changed the form from a pull-down menu to a scrolling list.

6. **Select a menu item. Hold down the Control key and select another menu item.**
   Only one item at a time can be selected.

Selecting Multiple Items

Only one item could be selected in the example above, making that example similar in behavior to a set of radio buttons sharing the same NAME= attribute. As with checkboxes, however, there are times when you want the question posed by a scrolling list to have more than one answer. To enable multiple-item selection, use the MULTIPLE attribute in the <SELECT> definition. The definition line looks like the following:

```
<SELECT NAME="Menu-Question6" MULTIPLE>
```

7. **Load** http://{*server*}/Chapter9/form3o.html.
   This form is a scrolling list with several items displayed.

8. **View the HTML source with View Page Source.**
   The <SELECT> line has been changed to resemble the example above. The attribute SIZE is not used here, but the scrolling list displays more than one item.

9. **Select a menu item. Hold down the Control key and select another menu item.**
   More than one item can now be selected here.

10. **Submit the form.**
    The result of this form is two values for the item Menu-Question6:

    • Menu-Question6=Option Text 1 (or whatever was selected)
    • Menu-Question6=Option Text 3 (or whatever was selected)

11. **Load** http://{server}/Chapter9/form4o.html.
    This form is a scrolling list with two items displayed and three items total. When MULTIPLE was used alone, all items were displayed. The number of displayed items can be controlled by means of the SIZE attribute.

Default Item Selection

Specifying default values can be done with pull-down menus and scrolling lists by adding the SELECTED attribute to the <OPTION> tag. An example is:

```
<OPTION SELECTED> Option Text 3
```

12. **Load** http://{server}/Chapter9/form5o.html.
    This scrolling list has the first and fifth items initially selected, as shown in Figure 9-12.

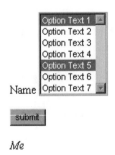

Figure 9-12   Sample Scrolling List with Multiple Items Selected

13. View the HTML source with View Page Source.

The form is similar to HTML Example 9-13.

HTML Example 9-13   Scrolling List Example with Default Items Selected

```
<SELECT NAME="Menu-Question6" MULTIPLE>

<OPTION SELECTED> Option Text 1

<OPTION> Option Text 2

<OPTION> Option Text 3

<OPTION> Option Text 4

<OPTION SELECTED> Option Text 5

<OPTION> Option Text 6

<OPTION> Option Text 7

</SELECT>
```

The `SIZE` attribute isn't specified in this list, but only five items are displayed. All the preselected items are displayed if the `SIZE` attribute isn't specified but the `MULTIPLE` attribute is used.

14. Submit the form.

The result of this form is two values for the item Menu-Question6:

- `Menu-Question6=Option Text 1` (or whatever was selected)
- `Menu-Question6=Option Text 5` (or whatever was selected)

15. Load `http://{server}/Chapter9/form6o.html`.

The form contains a pull-down menu that has the second item initially selected.

16. View the HTML source with View Page Source.

The attributes `SIZE` and `MULTIPLE` are not specified; thus, the display is again a pull-down menu. However, more than one item has the `SELECTED` attribute.

17. Submit the form.

The result of this form is the first selected value for the item Menu-Question6, `Menu-Question6=Option Text 2`. As with radio buttons, only the first item is returned when multiple items are selected but the `MULTIPLE` attribute isn't used.

Clearing Entries and Resetting Defaults

Each type of input form can set default values. This capability can save the user some time, or in the case of text entries, give the user an idea of what format to use. Default values are also useful when the user might opt to omit an answer to an important question.

What about the case where the user has filled out part of the form and wants to start over? This capability is provided by the TYPE="reset" attribute for the <INPUT> tag. By adding a reset button to your form, you allow users to erase or clear their partially completed form. An example of the reset button definition is:

```
<INPUT TYPE="reset">
```

As with the submit button, the text on the reset button can be changed with the VALUE attribute. An example is:

```
<INPUT TYPE="reset" VALUE="Clear">
```

1. **Load** `http://{server}/Chapter9/form1r.html`.
   This form has buttons, text boxes, text areas, and scrolling lists. At the bottom of the page is a button labeled clear.

2. **View the HTML source with View Page Source.**
   The HTML code looks like HTML Example 9-14.

HTML Example 9-14   A Full-Fledged Form Example

```
<html> <head>
<title> Form Template </title>
</head> <body>

<FORM ACTION="/cgi-bin/query.pl" METHOD="GET">
Question 1:Do you use the Web at work or at home?<P>
<INPUT TYPE="radio" NAME="Question1" VALUE="work"> At Work <P>
<INPUT TYPE="radio" NAME="Question1" VALUE="home"> At Home <P>
Question 2:Do you use Mosaic? <P>
<INPUT TYPE="radio" NAME="Question2" VALUE="yes"> Of Course <P>
<INPUT TYPE="radio" NAME="Question2" VALUE="no"> No Way!! <P>
Question 3: What OS's do you use?<P>
```

HTML Example 9-14   A Full-Fledged Form Example (Continued)

```
<INPUT TYPE="checkbox" NAME="Question3" VALUE="UNIX"> UNIX <P>
<INPUT TYPE="checkbox" NAME="Question3" VALUE="DOS"> DOS <P>
<INPUT TYPE="checkbox" NAME="Question3" VALUE="WinNT"> WinNT <P>
Question 4: What is your email address?
<INPUT TYPE="text" NAME="Question4" MAXLENGTH=25 > <P>
Question 5: What is your real name and address?
<TEXTAREA NAME="Question5" ROWS=3 COLS=10 >
</TEXTAREA> <P>
Question 6: What do you use the Internet for?<P>
<SELECT NAME="Menu-Question6" MULTIPLE>
<OPTION> Surfing
<OPTION> Obtaining Programs
<OPTION> Reading Netnews
<OPTION> Teleconferencing
<OPTION> Sending and Receiving Email
<OPTION> Playing MUDs
</SELECT> <P>
<INPUT TYPE="submit" VALUE="submit">
<INPUT TYPE="reset" VALUE="clear">
</FORM>

<address> Me </address>
</body> </html>
```

3. Enter some information.

4. Press the Clear **button to reset the form to its initial condition.**
   Notice that all fields clear, the buttons become unchecked, and scrolling lists and pull-down menus return to the first item.

5. **Load** `http://{server}/Chapter9/form1r.html`.
   This form has the same buttons, text boxes, text areas and scrolling lists, but there are now default values in the form's components.

6. **View the HTML source with View Page Source.**
   The HTML code looks like HTML Example 9-15.

HTML Example 9-15   HTML Source with Default Entries Defined

```
<html> <head>

<title> Form Template </title>

</head> <body>

<FORM ACTION="/cgi-bin/query.pl" METHOD="GET">

Question 1:Do you use the Web at work or at home?<P>

<INPUT TYPE="radio" NAME="Question1" VALUE="work" CHECKED> At
  Work <P>

<INPUT TYPE="radio" NAME="Question1" VALUE="home"> At Home <P>

Question 2:Do you use Mosaic? <P>

<INPUT TYPE="radio" NAME="Question2" VALUE="yes" CHECKED> Of
  Course <P>

<INPUT TYPE="radio" NAME="Question2" VALUE="no"> No Way!! <P>

Question 3: What OS's do you use?<P>

<INPUT TYPE="checkbox" NAME="Question3" VALUE="UNIX" CHECKED>
  UNIX <P>

<INPUT TYPE="checkbox" NAME="Question3" VALUE="DOS"> DOS <P>

<INPUT TYPE="checkbox" NAME="Question3" VALUE="WinNT"> WinNT <P>

Question 4: What is your email address?

<INPUT TYPE="text" NAME="Question4" MAXLENGTH=25
  VALUE="me@mydomain.com"> <P>

Question 5: What is your real name and address?

<TEXTAREA NAME="Question5" ROWS=3 COLS=10 >

FirstName LastName
```

HTML Example 9-15   HTML Source with Default Entries Defined

```
Street Address

City, State Zip Country

</TEXTAREA> <P>

Question 6: What do you use the Internet for?<P>

<SELECT NAME="Menu-Question6" MULTIPLE>

<OPTION SELECTED> Surfing

<OPTION> Obtaining Programs

<OPTION> Reading Netnews

<OPTION> Teleconferencing

<OPTION SELECTED> Sending and Receiving Email

<OPTION> Playing MUDs

</SELECT> <P>

<INPUT TYPE="submit" VALUE="submit">

<INPUT TYPE="reset" VALUE="Reset Values">

</FORM>
```

This is like Example 9-12, except that default entries have been defined this time. These are displayed in boldface in HTML Example 9-15.

7. Enter some information.

8. Press the Reset Values **button to reset the form to its initial condition.**
Notice that all fields return to their original default values.

Figure 9-13 illustrates the form in HTML Example 9-14 displayed on a Netscape browser.

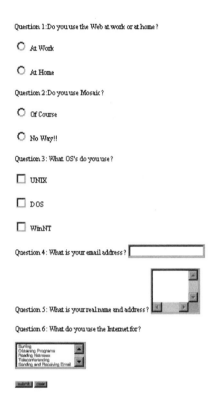

Figure 9-13   Full Form as Displayed on Netscape Navigator Browser

Multiple Forms on the Same Page

It is possible to put more than one form on a web page. The only restriction is that forms cannot be nested within forms. The drawback here is that each form must have its own submit button or alternative submission method. That submission method returns only the data for the form for which they are defined, *not* the other forms on the same page. There is no way to request common information that is shared between forms. A workaround is to obtain the information in a previous page and carry it through as hidden information or in the form of HTTP cookies. (See Chapter 11 for information about using cookies.)

If you need users to fill out both forms, they must complete one form, submit the results, and then go back to the page with the forms and complete the second form. This sequence can cause confusion on the part of the user. Multiple forms on a page should be used only when only one form of several will be returned. For example, a page which queries multiple Web search engines might consist of a separate form for each search engine.

To reduce user confusion:

- Visually separate the forms with a horizontal rule or similar device.

- Give clear instructions on when to use each submit button.

New in HTML 3.2: Sending a File with a Form

One addition to the HTML specification that has drawn little attention is the ability not just to gather data input by your users via the standard form fields and other widgets, but also to upload entire files. This process, called HTTP file upload, is accomplished with two new attributes:

- The `enctype="multipart/form-data"` attribute of the `<form>` tag itself enables the form actually to transmit the file through the CGI. The file's data are wrapped in a MIME boundary enclosure, so that the program identified in the `action=` attribute can parse the input stream and determine where the file starts and stops. (Any other elements in the form, such as text fields and radio buttons, are also sent to stdin this way, one field per "part" of the returned data.)

- The `type="file"` attribute of the `<input>` tag specifies that the browser render a text field in which the user can enter a filename (including path) to be uploaded. With the text field a Browse... button is displayed. When the user clicks on that button, he or she gets the operating system's standard "browse" dialog which lets a file on the local drive(s) be selected interactively, without having to type the filename in manually.

HTTP file upload can be accomplished *only* if the form's method is POST. Forms submitted with the GET method cannot upload files.

Note – Early versions of Microsoft Internet Explorer did not process HTTP file uploads correctly. What eventually became the HTML 3.2 file upload standard had actually been proposed by Netscape Communications several years earlier, and the Netscape browser has for this reason supported it for some time. MSIE 4.0 does support the feature, however.

The following steps assume that you are using the Netscape browser. If you have a different browser, follow along with the text and illustrations so that you understand what is happening.

1. **Load** `http://{server}/Chapter9/file_upload.html`.
   The page is displayed as shown in Figure 9-14.

HTTP File Upload

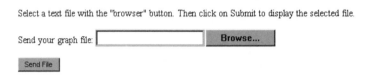

Select a text file with the "browser" button. Then click on Submit to display the selected file.

Send your graph file: [   ] **Browse...**

[Send File]

Figure 9-14   HTTP File Upload Example

2. View the HTML behind the page with View Page Source.

The portion of code which specifies a file upload appears in boldface in HTML
Example 9-16.

HTML Example 9-16   HTTP File Upload

```
<FORM ENCTYPE="multipart/form-data" ACTION="http://local-

host/cgi-bin/file_upload.pl" METHOD=POST>

Send your graph file: <INPUT NAME="userfile" TYPE="file"><p>

<INPUT TYPE="submit" VALUE="Send File">

</FORM>
```

3. Click on the button labeled Browse....

Under Windows 95, the dialoguebox which results looks like that shown in Figure 9-15.

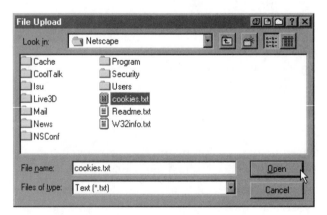

Figure 9-15   Browse Dialog on Windows 95

Depending on how your server software is set up, you may be able to click on the Submit button after selecting a text file in this step. If so, the text file you selected is passed through the CGI to the Perl script for processing, and simply displayed in your browser (embedded between two horizontal rules).

Note – A description of how to process file uploads is included in Chapter 10. If the Submit button in this example does not work, most likely the value of the form's `action=` attribute needs to be modified to conform to your system's configuration. See Chapter 10 for instructions on how to do this.

Summary

In this chapter, you learned:

- **Submitting forms** — Forms can be returned to the server for processing by:
  - A clickable image, `TYPE="image"`
  - A submit button, `TYPE="submit"`
  - A single text box, `TYPE="text"`

- **Buttons** — There are four types of buttons:
  - Radio – used in sets for yes or no answers
  - Checkbox – used for one or more answers
  - Submit – used to submit a form
  - Reset – used to return a form to default values

- **Text** — Can be input via two methods
  - Text boxes – used for single line input and where the input string needs length control. Text boxes have limited use for multiline text
  - Text areas – used for multiline text input

- **Pull-down menus and scrollable lists** — Accomplished with the `<SELECT>` tag and various options

- **HTTP file uploads** — Specified by using the new `enctype="multipart/form-data"` attribute of the `<FORM>` tag, and the new input type `file`.

9

Tags Used in This Chapter

Table 9-1   Tags Used in Creating Forms

Tag	Attributes	Description and Comments
`<FORM>`		
	`ACTION=`	Defines the cgi-bin script or program to execute with the incoming data.
	`METHOD=`	Defines whether the incoming data will be stored in the environment variable QUERY_STRING (GET method) or standard input (POST method)
	`ENCTYPE="multipart/form-data"`	Identifies the form as able to accept HTTP file uploads as well as regular form data
`<INPUT>`		
	`TYPE`	Defines the type of input field. (See Table 9-2.)
`<TEXTAREA>`		
	`ROWS`	Defines the height of the text area.
	`COLS`	Defines the width of the text area.
	`NAME`	Defines the variable name.
`<SELECT>`		
	`NAME`	Defines the variable name.
	`SIZE`	Defines the number of items displayed.
	`MULTIPLE`	Indicates that more than one item can be selected.
`<OPTION>`		
	`SELECTED`	Makes the item selected by default.

HTML for Fun and Profit

Table 9-2   Input Values and Uses

Input Type	Attributes	Description and Notes
submit		
	VALUE	Alters the text on the submit button.
reset		
	VALUE	Alters the text on the submit button.
image		
	SRC	Defines the URL for the image.
	NAME	Defines a variable name to be prepended to x and y when returning coordinates.
hidden		
	NAME	Defines the variable name.
	VALUE	Defines the value of the variable listed in NAME.
radio		
	NAME	Defines the variable name.
	VALUE	Defines the value of the variable listed in NAME.
	CHECKED	Indicates selected by default
checkbox		
	NAME	Defines the variable name.
	VALUE	Defines the value of the variable listed in NAME.
	CHECKED	Indicates selected by default.
text		
	NAME	Defines the variable name.
	VALUE	Defines the value of the variable listed in NAME.
	SIZE	Defines the number of characters in the returned value.
	MAXLENGTH	Controls the display size of the text box.
file		
	NAME	Defines the variable name.

Processing Data from Forms 10 ≡

In the previous chapter, you worked with the forms that gather data, and you were introduced to the script `query.pl` that lists the value(s) that each item in the form was set to. This chapter explains the scripts you have used thus far and introduces you to a sample script for processing the information that you received from the forms. In Chapter 7, we introduced you to Perl. Here, it comes into full play.

Some basic information about Perl here is repeated from Chapter 7 in order to reinforce it in the specific context of form handling.

Basic CGI Input and Output

Moving data between the CGI and the script is an important part of how the script is written. Remember, the output of the CGI is the input for the script, and the output of the script is the input for the CGI.

Input

Originally, all information was passed from the CGI to the script or program via environment variables. People began to create forms that returned a large quantity of information that overflowed the QUERY_STRING variable. A method was developed to pass the information from the form to the executing routine via the *standard input*, or *stdin* in UNIX terminology, because standard input doesn't have size limitations on what it can transfer.

The Perl script `testcgi.pl` was used in Chapter 7 to examine the variables that the executing routine received. The script, shown in Code Example 10-1, lists all the information that it received, both from environment variables and from stdin.

(By the way, note the first line of the script, a "comment" in the sense that it begins with the Perl comment symbol: `#!/perl`. A line such as this is essential for Perl scripts run on UNIX systems; it identifies the location on the server of the Perl interpreter. If you are running these examples on a UNIX host yourself, you will need to change the line so that it points to the correct path. On Windows platforms the line is not necessary because once the interpreter has been installed, the operating system automatically associates all .pl files with the correct path.)

Code Example 10-1   testcgi.pl Script

```perl
#!/perl

print "Content-type: text/plain\n\n";
print "CGI/1.0 test script report\n";

if ($ENV{'REQUEST_METHOD'} eq "POST") {
       $form = <STDIN>;
       print "$form \n";
} else {
print "ARGC is $#ARGV \nARGV element(s) passed:\n";

while (@ARGV) {
       $ARGV=shift;
       print "       $ARGV\n";
}
}
print "\n";


print "--------------- ENVIRONMENT VARIABLES FOLLOW: -----------
   ----\n";
print "AUTH_TYPE = $ENV{'AUTH_TYPE'}\n";
print "CONTENT_LENGTH = $ENV{'CONTENT_LENGTH'}\n";
print "CONTENT_TYPE = $ENV{'CONTENT_TYPE'}\n";
print "DATE_GMT = $ENV{'DATE_GMT'}\n";
print "DATE_LOCAL = $ENV{'DATE_LOCAL'}\n";
```

Code Example 10-1   testcgi.pl Script (continued)

```perl
print "DOCUMENT_NAME = $ENV{'DOCUMENT_NAME'}\n";

print "DOCUMENT_ROOT = $ENV{'DOCUMENT_ROOT'}\n";

print "DOCUMENT_URI = $ENV{'DOCUMENT_URI'}\n";

print "GATEWAY_INTERFACE = $ENV{'GATEWAY_INTERFACE'}\n";

print "HTTP_ACCEPT = $ENV{'HTTP_ACCEPT'}\n";

print "LAST_MODIFIED = $ENV{'LAST_MODIFIED'}\n";

print "PATH = $ENV{'PATH'}\n";

print "PATH_INFO = $ENV{'PATH_INFO'}\n";

print "PATH_TRANSLATED = $ENV{'PATH_TRANSLATED'}\n";

print "QUERY_STRING = $ENV{'QUERY_STRING'}\n";

print "QUERY_STRING_UNESCAPED =
  $ENV{'QUERY_STRING_UNESCAPED'}\n";

print "REMOTE_ADDR = $ENV{'REMOTE_ADDR'}\n";

print "REMOTE_HOST = $ENV{'REMOTE_HOST'}\n";

print "REMOTE_IDENT = $ENV{'REMOTE_IDENT'}\n";

print "REMOTE_USER = $ENV{'REMOTE_USER'}\n";

print "REQUEST_METHOD = $ENV{'REQUEST_METHOD'}\n";

print "SCRIPT_NAME = $ENV{'SCRIPT_NAME'}\n";

print "SERVER_NAME = $ENV{'SERVER_NAME'}\n";

print "SERVER_PORT = $ENV{'SERVER_PORT'}\n";

print "SERVER_PROTOCOL = $ENV{'SERVER_PROTOCOL'}\n";

print "SERVER_ROOT = $ENV{'SERVER_ROOT'}\n";

print "SERVER_SOFTWARE = $ENV{'SERVER_SOFTWARE'}\n";
```

Environment Variables

When the CGI started executing `testcgi.pl`, the CGI set the variables that make up the environment in which the script runs. Perl accesses these variables by referencing them with `$ENV{'`*env variable*`'}` or by setting a local variable in the script equal to the value of the environment variables, as in this line (*not* from the above script):

```
$DocRoot = $ENV{'DOCUMENT_ROOT'}
```

Note – Although the lines beginning with `print` in `testcgi.pl` look as though they contain assignment statements, they do not, because the the *string=environment variable* portion of the lines is enclosed in quotes following a `print` statement. Those lines simply display the text (after substituting for the environment variables) in the user's browser.

The information from a form submitted with the GET method has the item information stored in the variable `QUERY_STRING`. This information is stored in the format:

```
variable name=variable value
```

The information is referred to as *form variable information* to differentiate it from individual local or other variables. This form variable information is also stored in the ARGV variable, which stores the string of incoming arguments. The part of the script in Code Example 10-2 prints the variable information strings that were passed in to ARGV.

Code Example 10-2   ARGV Section of testcgi.pl – Used with the GET Method

```
while (@ARGV) {

       $ARGV=shift;

       print "     $ARGV\n";

}
```

Note – Perl code explanation – The @ sign at the start of a variable means that the variable is a list of items (an *array*, in programmerese). The $ sign at the start of a variable means that the variable is an individual item (a *scalar*). The example above says, "While there is anything left in the ARGV (with an @) array, move (i.e., shift) the leftmost item into the scalar variable ARGV (with a $), print this item, and start over by fetching the next item."

Standard Input

When the POST method is used to submit data from a form, the input comes from the standard input, as discussed previously. The part of the script shown in Code Example 10-3 reads this information and writes it out directly via the `$form` variable.

Code Example 10-3   Printing Form Variable Information with the POST Method

```
$form = <STDIN>;
print "$form \n";
```

Note – Perl code explanation – The <> as used in Perl indicates a stream of information from a source outside the current script, such as receiving input from a specified source or sending output to a specific source. This is also referred to as a file handle, even if a disk file is not used. <STDIN> is the definition for receiving a stream of information from stdin. If input comes from another source, such as a file, the source of the stream must be defined with an open statement. It is important to differentiate between the <> as used for file handles in Perl and as used for tags in HTML.

Parsing Input

The query.pl script returned information entered into forms in Chapter 9. The actual script is shown in Code Example 10-4.

Code Example 10-4   query.pl Script

```
#!/perl

print "Content-type: text/html\n\n";
print "<HTML><BODY> <H1>Query Results</H1>\n";
print "You submitted the following name/value pairs:\n";

if ($ENV{'REQUEST_METHOD'} eq "POST") {
      $form = <STDIN>;
} else {
      $form = $ENV{'QUERY_STRING'};
}
@pairs = split(/&/,$form);
print "<UL>";
while (@pairs) {
```

Code Example 10-4   query.pl Script (continued)

```
        $pair=shift @pairs;
        $pair =~ s/\+/ /g;
        print "<LI><CODE>$pair</CODE>\n ";
}
print "</UL>";
print "\n</BODY></HTML>";
```

In `query.pl`, the only difference between GET and POST data handling is the source of input to the `$form` variable. After the input is placed into the `$form` variable, the information is split into the individual elements of the `@pairs` list with:

```
@pairs = split(/&/,$form);
```

Note – Perl code explanation – The `split` function divides a scalar variable into an array variable, or a list of individual scalars, separating the component strings from one another at each occurrence of the character defined as the delimiter. In this case the & sign is the delimiter.

If the original input is:

```
name=Mary+Morris&email=marym&preference=UNIX
```

then the list now has three items that read:

```
name=Mary+Morris    email=marym      preference=UNIX
```

Each item of the `@pairs` list is then moved into the `$pair` variable with:

```
$pair=shift @pairs;
```

Converting URL Encoding

Spaces make for difficult data transmission and variable differentiation while transmitting the data. However, spaces aren't the only character that is hard to deal with during data transmission and variable processing. In Chapter 9, multiline text boxes returned a %0D%0A instead of a carriage return/newline. And since + marks a space, something else is needed to mark the occurrence of a literal +.

Actually, +, %, and & are the only nonalphabetic or nonnumeric characters that are used in the form variable information strings. All other special characters, including tabs, carriage returns, parentheses, and even the literal occurrences of +, &, and %, are encoded with a % sign and their numeric ASCII value. This is called URL encoding.

Now that the form variable information strings have been split apart, the + can be changed back to a space. This is done with:

```
$pair =~ s/\+/ /g;
```

Note – =~ is a specific operator in Perl. It indicates that the translation rule following it will be performed on the designated variable and that the output will be placed back into the same variable. In this case, the translation rule is s for substitute. This substitute syntax came from the sed command in UNIX. For more information on this substitution method, refer to *Programming Perl* (the so-called "Camel Book") by Larry Wall and Randal L. Schwartz (for publication details, see Appendix B), or see the man pages about sed on a UNIX system.

All the encoded characters must be converted back into regular characters during the variable information string processing. Some lines that could be added to the current script are:

```
$pair =~ s/\%0A/\/n/g;
$pair =~ s/\%2B/\+/g;
$pair =~ s/\%28/\(/g;
$pair =~ s/\%29/\)/g;
$pair =~ s/\%26/\&/g;
```

Note – Perl modules and individual scripts to split and unencode form variable information are widely and freely available. Use them instead of reinventing the wheel. (See Appendix B.) We mention the approach here merely to explain what happens behind the scenes.

Output

Just as the CGI interface uses the standard input to pass information to a script or program, standard output is used to pass information from the program or script back to the CGI and on to the client's browser. Remember two key things when writing your output:

1. **Include metainformation** — The client browser needs to have information about the type of information that the browser is receiving.

2. **Include HTML formatting** — If the information you are returning to the client is to be used as HTML, it must include HTML formatting.

MetaInformation

The client must have information about the type of information it is receiving. This information should be a text string in the format:

```
Content-type: {A MIME type}
```

The two example scripts above used the statement:

```
print "Content-type: text/html\n\n";
```

If this information isn't passed back to the client, peculiar things occur. Some client browsers offer you the opportunity to save the returning data to a file. Other browsers receive the data and don't display it. This is a small part of a program, but it is by no means trivial. Some servers offer alternative methods for ensuring that a header is printed; however, for the present, include content headers in all programs.

HTML Formatting

When you have defined the returning information as HTML, you need to add HTML formatting to the information that you send back. In Perl, this is usually done with a print statement and the format needed. For example, where Perl would specify a newline in plain text output with \n, the <P> or <BR> tags are used when an HTML document is to be returned.

The \n is used in the metainformation listed above because it defines the type of information returning, but it is not displayed because it is metainformation.

Sample CGI Script

The most common form is one that collects feedback. This example shows how information from a form can be gathered and used.

Feedback Form

Two parts are involved: gathering information and using it.

The HTML page gathers the information. An example is `feedback.html`, shown in Code Example 10-5.

Code Example 10-5   Feedback Form Script: Part 1

```
<html> <head>
<title> Feedback Form </title>
</head> <body>


<H1> Feedback Form </H1>
<HR>
<FORM ACTION="/cgi-bin/contact.pl" METHOD="POST">


Name: <INPUT TYPE="text" NAME="name" MAXLENGTH=50 > <P>
Email Address: <INPUT TYPE="text" NAME="email" MAXLENGTH=50 > <P>
Comments:
<TEXTAREA NAME="comment" ROWS=3 COLS=50 > </TEXTAREA> <P>
</FORM>
<HR>
<address> Me </address>
</body> </html>
```

The second component of the form process is the script that uses the information gathered by the web page. An example is `contact.pl`, shown in Code Example 10-6. (Note: This script cannot be used as is on all operating systems because it makes use of the `mail` command, which is not available on all systems. The script is included here for purposes of illustration only.)

Code Example 10-6   Feedback Form Script: Part 2

```
#!/perl
#
# Load environment variables
#
do '/WWW/cgi-bin/setenv.pl';
```

Code Example 10-6   Feedback Form Script: Part 2 (continued)

```
#
# Return Meta-Information
#
print "Content-type: text/html\n\n";


#
# Parse the variables to be used
#
$NAME='"$exeRoot/cgiparse" -value name';
$EMAIL='"$exeRoot/cgiparse" -value email';
$COMMENT='"$exeRoot/cgiparse" -value comment';


#
# Setup templates for output to log and email and HTML output
#
format COMMENTFORM =
    ===========================================================
    @<<<<<<<<<<<<<<<<<<<<<<<<<<<<<<<<<<<<<<<<<<<<<<<<<<<<<<<
    $NAME
    left this message about your web server
    @<<<<<<<<<<<<<<<<<<<<<<<<<<<<<<<<<<<<<<<
    $EMAIL
    @*
    $COMMENT
    ===========================================================


format STDOUT =
```

Code Example 10-6   Feedback Form Script: Part 2 (continued)

```
    <HR>

    Thank You,

    @<<<<<<<<<<<<<<<<<<<<<<<<<<<<<<<<<<<<<<<<<<<<<<<<<<<<

    $NAME

    <P> We will contact you at:

    @<<<<<<<<<<<<<<<<<<<<<<<<<<<<<<<<<<<<<

    $EMAIL

    <HR>

.


format MAILCOMMENT =

    =========================================================

    @<<<<<<<<<<<<<<<<<<<<<<<<<<<<<<<<<<<<<<<<<<<<<<<<<<<

    $NAME

    left this message about your web server

    @<<<<<<<<<<<<<<<<<<<<<<<<<<<<<<<<<<<<

    $EMAIL

    @*

    $COMMENT

    =========================================================

.


#
# Write the output to the appropriate places
#

open (COMMENTFORM,">> $logs/comments.log");

write (COMMENTFORM);

close (COMMENTFORM);
```

Code Example 10-6 Feedback Form Script: Part 2 (continued)

```
open (MAILCOMMENT,"|mail webmaster@finesse.com");
write (MAILCOMMENT);
close (MAILCOMMENT);


#
# Return a web page
#


select (STDOUT);
print "<html><head><title> Thanks for Your Comments </ti-
tle></head><body>";
write(STDOUT);
print "</body></html>";
```

Setting More Environment Variables

The first item of note in the script is the line:

```
do '/WWW/cgi-bin/setenv.pl';
```

This command executes the script setenv.pl. The results of setenv.pl are retained for use later in the script with the do statement. The setenv.pl script, shown in Code Example 10-7, sets environment variables beyond those known to the CGI. The CGI sets only the environment variables that it knows about from the httpd. Use setenv.pl to set all other variables that are needed for a script.

This method is also a handy way to make a set of scripts fairly portable by storing generic information in one place and referencing it from all scripts. Unfortunately, on a UNIX system, the #! ("she-bang") line that defines where to look for the Perl interpreter has to be coded into the individual script.

Code Example 10-7 Setting Other "Environment Variables" with setenv.pl

```
#!/perl

$ServerRoot = "/WWW";
```

Code Example 10-7 *Setting Other "Environment Variables" with setenv.pl (continued)*

```
$DocRoot = "$ServerRoot/Docs";

$cgiRoot ="$ServerRoot/cgi-bin";

$logs = "$ServerRoot/logs";
```

Parsing the Form Variable Information

In order to process form variables in a Perl script, their values generally need to be assigned to variables rather than processed "in the raw." Parsing routines are common and not that difficult to write, but their heavy use of regular expressions can make them confusing to beginners. A much more practical solution is not to roll your own but to make use of whatever resources are available to you on your OS and server.

In our example, the second section parses each form variable and assigns the information to a Perl variable by using the program cgiparse, included in the CERN server utilities distribution. By means of cgiparse, the section can be reduced to Code Example 10-8, shown below.

Code Example 10-8 *Using cgiparse*

```
#
# Parse the variables to be used
#
$NAME=`"$exeRoot/cgiparse" -value name`;
$EMAIL=`"$exeRoot/cgiparse" -value email`;
$COMMENT=`"$exeRoot/cgiparse" -value comment`;
```

Although we used cgiparse in this example, many other free or public-domain libraries of Perl code accomplish the same purposes. Check Appendix B for pointers to these resources.

Using Perl Formats

Perl uses *formats* to lay out information in a pleasing and organized form. A format is a block of Perl code that specifies the placement of text and variables. Each format starts with the format definition (a line such as format COMMENTFORM= in our example) and ends with a period. The terminating period must be the only character on the line, and it must be in the first column. A format is composed of general text, such as the information line "left this message about your web server," variables, and variable pictures. Variable pictures are strings of characters that define how a field should be laid out. The following characters are used in this script for variable picture formatting:

- @ — indicates the start of a new picture
- < — indicates that the text should be left-justified
- @*— indicates that the data may be multiline or more than one line in size

Other than variable names and these special characters, any other text in the format block (such as the rows of = signs in our example) is treated as text to be inserted as-is into the output stream. No newline characters need to be placed at the end of output lines; each line in the format block occupies its own line in the output (except for multiline data, of course, which takes up as many lines as necessary).

The format shown in Code Example 10-9 places the name variable on a line by itself and left-justifies it. Next, a text message is inserted. The e-mail variable is placed on a left-justified line by itself, and the comment is displayed until all information is printed.

Code Example 10-9   Using Formats

```
    =============================================================
    @<<<<<<<<<<<<<<<<<<<<<<<<<<<<<<<<<<<<<<<<<<<<<<<<<<<<<<<<
    $NAME
    left this message about your web server
    @<<<<<<<<<<<<<<<<<<<<<<<<<<<<<<<<<<<<
    $EMAIL
    @*
    $COMMENT
    =============================================================
```

Writing to Various Output Locations

The format is given the same name as the output variable to which the data will be written. Thus, the data laid out in the format STDOUT will be written to stdout, and the data in format COMMENTFORM will be written to whatever output COMMENTFORM is written to.

Code Example 10-10   Defining Format Outputs

```
open (COMMENTFORM,">> $logs/comments.log");

write (COMMENTFORM);

close (COMMENTFORM);
```

In Example 10-10 above, the output COMMENTFORM is set to append to the file comments.log in the defined logs directory. (The >> in the open statement specifies that the file is to be appended to rather than overwritten.) In the full example, there is an additional format output, MAILCOMMENT, which is currently usable in this form only on UNIX systems, because its output is piped to the UNIX mail command. Other operating systems have other facilities (such as sendmail) to perform the same function. Again, refer to Appendix B for suggested resources.

Search for Data

When your website is large, it is a good idea to let users search for the specific page(s) that meet their needs rather than load several pages to find what they are looking for. (You can include a menu of the site's main pages on every page in the site, but it is seldom practical to include *all* pages on such a menu.) Several data location programs, each with its own methodology, are available for each platform. They fall into two categories, search tools and indexed site databases.

Note – The term "databases" here is being used specifically to refer to databases of information about a website's documents, not databases of information that support a site's business or organizational purposes (such as databases of product information, conference registrants, and so on).

Search tools define a directory tree or list of directories to search for the specific word that a user wants to look up. Many common tools, such as agrep and htgrep, are based on the UNIX grep tool.

Site databases with indexes usually provide faster searching, and custom indexes, such as synonym indexes, make it easier to find a needle in a haystack. However, these databases require more maintenance. The indexes must be regenerated whenever you add new data to the site, and they can take up as much as 20 percent of the space of the data they are indexing. Most of the tools in this category are based on WAIS or the Z39.50 ISO standard. Refer to Appendix B for pointers to these products.

The basic process of creating searchable information is as follows:

- Install the indexing or search software.

- Create the indexes if you are using indexing software.

- Create a web page to call the search tool.

You can create a regular web page that has a form with a text field for a simple search. However, this process has been automated. A single tag can now do the work of three. You can use the <ISINDEX> tag instead of a form with a text field. The <ISINDEX> tag has the ACTION attribute, just like a form; the action points to a script or external program which performs the search. An example is:

```
<ISINDEX ACTION="/cgi-bin/newwais.pl/wwwserver">
```

This example in Figure 10-1 creates a search prompt.

This is a searchable index. Enter search keywords:

Figure 10-1   Search Prompt Created with <ISINDEX> Tag

Depending on your site's policies, it may also be useful to know that some commercial Web search engines (such as Excite! and HotBot) offer a service that lets you use their resources as the ACTION attribute, in exchange for the publicity that placing the search engine's logo on your pages generates.

Summary

In this chapter, you learned:

- How to handle input from web forms.

- How to direct the output to the client via stdout, to a file, and, on UNIX systems, to e-mail.

- How to create a feedback form.

- How to create a search prompt.

Tags Used in This Chapter

Tag	Attribute	Description
`<ISINDEX>`		Creates a prompt to gather a request for searching.
	`ACTION`	Defines the script or program called to complete the search.

10

HTML for Fun and Profit

Client-Side Processing 11 ☰

Earlier chapters of this book have presented various techniques of driving the user's client—the browser—from the server. A wholly server-based website is a good approach to delivering content for numerous reasons: control, stability, the generally greater computing power of servers relative to local workstations or PCs, and a multitude of server-based tools such as http itself and the CGI.

As the Web has exploded in the last two to three years, though, increasing attention has been given to offloading to the client some of the processing burden normally placed on servers and on the network as a whole. For example, when a user submits a form, why should the data have to be validated at the server end, after transmitting it all and perhaps requiring a "Sorry—your responses are not correct; please reenter and repost them" cycle?

Also, while growing commercial use of the Internet has resulted in many excellent new services (and 'Net-based versions of older ones), privacy advocates are with some justification concerned about the growing concentration of personal data kept on-line, for example, in server-based databases.

This chapter provides an overview of several fairly new mechanisms for addressing these problems. We will present information particularly on two of these tools (cookies and JavaScript) and brief discussions of two others (Java and VBScript/ActiveX).

Note – The technologies covered in this chapter, as of this writing, are *generally* accepted for use in the form and to the extent described. However, these are evolving technologies in various stages of review and approval by the standards organizations. Check the resources in Appendix B for information about the current status of proposals related to specific client-side technology.

HTTP Cookies: Halfway to Client-Side

The Web is by nature a *stateless* environment, thanks to the request-response model inherent in http itself. When you request a document by clicking on a hyperlink, the document is fetched from the corresponding URL and delivered to your browser—after which the server forgets that you exist, let alone that you ever requested that document (or any other). When you submit a form to a server, a CGI program on the server processes the form data, performs some action (such as placing an order for a purchase), and then forgets about you and your data. The server, in short, does not maintain knowledge of the state you and your browser were in on your last visit.

Various remedies have been developed for this "forgetfulness," using technology such as hidden form variables (to pass form data from one document to another) and server-based databases (for retaining data beyond the current session). As stated above, though, these server-side state-preservation devices have a number of drawbacks. To reiterate, they:

- Require that the processing resources of the web server be used for purposes other than serving web documents.

- Potentially require large quantities of disk space for retaining state data for thousands of users—many of whom will never (or seldom) be back for subsequent visits.

- Can expose private information to potential misuse or abuse by corporations, governments, and unscrupulous individuals. Adding security mechanisms like encryption minimizes but does not eliminate this exposure, especially if the data resides in centralized databases.

Cookies—originally developed for the Netscape Navigator browser version 1.1—were developed to address these concerns, particularly those involving preservation of state. Because they still require some processing by the server, cookies are not a 100 percent client-side technology. However, the preservation of state occurs on the client machine.

What Is a Cookie?

Briefly, a cookie is a single data element created by a web server-client interaction and stored on the user's local workstation or PC. The cookie contains not only the data itself, but also information—meta-information—*about* the cookie, such as how long it will be effective and which server may request delivery of the data. A cookie's data can optionally be encrypted and/or transmitted only over a secure connection, which would be desirable, for instance, when storing a user password for entering a site.

Since Netscape Communications first established the cookie mechanism, the company's browser has kept all cookies in a single file, named `cookies.txt`. (With the recent Netscape Communicator 4.0 release, each user of a workstation or PC can have his or her own `cookies.txt` file.) The exact format of this file is not terribly important to understand in order for a web developer to use cookies; but for the curious a sample of one appears in Code Example 11-1.

Code Example 11-1   Excerpt from a Sample `cookies.txt` *file*

```
# Netscape HTTP Cookie File
# http://www.netscape.com/newsref/std/cookie_spec.html
# This is a generated file!  Do not edit.


.somecompany.com  TRUE /main      FALSE900160050 user       JohnS
.somecompany.com  TRUE /software  TRUE 900160059 lastpurchFileEdit
```

The file begins with a three-line header of general information. The URL in the second line is that of the Netscape document which spells out the company's specification for the cookie "protocol." Following the header is a blank line, followed by a list of the individual cookies themselves, one cookie per line. Each cookie consists of seven "fields" separated from one another by a tab character. These fields are:

- Identity of the **server** which is allowed to access the cookie's data.

- A Boolean (true/false) flag which indicates whether the cookie is accessible by all machines in the domain represented by the first field (TRUE), or only by the machine which set the cookie on which the cookie-setting document itself resides (FALSE).

- A **path** on the designated server: When you access a document in this directory, or any of its subordinate directories, the cookie's data will be sent to the server.

- A Boolean flag: True if the transmission of the cookie is **secured** (via the Secure Sockets Layer protocol, or SSL), false if not.

- The **expiry date/time** of the cookie, expressed in milliseconds since the start of a standard "epoch" (January 1, 1970). Note that when you set the cookie (see below for an example), you don't supply this value in the form stored here—just as a regular date and time. After this date, the cookie will no longer be set or retrieved.

- The **name** of the cookie itself.

- The **value** of the specified cookie. Together with the preceding field, this field is analogous to the name/value pairs discussed in Chapter 10.

What the first cookie in Code Example 11-1 says, in effect, is: "Whenever this user visits the **somecompany.com** site and goes to its **/main** directory (or any of its subordinates), send the **unsecured username 'JohnS'** to the server. Do this until the given **expiration date/time**." (If the user accesses the site after that time, it will appear to the server that the cookie had never been set.)

It should be obvious from this sample that cookies, used judiciously, can be a powerful aid in regard to both minimizing housekeeping details and enriching the user's experience of your website.

Note – Microsoft's Internet Explorer (MSIE) browser also supports cookies, with some differences in the way it handles individual data items. For example, MSIE requires that the domain be set in all lowercase, whereas this doesn't seem to matter in the Netscape browser. More importantly, cookies set from within MSIE do not get placed in a single `cookies.txt` file. Rather, each cookie is placed in a file of its own, one "field" per line, and all the individual cookie files are kept in a `\Cookies` directory (typically a subdirectory of the operating system's own directory, e.g., `\Windows\Cookies`).

Setting a Cookie

You will recall from earlier chapters that a CGI program or script sends to the browser not only the body of the data to be displayed, but also a response header (the content-type definition). The value of a cookie is also set with a response header, called `SET-COOKIE`. The format of this header is:

```
Set-Cookie: name=value; Expires=date; Path=path; Domain=domain; secure
```

Values shown here in italics correspond to items in the `cookies.txt` file as described above. (*Secure* has a value of `SECURE` or is not specified at all, depending on whether the transmission of the cookie's data must occur made over SSL.) Only the *name* and *value* parameters, in theory, are required; however, specifying all parameters, except perhaps *secure*, is a better practice. You should also specify the parameters in the order shown.

Other "gotchas" pertaining to the Set-Cookie header:

- If you do not specify the expiry date, the cookie is temporary (retained during the current session but not saved beyond that).

- If you don't supply a path, the browser is supposed to set the value to whatever the path of the original request was.

- The `domain` parameter must include at least two periods, which is to say that you can't simply specify a domain of `.com`, `.org`, and so on. (There is one exception to this rule, in the case of certain PC-based server software such as WebSite. When setting a cookie from a local document on that server, `domain` may appear, for example, as `localhost` without any periods at all.) For a domain consisting of just two components (like `.somecompany.com` in the above example), the cookie will apply to `www.somecompany.com`, `worldbiz.somecompany.com`, and so forth. Note that Internet Explorer has reportedly had difficulties if the domain includes any uppercase letters.

- A cookie with the same name, path, and domain as a cookie already stored on the user's system will overwrite the existing cookie. (Note, however, that according to the Netscape specification, you can *delete* a cookie by setting a new one to the same name, path, and domain, and specifying an expiry date in the past.) If these three parameters, taken together, are unmatched in the `cookies.txt` file (or any of the `\Windows\Cookies` files, for MSIE users), the cookie is simply added.

- The Netscape cookie specification says that up to 300 cookies can be kept in `cookies.txt`, and that a maximum of 20 cookies can be kept for each domain. When these limits are exceeded the browser should delete the "least recently used" cookie before adding the new one.

- Each cookie is limited to no more than 4 KB in size. If longer than 4 KB, it is trimmed to that length. (This should ensure that at least the *name* and *value* parameters "make the cut.")

An example of a Set-Cookie header would be:

```
Set-Cookie: bgcolor=magenta; expires=Sunday, 27-Jul-1997 23:59:59
         GMT; path=/; domain=.yourdomain.com
```

Or, in Perl:

```
print "Set-Cookie: bgcolor=magenta; expires=Sunday, 27-Jul-1997
         23:59:59 GMT; path=/; domain=.yourdomain.com\n";
```

A good place to issue the `Set-Cookie` directive is before the content-type.

Here is the `cookies.txt` record resulting from the above Set-Cookie response header:

```
.yourdomain.com FALSE / FALSE 870048000    bgcolormagenta
```

Retrieving a Cookie

Obviously, storing persistent data is of little use if they cannot be recovered from the user's system. This is a simple task, as the browser returns the information to the CGI automatically as soon as the user accesses a document anywhere in the designated path. Your CGI program/script does not need to (indeed, cannot) explicitly request the cookie.

This returned cookie is in the form of a *request header* from the browser to the server and accessible with the HTTP_COOKIE environment variable. Contents of this variable are the *name=value* pairs of all cookies set for that domain and path; the metainformation about the cookies (expiry and so on) is not returned. Multiple *name=value* pairs for the same domain and path are delimited by semicolons. To use the HTTP_COOKIE data, your script must parse it into its component *name=value* pairs, storing them in other variables.

The following steps will walk you through two forms, one of which is dynamically generated by a Perl script which both sets and uses the value of a cookie. Note that in this case the script does not supply a domain parameter, since that will vary with whatever server you are using. (The Set-Cookie header's default domain value is the domain of the server on which the script runs.)

1. **Load** http://*{server}*/cgi-bin/use_cookie.pl **in your browser.**
   The script (shown below in Code Example 11-2) generates a simple form displaying the current value of the bgcolor cookie, and asking you to select a background color. The first time you run this script, the bgcolor cookie will be blank because it has not yet been set.

Code Example 11-2 use_cookie.pl

```
#!/perl/perl

print "Content-type: text/html\n\n";
print "<html>\n";
print "<head><title>Cookie Confirmation</title></head>\n";
@cookies = split(/=/,$ENV{'HTTP_COOKIE'});
print "<body>\n";
print "<H1>Cookie Confirmation</H1>\n";
print "<hr>\n";
print "Current cookie list (less '=' signs) for this domain/path: ";
while(@cookies) {
```

Code Example 11-2 use_cookie.pl (continued)

```perl
    $cookie=shift @cookies;
    print "<CODE>$cookie</CODE> ";
}
if ($cookie eq "") {
    print "<P>The <CODE>bgcolor</CODE> cookie hasn't yet been set for
        this domain/path.";
}
else {
    print "<P>The last background color you chose (per the above
    cookie list) was <b>";
    print $cookie;
    print "</b>.\n<P>";
}
print "When you click on the button below, your browser window's
  background color should be set accordingly.<P>\n";
print "<FORM action='/cgi-bin/set_bgcolor.pl' method='get'>\n";
print "<select name='bgcolor'>\n";
print "<option>Yellow\n";
print "<option>White\n";
print "<option>Gray\n";
print "<option>Magenta\n";
print "</select>\n";
print "<input type='submit' value='Set Color'>\n";
print "</select><br>";
print "</form>\n";
print "</body></html>\n";
```

2. **In a text editor or using** more, **display the contents of the** use_cookie.pl **Perl script (see Code Example 11-2).**
   The script parses the data in the bgcolor cookie, if any, and uses it to set the generated document's title, a level-one header, and the background color of the page. If the cookie is not yet set, the document's text states instead that that is the case.

3. **Set your browser's options/preferences so that you are warned whenever a page attempts to set a cookie.**
   This will enable you to see the value of any cookies set for this domain/path, as well as the expiry date and other information. In Netscape Navigator 4.0, this is done with the Edit->Preferences menu. Click on Advanced in the left pane of the Preferences window and be sure the box labeled "Warn me before accepting a cookie" is checked. For other browsers, check your documentation.

Note – You need to be aware of the various ways in which users can control the setting of cookies on their machines. Depending on the browser, they may simply accept the default (to accept all cookies); to be warned whenever a cookie is about to be set (as in this step); to accept cookies which may be returned only to the server that sets them; or not to accept any cookies at all. Given the privacy concerns about indiscriminate use of cookies, you should *not* make your site's behavior entirely dependent on the user's willingness to accept cookies.

---

4. **Return to the browser display. Select a color from the drop-down option box and click on the** Set Color **button.**
   As shown in the action= attribute of the <FORM> tag in the document generated by the use_cookie.pl script, clicking on the Set Color button invokes another script, set_bgcolor.pl. The first thing that happens (assuming you performed step 3) is that your browser asks if you will accept the cookie. Note the information displayed in this dialog box and click on OK. Then set_bgcolor.pl simply takes the value of the bgcolor cookie (passed to it from use_cookie.pl) and sets the background color of the document which it generates (and incidentally displays the name of the color in a header and the document's title bar).

5. **Note that the contents of the browser window vary depending on the color you selected.**
   Because this script does not read the HTTP_COOKIE environment variable but merely reads the query string passed to it from use_cookie.pl, your screen will be customized regardless of whether you clicked on OK or Cancel in the preceding step. However, if you clicked on Cancel, the cookie will not actually be set. You can confirm this by rerunning the previous step, clicking on Cancel, and then using your browser's Back and Reload features to see the current actual cookie value.

Note – Cookies are saved to the client hard drive when the user exits the browser. If you open `cookies.txt` in a text editor while the browser itself is still open, you will see that the cookie has not yet been set/updated.

6. Optional: Delete the `bgcolor` cookie.
It is possible to delete a cookie by using a text editor to remove the corresponding line from the cookies.txt file. This risks damaging real cookies containing possibly useful information, however. A safer (and more educational) course of action is to force the browser itself to remove the cookie by changing the expiry date in the `Set-Cookie` directive to a date in the past.

To do so, with a text editor open the file `Chapter_11/set_bgcolor.pl`. Change the line containing the `Set-Cookie` directive to:

```
print "Set-Cookie: bgcolor=$bgcolor; expires=1-Jan-1970 00:00:01 GMT;
    path=/\n";
```

You can use any other past date/time to achieve the same effect.

Save the modified `set_bgcolor.pl` script to your server's cgi-bin directory and open the script in your browser by entering `http://{server}/cgi-bin/set_bgcolor.pl` as the URL field. The page will display once with the previously set background color.

JavaScript: Freeing the Client from the Server

That's an exaggeration, of course: A browser completely uncoupled from the web would be like a television set with no antenna or cable box.

On the other hand, a television set that couldn't do anything without first consulting a broadcast source would be of extremely limited intelligence, let alone practical use. Such a set would rely on the broadcaster or cable company to tell it what volume to set the audio at, for example.

Enter JavaScript. We do not cover it here to suggest that it is the first, or necessarily the best, tool for controlling the web client *from* the client; it is however quite simple to learn and use, especially if you have been following our Perl-based CGI programming examples.

What JavaScript Is Not

First, to head off a potential misunderstanding: JavaScript has almost nothing to do with Java (another client-side programming language, covered in limited form later in this chapter).

It does not, in its current form, offer much help at all in regard to manipulating things *outside* the browser, such as files on the user's hard drive.

Finally, it is not a cure-all for web application difficulties. In particular, using JavaScript does not free you from understanding basic programming concepts, different browsers' characteristics, or the basics of http. And because even users of JavaScript-capable browsers can opt *not* to run JavaScript programs, you probably are not off the hook in the area of providing alternative "dumbed-down" interfaces to your slick JavaScript pages.

What JavaScript Is

As you might guess from the name, JavaScript (like Perl) is a *scripting* language. That is, JavaScript programs do not run in compiled form on the target computer, but by being interpreted (in this case, by the browser itself rather than by an interpreter on the server).

One thing that distinguishes JavaScript from many older languages such as Fortran, Basic, and C is that it is object based. JavaScript code can manipulate plain old variables in the same way that the older languages can; however, it is also intelligent about real *things* (and the things that those things are made up of). It knows that the user has a browser, for example, and that the browser has a window, and that in that window might be elements of a form (checkboxes, selection lists, and so on), and that these elements behave in certain ways (and can be induced to behave in others). We will have much more to say about JavaScript objects in the next section of this chapter.

There is such a thing as server-side JavaScript, but by far most of the attention paid to the language has resulted from its client-side capabilities. One benefit of these capabilities for a Web developer is that he or she does not need to set up a test server environment on a PC to duplicate that of the target server. Installing a server package to correctly run CGI programs and scripts can be overwhelming and error prone for a newcomer; there is no such difficulty for a JavaScript programmer. This assumes the availability of a JavaScript-compatible browser, of course—but considering that JavaScript is supported by both Netscape and Microsoft products, this should not prove too much of a burden.

JavaScript, originally known as LiveScript, was developed by Netscape for use in its Navigator version 2.0 browser, released in January 1996. With Sun Microsystems (developers of the wildly popular Java language), Netscape collaborated on the changeover from LiveScript to JavaScript. It is anticipated that the language will be standardized (and become truly open) in the near future, as it is merged with a similar language developed by the European Community, ECMAScript.

Note – In a somewhat typical confrontation between browser competitors, Microsoft and Netscape support slightly different versions of JavaScript. Microsoft's, called JScript, has some variations on the basic Netscape theme but it is effectively identical to JavaScript. Microsoft's Internet Explorer will not choke on almost any JavaScript code.

Like Java, JavaScript owes much of its syntax to the C and C++ languages (especially C). If you've had any exposure at all to those languages, you will find programming in JavaScript a natural extension.

JavaScript Uses

You can use JavaScript in many of the same situations in which you would use CGI programming. Because of its client-side orientation, however, JavaScript is particularly well suited to situations in which you want to control or respond to user behavior independently of anything that absolutely must take place on the server.

Typical uses of JavaScript include:

- Validating user input on HTML forms before issuing the GET or POST request to a server-side CGI process. You can validate user input with Perl or another CGI language, but this is such a powerful (and relatively simple) feature of JavaScript that it may seem a shame to waste network (and user!) time and resources by transferring the input, and error messages, back and forth across the http connection.

- Cookie processing. Setting and retrieving cookie data with JavaScript is very simple.

- Defining and controlling frames and windows.

- Customizing the user's multimedia experience of your website based on the browser plug-ins available on his or her system.

- With server-side JavaScript, establishing "user profiles" to give them each a different, customized view of your documents and to interact with many of the most popular SQL- and ODBC-based database systems.

Programming in JavaScript

Unlike CGI programs and scripts, JavaScript code is entered directly into the body of your HTML document. It is set off from the rest of the document with `<script>` and `</script>` tags.

Note – The W3C introduced this new HTML container in version 3.2, although it was supported earlier, without the official blessing, by both Netscape and Microsoft. The HTML 3.2 specification says that the container is reserved for future use, which means essentially that not only the formalization of a JavaScript standard but also the issue of the `<script>` tag's attributes has not yet been resolved. It is likely that there will be at least one attribute, `language=`*name*, to distinguish JavaScript from other in-line scripting languages. You are encouraged to use `language="JavaScript"` as an attribute to the `<script>` tag for all JavaScript code. (Note that the HTML 4.0 working draft goes a step further, recommending that you use the `type=`*name* attribute instead of `language=`*name*).

The code sample in JavaScript Example 11-1 illustrates some other key points to know about JavaScript coding. Don't worry about the details of each JavaScript instruction for now; simply examine the code for structural and syntactic elements.

JavaScript Example 11-1   A Basic JavaScript Program

```
<html>
<head><title>Basic Dull JavaScript</title></head>
<body>
<script language="JavaScript">
<!-- Hide the script itself from non-JavaScript-aware browsers.
document.write("<h1>Welcome to Your Current Time</h1>");
currtime = new Date();
document.write ("It is currently "+currtime + " where you are.");
// Unhide the remainder. -->
</script>
</body></html>
```

Note the following about Example 11-1:

- Non-JavaScript-aware browsers will ignore the `<script>` and `</script>` tags (browsers always ignore unrecognized tags). However, if you do not enclose the body of the script itself within comments (the `<!--` and `-->` codes), the script will be *displayed* by such browsers. Although a blank document may perplex users of such browsers, a document displaying JavaScript code will almost certainly alarm them.

- There is no "pure HTML" within the `<script>` container. As with Perl scripts, the embedded HTML is generated in the document using a "command" (here, `document.write` instead of Perl's `print`).

- Single-line or within-a-line JavaScript comments begin with a double slash // and continue through the end of the line. (If your comments extend over multiple lines, you can begin them with /* and end them with */, as in C. This is at some risk to maintainability, however—it is very easy to omit either the start or the ending comment string, or to add an extra one.)

- No JavaScript processing occurs anywhere except within the `<script>` container.

- As in Perl scripts, JavaScript command lines terminate with a semicolon.

- Although not necessarily obvious in the example, JavaScript is case sensitive. Changing the capitalization of JavaScript reserved words (such as `document`, `write`, `new`, and `date`) will generate a JavaScript error message. In the case of variables (such as `currtime` in the example), you can capitalize them however you want—but if you want your program to behave as expected, you must capitalize each variable the same way whenever you refer to it. This is a marked departure from the syntax of HTML itself, but consistent with syntactic conventions in many other programming languages (including Perl and C).

- The whitespace between JavaScript elements is not significant. For example, you can use or omit a space between the `document.write` command and what follows it; similarly, the space around the string concatenation operators (+ signs) in the second `document.write` line in the example.

Perhaps most importantly, because the JavaScript code is directly entered in the HTML document and processed directly by the browser, you do not need any special software to create and test it—a simple text editor and a browser suffice, just as with the HTML code alone.

Note – Many current-generation HTML-editing software packages provide direct support for JavaScript entry, such as wizards and other tools for performing common JavaScript tasks. See Chapter 14 for more information on some of these packages.

Objects, Methods, Properties

You get in your car and start it up (perhaps fluttering the gas pedal; it's a bit cranky first thing in the morning). You turn on the radio, adjust the volume, and you're off. That scenario comprises nearly all you need to know about objects, methods, and properties—the cornerstones of JavaScript programming.

- *Objects* are the things the program manipulates. (Your car is an object; so are the gas pedal and radio—which are actually subordinate objects of the car.)

- *Methods* are the actions applied to the objects by the program. (You start the car, tap the gas pedal, press a button or turn a knob to adjust the volume up or down.)

- And *properties* are the characteristics of objects, characteristics which can be affected by methods and other actions, such as assignment with an = sign. (The radio's volume is loud, inaudible, or just right.)

The JavaScript language includes over two dozen standard objects, arranged in a hierarchy (like the `car->radio->volume control` hierarchy). Among these "things which the program manipulates" are obvious ones such as `document`, `frame`, `window`, and `form`, and some perhaps not-so-obvious ones such as `history` and `Math`. Each object type has its own unique properties and methods that control the behavior of the user's browser. (For a complete list, please refer to Appendix A.)

Event Handlers

You already know that HTML and servers can interact in some ways, such as when the user clicks on a hypertext link or a form's Submit button. JavaScript extends this awareness of user behavior with what are called event handlers—effectively little subprograms which kick in depending on what the user is doing at a given moment.

The events which a JavaScript-enabled document can react to vary depending on the object with which the user is currently interacting. They include such common GUI events as `onClick` (which happens when the user clicks on the object), `onMouseOver` (when the user's mouse cursor passes over the object), and `onBlur` (when the cursor leaves a text field, for example—the object is said to have "lost focus," hence the name of the event). This is analogous to the way that a hypothetical "`onPress`" event might be handled differently when the driver presses on the gas pedal and presses the radio's on/off switch: You do not normally (we hope!) want the car to accelerate when you turn on the radio.

A JavaScript Example

In the example below, we demonstrate some elementary features of JavaScript objects, methods, properties, and event handlers. (A greatly detailed discussion of JavaScript is beyond the scope of this book, but we encourage you to explore this powerful resource for Web developers, starting with some of the resources listed in Appendix B.)

1. **Load** `Chapter_11/javascript.html` **in your browser and view the document source.**

The code is shown in JavaScript Example 11-2.

JavaScript Example 11-2   Reacting to User Behavior

```
<html>
<head><title>Responding to User Behavior with
  JavaScript</title></head>


<script language="JavaScript">
<!-- Hide the script itself from non-JavaScript-aware browsers.
  function chgColor(newcolor) {
      if (document.bgColor != newcolor) {
        document.bgColor = newcolor;
      }
  return;
  }


  function showStartTime() {
      var currtime = new Date();
      var currHrs = currtime.getHours();
      var currMins = currtime.getMinutes();
      var currSecs = currtime.getSeconds();
      var disptime = "" + ((currHrs <= 12) ? currHrs + ":" :
        ((currHrs - 12 >= 10) ? currHrs - 12 : "0" +
        (currHrs - 12) + ":"));
      disptime += ((currMins >= 10) ? currMins + ":" : "0" +
        currMins + ":");
      disptime += ((currSecs >= 10) ? currSecs : "0" + currSecs);
      return disptime;
}
// Unhide the remainder. -->
</script>


<body>
<script language="JavaScript">
document.bgColor = "#ffffff";
```

```
</script>
<h1>Responding to User Behavior with JavaScript</h1>
<a name="top">This script makes use of some of JavaScript's
document-formatting capabilities
to demonstrate how you can dynamically change the appearance of a
document based solely on the ways that the user is interacting with
the
browser window.
<P>
<blockquote>
<form name="currform">
  <input type="button" name="YellowButton"
     value="          Yellow          " onclick="chgColor('#ffff00')">
  <input type="button" name="WhiteButton"
     value="Back to White" onclick="chgColor('#ffffff')">
</form>
<P>
With the <a href="#top" onclick="chgColor('#c0c0c0')")">gray</a>
link, the background color changes to gray when you click the link.
With
the <a href="#top" onMouseOver="chgColor('#ff00ff')">magenta</a>
one, on
the other hand, it changes to magenta when your cursor simply moves
over
the link.
</blockquote>

<script language="JavaScript">
<!-- Hide the script.
  document.write("<h3>You started looking at this page at <em>" +
     showStartTime() + "</em>.</h3>");
  // Stop hiding. -->
```

```
</script>

</body></html>
```

Here are some key elements to notice:

- Structurally, the document consists of a document head and title in HTML, a JavaScript code block, a body tag, a second (short) JavaScript code block, some HTML to define a level-three heading and an HTML form as well as some straight text (with two hypertext links), a third JavaScript code block, and the concluding `</body>` and `<html>` tags. The key thing to observe here is that you can include more than one JavaScript block in a document.

- The first JavaScript code block defines two *functions*, `chgColor` and `showStartTime`. Functions (in JavaScript terms) are reusable code that can be called repeatedly, thereby eliminating the need to repeat entire sections of code (and perhaps introduce errors). Note that the contents of each function are enclosed in curly braces `{}`.

- The `chgColor` function receives one argument, `newcolor`. Every time `chgColor` is invoked in this document—as long as the current background color is different from `newcolor`—it changes the document's background color. The word `document` is a JavaScript reserved word: It is an **object** that identifies whatever the current HTML document is. Similarly, `bgColor` is a built-in **property** of the `document` object. You can "read" all properties (as in the `if` statement), and you can "write" most of them as well (as in the statement following the `if` test, which actually sets the `bgColor` property).

- The `showStartTime` function does not receive any arguments; all the data it needs are available internally. The various steps in this function define variables to be used in breaking up the current date and time into a standard 12-hour representation of the time, in HH:MM:SS format. Most importantly for the purposes of this example, it *returns* the formatted time string to whichever JavaScript statement invoked the `showStartTime` function. This returned value can be used by the invoking statement in whatever way it wants. Also note the items such as `getHours()` and `getMinutes()`. These are **methods** which, in this case, operate on the JavaScript `Date` object (as well as on objects, such as variables, which derive from it).

- In the main section of HTML code, you should note several new attributes to previously introduced tags. These attributes, `onClick=` and `onMouseOver=`, define **events** for which the JavaScript author has provided some special processing (known as **event handlers**). Different elements of the user interface come with different events; for example, you can provide an `onMouseOver` event handler for hyperlinks but not for form buttons. The value of the event attribute is the name of a JavaScript function—chgColor, in this case—including any arguments which the function expects to receive. Browsers read and process all HTML documents from start to finish; for this reason it is critical that you define all of your JavaScript functions somewhere in the document *before* they are invoked, otherwise JavaScript will tell you it cannot find a function by that name.

- The final JavaScript block simply issues a document.write to display the text as formatted by the showStartTime function. The value returned by that function is simply inserted into the displayed text in place of the function call. (Since showStartTime is called only once in this document, its code could simply be moved down to this JavaScript block; however, this illustrates the manner in which to invoke a function.)

2. **Close the View Page Source window and return to the browser display. Observe what happens as you interact with various elements of the page.**
   Relate the changes in the document to the JavaScript code shown in Example 11-2.

Beyond Basic Client-Side

CGI and JavaScript programming can solve many of the problems associated with static HTML documents. Nevertheless there are many perceived limitations to these solutions, and a number of "solutions to the solutions" are in various stages of development and standardization at this time. Among the most promising are Sun Microsystems' Java programming language, and Microsoft Corporation's VBScript and ActiveX initiatives.

Both Sun's and Microsoft's enhancements of client-side standards are enormous topics, supported by entire libraries of reference books, tutorials, and Internet resources (newsgroups, Web and ftp sites, and mailing lists). Our overview here will necessarily be brief but, as always, you are encouraged to consult the resources listed in Appendix B for details.

(Also, as you may be aware, Java and VBScript/ActiveX are given much media attention and attract more than their share of die-hard opponents and proponents. Our material on these topics will probably not be deep enough for you to form your own opinions, let alone win any arguments.)

Java

Based primarily on C++, the Java programming language is large and extremely powerful. It shares with C++ and JavaScript an affinity for handling objects, methods, and properties, as well as user events. Java is truly object *based*, though, unlike JavaScript (which is merely object *oriented*); this enables its built-in capabilities to be extended easily and powerfully.

Unlike Perl and JavaScript, Java is not interpreted directly by the browser: If you look at a Java program in the form in which it runs in your browser, you don't see "readable" text. But unlike many other languages—C, C++, Fortran, Cobol, and others—Java applications are not distributed and run in true compiled form, either.

Instead, the Java programmer enters his or her code with a text editor (if really ambitious) or with a Java development environment. (Sun makes one of the latter, called the Java Development Kit, or JDK.) The programs are then "pseudocompiled" into, and ultimately distributed in, something called *bytecode* form. The bytecode is compiled on-the-fly by a software component called the *Java Virtual Machine*.

The major browsers come with built-in Java Virtual Machines. More importantly—and the source of much of the excitement about Java—JVMs are also available *outside* the browser environment, running as applications on a wide variety of operating systems. This means that full-blown Java applications can with some restrictions be run either from within the browser or "naked," without the browser wrapper at all. Indeed, many software vendors and other corporations are converting their applications wholesale to Java for this reason. (At the time this was being written, there was even talk of using Java to program "smart cards" and household appliances.)

Imagine a word processor written entirely in Java, for example. The product's vendor could write the code once, making it instantly portable to any platform with its own Java Virtual Machine. True word processing functions could be made available, for that matter, in a web page viewed with a Java-capable browser. The distinction between "what I can do on the Web" and "what I can do on my standalone PC" would diminish, perhaps even disappear entirely.

Note – Technically, a Java *application* is a Java program that runs outside a web browser; this is distinguished from a Java *applet*, one which is intended strictly for web use. In this brief discussion we use the term "application" to cover both kinds of Java-based programming, although of course we are most concerned here with web-based applets rather than purely local applications.

A particularly important feature of Java is that it explicitly supports *multithreading*. This is analogous to juggling many balls at once and having each ball behave differently from the others at the same time. The Java programmer can assign one "thread" to the processing of the user's keyboard input, for example, so that no matter what else the CPU is up to the display of keyed-in text does not slow down.

Aside from its object orientation and multithreading capabilities, Java includes excellent support for features (often overlooked in new languages, especially cross-platform ones) such as:

- Garbage collection (the management of memory allocation).

- Verification: Java bytecode is examined by the JVM for possible security leaks before being executed.

- Memory-leakage control: When a Java program has finished using an object, the object goes away—it does not remain in memory, getting in the way of other processes that could make use of the memory.

There are some downsides to this revolution.

First, as of this writing, Java applications cannot access the user's local environment in any way familiar to most developers for client platforms. This is a byproduct of the Java developers' laudable decision to make Java secure; Java is said to run in a "sandbox" in which it can know about everything internal (and everything available to it on the Web) but cannot affect the user's environment in various useful but potentially dangerous ways. For example, a Java program can give the user the option of downloading a shareware program from an ftp site, for example, but can't download the file behind the scenes, on its own.

Note – Some work is occurring (in Sun's own JavaSoft division and elsewhere) to relax this restriction in new versions of Java. This is a delicate balancing act, however; it remains to be seen whether there can ever be any fully satisfactory solution to the power-vs.-security dilemma.

A second drawback is that—again, as of this writing—Java applications still run relatively slowly. To some extent (at least for web-based applications) this is a simple matter of "waiting to get what you need to run," as with nonstreaming multimedia (see Chapter 4): The Java bytecode must be downloaded completely before the Java Virtual Machine can interpret and run the program.

However, even with Java applications that are run directly on the user's machine (with no download required), there is still a performance penalty. This is due to the necessary intervention of the Java Virtual Machine. No matter how finely optimized for each platform, the JVM still must read the bytecode and "compile" it before actually running it. If the application is simple, the performance lag can be of little or no consequence; if large and complex, it can virtually negate the application's practical usefulness. Java programmers have a variety of performance-optimization techniques available to them; further, Java vendors have introduced products that include "just-in-time" compilers to accelerate the JVM's processing of bytecode. The lag still persists, however, and it is unlikely that Java applications will ever run as fast as those developed specifically for a given OS as long as the JVM's preprocessing is required.

Finally, much of the Java controversy centers around the very portability that is one of Java's hallmarks. If tools for building a user interface result in an identical application across all platforms, goes the question, will the application ever be able to take advantage of Platform X's peculiar strengths (whatever they may be)?

Microsoft Client-Side Technologies: VBScript and ActiveX

In the few years that the Internet, particularly the Web, has become a major attractor of media, business, and consumer interest, Microsoft Corporation has released a flurry of new technologies in an effort to obtain and keep a share of the new market. Giving away the Internet Explorer browser with every copy of Windows 95/NT has been just the tip of the iceberg.

Much of the controversy about Microsoft's presence as a Web-related software vendor is due to its Windows-centric view of new technologies. While this is understandable—Microsoft after all *is* the Windows company—this predisposition alarms many who value the Internet as a place where standards become so by common consensus, not because they are declared as "standards" by their vendors (however powerful the vendors may be).

The VBScript language for web developers is a good case in point. Although Microsoft (as described earlier in this chapter) supports JavaScript in its browser (especially the Microsoft variant called JScript), the company has also adapted its popular Visual Basic language for use in web pages. VBScript thus leverages the existing base of Visual Basic developers, enabling them to transition smoothly into the web authoring world.

Note – Microsoft's support of *Java* has been much more ambiguous than that of JavaScript. For a while, company officials derided Java as "just another programming language." More recently, they announced that Java as a programming language is wonderful and that they intend to go full-speed ahead with releasing Java development kits and other Java tools of their own. Most critically, they find fault with the Java write once/run anywhere approach, since if widely adopted that approach would result in fewer applications being written specifically for the Windows product line.

Like JavaScript, VBScript is interpreted by the browser after having been embedded directly in the HTML source document. It uses the same `<script>` tag to bracket the script code—here of course the attribute is `language="VBScript"`—and is object based, supporting objects, methods, properties, and event handlers. Otherwise the languages (with some superficial similarities) are unrelated. New proprietary HTML features support VBScript (and distinguish it from JavaScript). For example, in a VBScript document, buttons can be defined without enclosing them in a `<form>` container, and the `<input>` tag has been extended with a new attribute, `language="VBScript,"` to associate form elements with VBScript programs.

One of the biggest advantages of VBScript programs is the ability they give Web authors to embed OLE—Object Linking and Embedding—objects and custom controls in Web pages. OLE is Microsoft's technology for building "superapplications" from various bits and pieces of existing applications. For instance, a Microsoft Word document can contain a Microsoft Excel spreadsheet, allowing the user to enter data and formulas in the spreadsheet without opening up and running a completely separate instance of Excel. Custom controls are the various GUI "widgets"—buttons, scrollbars, calendars, as well as many more exotic ones such as database-like grids—familiar to users of the Windows environment. Microsoft has grouped all its OLE technologies under the term *ActiveX* since their introduction to the Internet environment.

The potential to use ActiveX technology in web pages is exciting, even among some developers and users otherwise opposed to Microsoft. Many ActiveX objects can even be embedded in documents intended strictly for display in Netscape's browser, by using a browser plug-in. So why not embrace the use of VBScript, with its built-in affinity for ActiveX, rather than JavaScript?

The reason is that to date, no browser other than Microsoft Internet Explorer can process VBScript code. If you are developing for an intranet which your users are guaranteed to be accessing via MSIE, this should not be an issue—in such an environment there is almost no reason *not* to use VBScript.

Most of us however are more concerned with making our websites accessible to all users, regardless of their browser. Until and unless MSIE becomes almost exclusively the Web browser of choice, you should be wary of using VBScript in your Web development efforts.

Summary

In this chapter you learned:

- The advantages of processing elements of a web document in the client rather than the server.

- How to set and retrieve cookies to maintain state across sessions.

- How to build a basic JavaScript program and incorporate it within a web document.

- The pros and cons of using advanced client-side technologies such as Java, VBScript, and ActiveX as web development tools.

Cookie Processing

Table 11-1 Cookie Processing

CGI Directive/Element	Option	Description
Set-Cookie		
	name=value	Gives the cookie a name and assigns its value.
	expires=date	Sets the expiry date for the cookie.
	path=path	Defines the path on the designated domain for which the cookie can later be retrieved.
	domain=domain	Identifies the server permitted to retrieve the cookie.
	secure	Indicates whether the cookie is to be transmitted only via a secure socket connection. (Value secure, or omitted.)
HTTP_COOKIE		Environment variable containing semicolon-delimited list of all cookies available on the current page.

JavaScript Elements

Table 11-2 JavaScript Elements

JavaScript Element	Option	Description
`<script>`	`language="JavaScript"`	Opens a JavaScript code block.
`</script>`		Closes a JavaScript code block.
`;`		JavaScript statement terminator.
`document`		The JavaScript object corresponding to the currently open web document.
	`.write`	Returns a line of text (possibly with HTML) to the user's browser.
	`.bgColor`	The background color for the current web document.
`Date()`		The JavaScript object corresponding to the current date/time.
`//`		Marks an in-line JavaScript comment.
`onClick=` *eventhandler*		The name of the JavaScript event handler which reacts to a user mouse-click on a given object.
`onMouseOver=` *eventhandler*		The name of the JavaScript event handler which reacts to the presence of the user mouse cursor when placed over a given object.
`function` *name*()		Defines the start of a JavaScript function.
`var varname`		Defines a JavaScript variable.
	=value	Initializes a JavaScript variable.
	`new`	Establishes a new instance of a JavaScript object.

Table 11-2 JavaScript Elements (continued)

dateobject	`.getHours`	Returns the "hours" portion of the indicated date object.
	`.getMinutes`	Returns the "minutes" portion of the indicated date object.
	`.getSeconds`	Returns the "seconds" portion of the indicated date object.
=		JavaScript assignment operator.
+		JavaScript add/concatenate operator (depending on whether processing numeric or string date).
+=		Add/Concatenate the following value to that of the current value of a variable.
!		JavaScript negation operator (e.g., != interpreted as "is *not* equal to").
(*condition*) ? *truevalue* : *falsevalue*		If *condition* is true, use *truevalue*, otherwise use *falsevalue*.
`return`		Ends a function.
	value	With `return` statement, passes the indicated value back to the JavaScript code which invoked the function.

11

Style Sheets   12 ≡

Style sheets can give you a typographically sensitive way to improve the look of your HTML formatting. In this chapter we provide examples and exercises to help you develop style sheets that you can apply to any web document you create. To make the style sheet examples function correctly, you will need a browser capable of handling style sheets such as Microsoft Internet Explorer 3.0, Netscape Navigator 4.0, or equivalent, although a server is not necessary. The usual View Page Source feature of your browser will work for viewing the HTML examples in this chapter, but the external files are best viewed with a text editor.

The style sheet standard is incorporated in a W3C recommendation, which you can find at:

```
http://www.w3.org/pub/WWW/TR/REC-CSS1
```

We cover the basics of style-sheet handling in this chapter. We encourage you to explore some of the more advanced features on your own, beginning with the above W3C document and other resources pointed to in Appendix B.

Note – Screen shots in this chapter all use Microsoft Internet Explorer (MSIE) rather than Netscape Navigator as the browser. In the case of style sheets, there are one or two cases in which MSIE renders the screen differences more visibly than does the Netscape product.

What Are Style Sheets?

A style sheet is a collection of formatting instructions that allows you to specify font sizes, column widths, leading (pronounced "ledding"—how closely a line of type is packed relative to the lines above and below it), and even color of type and the background it is set upon. By saving this collection of instructions separately, you have a style sheet that you can apply throughout a document—even a set of multiple documents—simply by altering the corresponding style sheet.

You can develop style sheets for different purposes. For example, you might want some text to appear in a corporate format complete with graphics, and then have the same text appear in a plainer, correspondence format. Style sheets separate the text from the formatting instructions, and make the process of revising your page(s) much easier and less error-prone. You are less likely to miss a set of closing brackets, for instance.

Style sheets can be either used inside a Web document, or *linked*—that is, external to the documents that employ those styles. Linked style sheets are preferable for clarity, as they avoid cluttering up the document itself with formatting instructions. A style sheet overrides the way a user's browser displays text, and you can change the *formatting* of every document on your web site without touching a single one.

Note – Style sheets go a long way toward freeing the webmaster from the limitations of HTML as a design tool. With both the Internet Explorer and the Netscape browsers, however, users can opt *not* to use style sheets by altering their preferences—in which case they will see your document as if your pages had no styles at all to be applied. Bear this in mind when designing your pages with style sheets. Test your styled pages with style sheets turned off in the browser.

Style Sheet Syntax

There are several ways to incorporate style sheets into your web documents, as we will show below. However the style sheets are referenced by documents on your site, though, the basic syntax for specifying document style is the same.

Each style specification is called a *rule*. A rule is a simple line of text which follows this basic syntax:

> *selector { property: value }*

Most commonly, what is called a "selector" is an HTML tag, without the surrounding greater-than/less-than characters, < and >. Any HTML tag can be used as a selector. *Property* is, roughly speaking, a visual (or other) attribute that the selector will have when rendered by the browser. And *value* (like the value of a straight HTML attribute) defines the specific rendering of the property. (Notice that the property-value pairs are separated from the rest of the rule by "curly braces," { and }, and that they are separated from each other by a colon. If you want, you can include more than one property-value pair in the same rule—separate them from one another using semicolons.)

For a simple example, if you want all text enclosed within an HTML <h3> container to be displayed in italics, you could use this rule:

```
h3 { font-style: italic }
```

Any document which includes or otherwise references this rule would display its level-three headings the same way. If you later decide to remake the look of your pages so that all level-three headings display in small caps, in a sans-serif font, you just change the rule to something like this:

```
h3 { font-variant: small-caps; font-family: sans-serif }
```

Each line within a style sheet has to end with either a semicolon or a closing }. (You would end the line with a semicolon only if you are defining more than one property-value pair. Each rule itself is always terminated by the closing brace.) If you want to include comments in your style sheet, enclose them within /* and */ characters (which is identical to the C programming language's commenting convention).

Internal Style Sheets

Throughout this chapter, we will use the same basic HTML document, simply changing the style-sheet notation and rules as necessary for the point being demonstrated. Code Example 12-1 shows the entire file.

Code Example 12-1 shows how to format text using a style sheet embedded *in* the document using <STYLE> tags. As with all HTML documents, we begin with <HTML> and <HEAD>. Since the purpose of a style sheet is to specify fonts, type is a mandatory attribute. Complete internal style sheets should always go in <HEAD>. (Obviously, if you put them in later you risk having some elements displayed in the browser's default styles.) Note that in order to accommodate browsers that don't know how to treat the style sheet, use HTML comments to hide it. Otherwise the rules will be displayed in such browsers' windows.

Code Example 12-1   The Basic Style Sheet — ssex1

```
<HTML> <HEAD> <TITLE>Stylesheet Basics Examples</TITLE>
<STYLE TYPE="text/css">
<!--
  H1 { font-size : 48pt }
-->
</STYLE></HEAD>
<BODY>
<H1>Stylesheets</H1>
Stylesheets are a method of controlling the presentation aspects of a
web page.
<H2>Web Designer's Viewpoint</H2>
```

```
The goal of the original designers of the web was to create HTML as a
languagethat did <EM>content</EM> markup, or just define the types
of
elements that there were on the page such as:
<UL>
<LI>paragraphs,
<LI>headings,
<LI>lists.
</UL>
Each browser was then supposed to render these elements as the
browser
designer saw fit.
<H2>Content Creator's Viewpoint</H2>
<P>However, content creators had already had quite a bit of
experience
with desktop publishing systems, and they wanted presentation
control.</P>
<P>In the interim between the advent of wide-spread browser use and
the integration of
stylesheets in those browsers, tags were created to add presentation
aspects to HTML. This was not a good thing to do for several
reasons:</P>
<OL>
<LI>The look and feel of a web site was not consistantly maintained
because multipledevelopers did their own thing, instead of using a
single master template or stylesheet.
<LI>Changing the look and feel of a web site requires editing
<EM>all</EM> of the oldfiles to change the look and feel, regardless
if
there are ten or ten thousand pages.
<LI>Kludges or attempts to use tags for things that they weren't
designed for sometimes backfired on the wide variety of browsers
available.
</OL>
</BODY></HTML>
```

Note the following about the above <STYLE> tag and the contents of the style sheet itself:

- The TYPE= attribute specifies a MIME type of text/css. (The css refers to cascading style sheets, described below.) This is similar to the Content-type: text/html declaration covered in the chapters on CGI programming. Like that declaration, it puts the browser on notice that what follows is a particular kind of content to be treated in a particular way different from plain text.

- All <H1> tags in this document will be displayed the same way, in 48-point type. Other than the size, the level-one headings will be rendered according to the user's preferences (or the browser's default, if not overridden by the user).

- No other tags beside the level-one headers will be treated in any special way.

Linked Style Sheets

Instead of incorporating the style sheet into the document itself, it is preferable to create a separate external style sheet and link the HTML document to it. This enables the style sheet to be used by more than one document. The following example shows how to create a <LINK> for style sheets.

The link is declared in the line:

```
<LINK REL="STYLESHEET" TYPE="text/css" HREF="ssmain2.css">
```

incorporated into the head of the document. Required attributes to <LINK> are REL, TYPE, and HREF.

LINK gives a name to the external style sheet, while REL. TYPE identifies its characteristic, just as in the <STYLE> tag in Code Example 12-1. HREF is the specific reference point—the file containing the style rule(s) to be applied to this document. To produce exactly the same result as in Code Example 12-1, the file ssmain2.css would contain a single rule:

```
H1 { font-size : 48pt }
```

Code Example 12-2 shows how the internal style sheet of Code Example 12 might be altered to become a linked style sheet.

Code Example 12-2 Linking an External Style Sheet—ssex2.html

```
<HTML> <HEAD> <TITLE>Stylesheet Basics Examples</TITLE>
<LINK REL="STYLESHEET" TYPE="text/css" HREF="ssmain2.css">
```

12

Code Example 12-2 Linking an External Style Sheet—ssex2.html (Continued)

```
</HEAD>
<BODY>
                (etc.)
</BODY></HTML>
```

Cascading Style Sheets

The word "cascading" in the phrase "Cascading Style Sheets" (CSS) refers to the way in which styles are assigned a hierarchy. The author indicates this is the best way to view the page, the reader's browser defaults to another. The order of preference is what creates the cascade; usually the author's formatting takes precedence over the reader's, and in-line formatting takes precedence over whatever is specified in the <STYLE> block. If more than one style is specified for the same selector, the last one "wins." With Internet Explorer, the rules specified in linked style sheets take precedence over those in an embedded style sheet.

To link an external file, create a file with your style definitions, as in these examples, save it with a .css extension, and link it to your web page as shown in Code Example 12-2.

Note – If you use a linked style sheet, Internet Explorer 3.0 requires you to register the Internet Media (MIME) type for style sheets (text/css) on the user's server. See Appendix A for more information about MIME types.

Setting Font Properties

Fonts are a different way of describing typefaces. A serif typeface like Times Roman, and a sans-serif typeface like Helvetica are both fonts. (What may be a little less obvious is that a slanted serif typeface is called *italics*, but a slanted sans-serif is called *oblique*.)

Changing Typeface or Font Family

The next example (illustrated in Figure 12-1) defines different font families to be used for heading level one (H1) and heading level two (H2).

1. **Load** Chapter12/ssex3.html.

2. **View the HTML source with View Page Source.**
   Notice that the <LINK> line now refers to HREF="ssmain3.css".

---

3. Look at `ssmain3.css` **with your favorite text editor.**
Notice that `H1  font-family` is `arial`, `H2` is designated as `times` (Times Roman), and *inherits* a size of 24 points from the previous example.

This notion of *inheritance* is fairly simple: It just says that if you do not specify in a style sheet a property for one tag embedded within another, but you *have* done so for the parent tag, then the embedded one assumes (inherits) the same characteristic as its parent. For example, if you've set the color of all text in list items to blue using a style sheet, and in a particular list item you use the <em> tag for emphasis, *that occurrence* of the <em> tag will also be in blue (even if you have not defined a rule that renders <em> tags thusly). Understanding how inheritance works can make your style-sheet work much simpler, as it eliminates the need to replicate styles across all tags that might be used together.

This is `ssmain3.css`:

```
H1 {font-family : arial}

H2 {font-size : times}
```

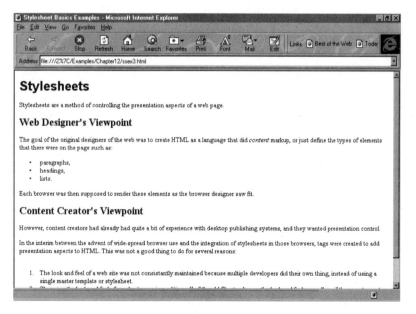

Figure 12-1   Varying Font Families—ssmain3.css

Specifying Font Alternatives

Sometimes the font you want to use may not exist on a particular platform. For example, the Arial font is common to machines based on Microsoft operating systems. Most systems have Helvetica. In a style sheet, you can specify a generic font family such as sans-serif, for which the system will choose the font, or you can specify a specific font family such as Garamond.

Note – We are still in a transitional period when it comes to the use of specific fonts: If a user does not have the font installed on his or her machine, your carefully orchestrated "look" will be ignored (at least insofar as that specific font is concerned). Microsoft and Adobe have proposed a technique of "embedding" fonts in Web documents so that they can be downloaded to anyone who doesn't already have them, but this proposal has not yet been formally ratified.

You can specify your fonts in such a way that if the first one is not available to the user, then use the second; if the second is also not available, then use the third; and so on. If none of the fonts are available the text will then be rendered according to the browser default/user's preference. When deciding which of several fonts in a rule to use, the system precedence is from left to right.

1. **Load** `Chapter12/ssex4.html`.

2. **View the HTML source with View Page Source.**

3. **Look at** `ssmain4.css` **with your favorite text editor.**
   As you can see in Figure 12-2, in this example all headings will be rendered in specific fonts in the order of preference, and for each font specification, the generic font is specified last. The system will try to use the fonts in the order specified, and if all else fails, will use whatever the generic font is for sans-serif, serif, or monospace on that particular system. This is `ssmain4.css`:

   ```
   H1 {font-family : arial, helvetica, sans-serif}

   H2 {font-family : palatino, times, serif}

   CODE {font-family : courier, monospace}
   ```

It is a good practice to specify common and generic fonts as a final choice to replace specialty fonts if the latter are unavailable. This ensures that at least the display will approximate your intentions, even if the specific look can't be duplicated.

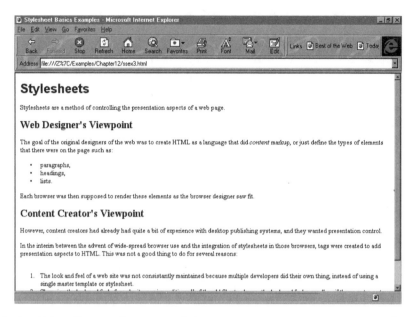

Figure 12-2   Specifying Alternate Fonts—ssmain4.css

Modifying Font Characteristics

Font characteristics can be modified relative to values they inherit from other font types on the page. However, you can change the font weight of a specific instance of data by explicitly setting it in that particular case. For example, the EM tag can be made bold as shown here.

1. **Load** Chapter12/ssex5.html.

2. **View the HTML source with View Page Source.**

3. **Look at** ssmain5.css **shown below.**
   Notice that it is H1 that changes weight in this brief example. This is ssmain5.css:

   ```
   EM {font-weight : bold}
   ```

Figure 12-3 shows the effect of changing the weight of a font.

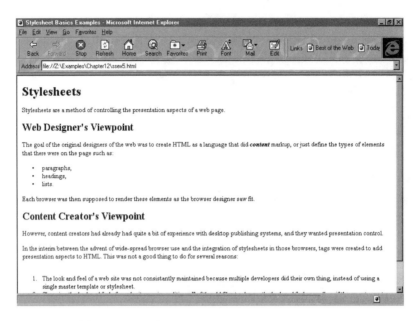

Figure 12-3   Creating a Bold in Font Weight—ssmain5.css

Changing Font Style

When you change the weight of a font, it is clear that bold is heavier than regular. However, to create slanting type you need to change the style, such as: H2{font-style:italics}. Slanting type, whether italic or oblique, demands a change in font style.

1. **Load** Chapter12/ssex6.html.

2. **View the HTML source with View Page Source.**
   Notice that the <LINK> line now refers to HREF="ssmain6.css".

3. **Look at** ssmain6.css **with your favorite text editor.**
   This is ssmain6.css:

   ```
   H2 {font-style : italics}
   ```

Figure 12-4 shows how changing font style to italics affects the look of the document.

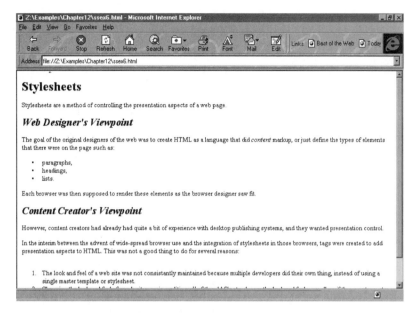

Figure 12-4   Changing Font Style—ssmain6.css

Changing Font Size

Being able to pick the precise size of font to emphasize your message makes a difference in designing readable pages. Traditionally, font sizes are measured in *points* (covered in more detail below in Changing Line Heights); however, other units of measure sometimes show up in connection with fonts. The complete list of options appears in Table 12-1.

Table 12-1   Measurements of Font Display

Unit	Abbrev.	Measure Description	Examples
point	pt	Unit of height of a font or leading. Also used to measure margins.	`{font-size: 24pt}` `{line-height: 30 pt}`
em	em	The width an m character takes in that particular font.	`6 ems`
pixel	px	Size of a dot on the screen, so varies with screen resolution.	
inch	in	Used for margins.	`{margin-right: 1.5in}`
centimeter	cm	Alternate for margins and other areas.	`{margin-left: 2cm}`

Realize that specifying a font size in pixels can lead to strange variations on different screen resolutions. In fact, any way of specifying fonts that assumes specific browser or screen characteristics should be avoided. It is best to stick to the more conventional fixed-value font sizes for now.

1. **Load** `Chapter12/ssex7.html`.

2. **View the HTML source with View Page Source.**
   Notice that the `<LINK>` line now refers to `HREF="ssmain7.css"`.

3. **Look at** `ssmain7.css` **included here to see how the various font changes are accomplished.**

   ```
   H1 {font-size : 48pt;}
   H2 {font-size : 24pt;}
   ```

Figure 12-5 shows the effect of font size changes.

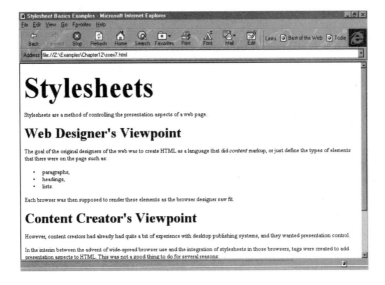

Figure 12-5 Varying Font Sizes—ssmain7.css.

Changing Line Height

The size of the font itself is important, but another contributor to readability is the space between the lines of type (the leading). This space, as well as font sizes, is usually given in terms of *points*—a printer's term—with 72 points equaling one inch. Traditionally, leading has been 2 points for a 10-point type; in order to accomplish this with style-sheet

HTML for Fun and Profit

rules you would specify not only `{font-size:10pt}`, but also `{line-height:12pt}`. (A line height of 12 points, less 10 points for the type itself, leaves 2 points of leading.) Clearly, the larger the font size, the greater the difference between font and line height.

1. **Load** `Chapter12/ssex8.html`.

2. **View the HTML source with View Page Source.**
   Notice that the `<LINK>` line now refers to `HREF="ssmain8.css"`.

3. **Look at** `ssmain8.css` **with your favorite text editor.**
   The file `ssmain8.css` is included below for your convenience.

   ```
   P {line-height : 16pt;}
   ```

In this example, the line height of 16 pt affects `H1` and `H2` most noticeably.

Figure 12-6 shows the effect of changing space between lines.

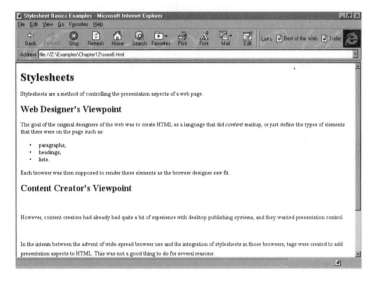

Figure 12-6   Changing Line Height—ssmain8.css.

Putting It All Together

Instead of making separate declarations for font family, size, line height, and so forth, it is simpler to put them all together in one place. The next example demonstrates how to put multiple font definitions in one set of brackets.

Note – Remember to end each line with a ; or closing }.

You can put other definitions such as nonfont definitions here as well.

1. **Load** `Chapter12/ssex9.html`.

2. **View the HTML source with View Page Source.**
   Notice again, that the `<LINK>` line now refers to `HREF="ssmain9.css"`.

3. **Look at** `ssmain9.css` **with your favorite text editor.**
   The file `ssmain9.css` is included below to save you time.

   ```
   P {font-family: Arial, Helvetica, Sans-serif;

      font-size: 12pt;

      line-height: 20pt}
   ```

Notice the effect of increasing the paragraph line height to 20 points on a font size of 12 points.

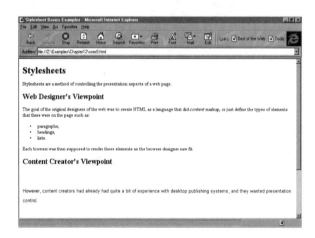

Figure 12-7   Multiple Definitions in One Set of Brackets—ssmain9.css

Complex Font Definitions

When you are declaring complex or precise font designations, order is important. This example shows a complex font definition. Unlike the previous example, this one is for font information only. (Some browsers cheat and allow color in this definition, but that can lead to a variety of random and even unpleasant effects.) After following the steps, note Figure 12-8 for comparison.

1. **Load** `Chapter12/ssex10.html`.

2. **View the HTML source with View Page Source.**
   Notice again, that the `<LINK>` line now refers to `HREF="ssmain10.css"`.

3. **Look at** `ssmain10.css` **below to see how this is accomplished.**

   ```
   P {font: bold italic 12pt/20pt "Arial, Helvetica, Sans-serif"}
   ```

Note – Text "contained" by paragraph tags is affected by font definition. Text not contained by `<P>` is not affected. `<P>` must be used as a container, that is, including the closing `</P>` tag, with style sheets to make formatting carry through. This is a departure from the more relaxed (and more common) practice of omitting the stop tag at the end of paragraphs.

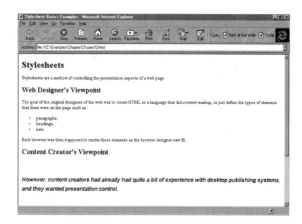

Figure 12-8   Complex Font Definition—ssmain10.css

Setting Colors

Every text element has both a foreground and a background color associated with it. Most of these colors are by default. In the next example, we set H1 text in green, H2 in blue, and body color in brown. *These are all foreground colors*—that is, the color of the text itself. All elements in the document BODY will be in brown, unless overridden by other cascading rules.

1. **Load** `Chapter12/ssex11.html`.

2. **View the HTML source with View Page Source.**
   Notice again, that the `<LINK>` line now refers to `HREF="ssmain11.css"`.

3. **Look at** `ssmain11.css` **below to see how this is accomplished.**

```
H1 {color: green}

H2 {color: blue}

BODY {color: brown}
```

The range of standard colors can be found in a default palette, which is the best practice. Microsoft's default palette can be found at:

```
http://www.microsoft.com/workshop/author/roberth/set1/iecolors.htm
```

Netscape's default palette can be found at:

```
http://developer.netscape.com/library/documentation/htmlguid/
    colortab.htm
```

You can also set the colors using hex (RGB) designations to correspond with the default colors. The next example designates `H1 color:#0000CC`, `H2 #003399`, and `BODY #0099ff`. The # symbol indicates the value is in hexadecimal notation. Named colors are generally simple—`red`, `blue`, `green`, `black`, `white`, `brown`, or `yellow`.

1. **Load** `Chapter12/ssex12.html`.

2. **View the HTML source with View Page Source.**
   Notice again, that the `<LINK>` line now refers to `HREF="ssmain12.css"`.

3. **Look at** `ssmain12.css` **below to identify the hexadecimal color notation used for text in** `ssex12.html`.

```
H1 {color: #0000CC}

H2 {color: #003399}

BODY {color: #0099ff}
```

Setting Foreground and Background Colors

Since you cannot guarantee what default background color the user's browser will use, there is a potential for declaring white type on a white ground, for example, making it impossible to read. Being able to declare background color is a useful control. The next example shows how to set foreground and background colors. The background color covers the area directly behind the type. Where there appears to be no background, the designated background color is the same as the browser's default background.

Note – BODY background in style sheets is not equivalent to the background of document. It affects *only* the background color displayed behind text.

1. **Load** `Chapter12/ssex13.html`.

2. **View the HTML source with View Page Source.**
   Notice again that the `<LINK>` line now refers to `HREF="ssmain13.css"`.

3. **Look at** `ssmain13.css` **below to identify the hexadecimal color notation used for both text and background in** `ssex13.html`.

   ```
   H1 {color: #0000CC;

       background: #FFFFFF}

   H2 {color: #003399}

   BODY {color: #0099ff;

       background: #C0C0C0}
   ```

4. **Compare the effect of** `Chapter12/ssex14.html`.

5. **Look at** `ssmain14.css` **to see the contrasting effect where the browser's default background shows up blocks around the body text alone.**

   ```
   BODY {color: #0099ff;

       background: #C0C0C0}
   ```

Setting Background by URL

It is possible to set background using the URL of an image to display in the background. The next example, illustrated in Figure 12-9, shows the BODY background as URL(bkg.gif).

1. **Load** `Chapter12/ssex15.html`.

2. **View the HTML source with View Page Source.**
   Notice again that the `<LINK>` line now refers to `HREF="ssmain15.css"`.

3. **Look at** `ssmain15.css` **below to identify how the URL is used to set body background in** `ssex15.html`.

   ```
   H1 {color: #0000CC;

       background: #FFFFFF}

   H2 {color: #003399}

   BODY {color: #0099ff;

       background: URL(bkg.gif)}
   ```

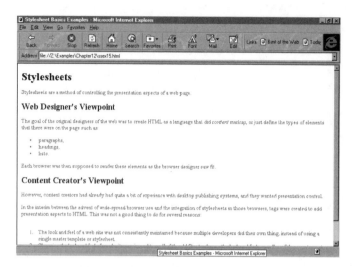

Figure 12-9   Setting Background Color Using a URL—ssmain15.css

Changing Text Properties

Besides changing the size, color, and background of text, it is important to have control over how text is displayed on the page—whether it is aligned on the left, right or centered, or justified like a newspaper column, what kind of margins appear around the text, and other options.

Indenting Text

Sometimes you may simply want one line of text indented. This example shows how to indent the first line of block of text as shown in `ssmain16.css`:

```
P {text-indent: 20pt}
```

Figure 12-10 shows the result.

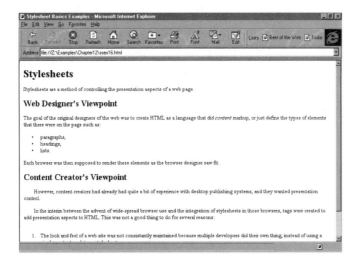

Figure 12-10 Indenting a Single Line of Text—ssmain16.css

Aligning Text

Our next example (see Figure 12-11 for the result) shows how text can be aligned. Default alignment is `left`—all text lines up on the left. Other options are `center`, `right`, and `justified`, although the latter is implemented rather inconsistently.

1. **Load** `Chapter12/ssex17.html`.

2. **View the HTML source with View Page Source.**
   Notice again that the `<LINK>` line now refers to `HREF="ssmain17.css"`.

3. **Look at** `ssmain17.css` **below to identify the alignment used for text in** `ssex17.html`.

   ```
   H1 {text-align: center}
   ```

   ```
   H2 {text-align: right}
   ```

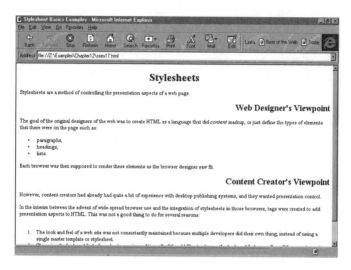

Figure 12-11 Aligning Text—ssmain-17.css

Creating Margins

Margins introduce "air" into your document, preventing a crowded look. This example (illustrated by Figure 12-12) shows how to create margins. Options are: `margin-left`, `margin-right`, `margin-top`, `margin-bottom`, and `plain-margin` (implemented inconsistently). Notice that margins can be declared in points, inches or centimeters—any of the increments outlined in Table 12-1.

1. **Load** `Chapter12/ssex18.html`.

2. **View the HTML source with View Page Source.**
   Notice again that the `<LINK>` line now refers to `HREF="ssmain18.css"`.

3. **Look at** `ssmain18.css` **below to see how the margin identifications are accomplished.**

   ```
   BODY {margin-left: 40pt;

      margin-right: 40pt}

   P {margin: 50pt}

   H1 {margin-top: 50pt}
   ```

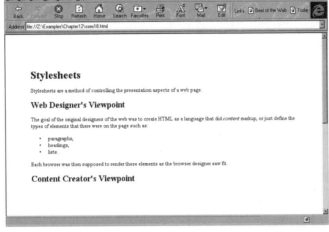

Figure 12-12 Declaring Margins—ssmain18.css

Creating Fancy Text Options

Text decoration offers some options that may not be ideal. For example, you can underline text that is not a link, or remove the underline from linked text. This should only be used when other link identification cues are obvious. This example (see Figure 12-13) shows H1 set as `text-decoration: underline`, and LI `text-decoration: line-through`.

1. **Load** `Chapter12/ssex19.html`.

2. **View the HTML source with View Page Source.**
   Notice again that the `<LINK>` line now refers to `HREF="ssmain19.css"`.

3. **Look at** `ssmain19.css` **below to identify text-decoration implementation used in** `ssex19.html`.

   ```
   H1 {text-decoration: underline}

   A {text-decoration: none}

   LI {text-decoration: line-through}
   ```

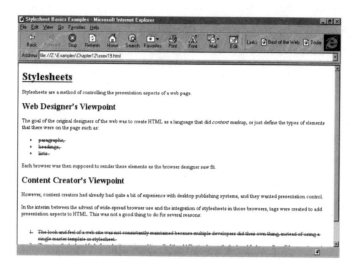

Figure 12-13 Fancy Text Options

Summary

In this chapter, you learned:

- What style sheets are, and why they are useful.

- The basic syntax of style sheet rules.

- The difference between internal (embedded) and external (linked) style sheets.

- How to code style sheet rules for font properties such as font family, style, margins, and color.

Style Guides 13 ☰

The market is wide open for the companies that rent space on web servers. Costs can range from $10 to over $1000 per month. One of the key selling points touted for the more costly web hosting providers and site-design firms is that they can offer better design skills to their customers. Unfortunately, cost isn't always related to design quality. (For that matter, design *skill* is no guarantee of design *quality*.) This chapter discusses some standard style and design techniques that you can apply in building your own site and, should the need arise, evaluating the work of others who propose to do it for you.

Content, Content, Content—and Don't Forget Content

Some discussion of page design is a matter of taste: One person's meat is definitely another's poison. Yet it also seems beyond argument that a site's design must support its content—its purpose.

Consider the humble telephone directory (the printed kind, not the look-up-a-number ones you can find on the Internet). Page after page of tiny black text on off-white background. And consider what would happen were the phone company to hire one of the thousands of web page designers who "know" that the best way to be an information resource is to get people's attention: chaos. In the first place, the phone book would be 20 times its current size, what with all the pictures. The background colors would jar the eye (and perhaps make the text completely unreadable for the color blind). Listings might be placed in random rather than alphabetical order. Phone company revenues would soar, as a result of the sudden surge in directory-assistance calls.

The important thing to note here is not that a jazzed-up look is necessarily wrong in and of itself—but that it has no place in some (maybe even most) contexts.

At the other extreme is the site whose design and purpose are inseparable. An on-line gallery of contemporary art might be structured, for example, as a kind of conceptual-art experience designed to challenge a visitor's preconceived notions of continuity. The Web presence of a print publication whose target audience are teenagers and young adults with a heavy interest in technology might naturally attract heavier traffic with a Tommy Hilfiger look than with one straight out of Brooks Brothers or L.L. Bean.

Most likely, your site will fall somewhere between these extremes. Always feel free to consider the latest and greatest multimedia and page makeup extensions, but never (unless your site is *selling* them) use them for their own sake.

Document Layout

Effective web documents share much in common with the more traditional kinds. But they are also in many respects of a different order altogether. Keep in mind both the similarities and differences as you design the general appearance of your pages.

Creating a Common Document Look with Templates

Users obtain more information if they know where to look for it. Documents should have a consistent look and feel. You should consistently put information in the same structural format. To begin with, you should create a template that includes the standard HTML formatting tags, a common titling methodology, and a set of navigation links. If your server allows SSI, covered in Chapter 8, you can build this template with an eye toward using that feature (which greatly simplifies the redesign task and the need to add new content, such as new site sections that must be added to a table of contents, when the time comes). If SSI is not an option, at the very least you should have a basic "empty document" which includes all the common structural elements and none of the variable text. This template will become the model on which all your pages will be constructed.

Finally, of course, by far the simplest solution to creating (and later modifying) your site's appearance as a whole is by using style sheets. These are covered in detail in Chapter 12.

Navigation around Your Site

When documents form a set, there can be more than one way to step through the documents. They may have a linear progression ("Read this page first; then go on to this page; then this one," and so on). They may have a group of overview documents that can call up task- or object-specific information. Whatever structure is implied in the documents should be reflected in the navigation tools offered to the user.

These tools are usually a set of links within each document and between related documents. There is a wealth of graphical images to use for these links. However, to accommodate the use of browsers with Delay Image Loading, every navigational image should also have a text-based link in addition to the image link. The link can be created such that the anchor encompasses both the image and the text of the anchor as one link. An example of this is:

```
<a href=/><img src="/images/home.gif">Return to the Home Page</a>
```

In addition, all in-line images should have the ALT attribute defined for the text-only browsers. An example is:

```
<a href="/">

<img src="/images/home.gif" alt="Return">Return to the Home Page

</a>
```

All document sets should have some navigational control. Related documents should have even more control. The most commonly used controls are described below.

- **Go to Top** — When a document is more than two screen pages in length, a Go to Top link should return the user from the bottom to the top of a document. In documents that run more than 10 screen pages in length, this control might be placed at the end of a main section or level-two heading. To accomplish this, use a named anchor at the top of the document and a pointing anchor that starts with a # sign to avoid reloading the current document. For example, this identifier can be placed just after the <BODY> definition:

```
<a name=top>
```

The following tag can then be placed at the bottom of the document, and in cases of very large documents at the end of one section, just before starting the header for the next section:

```
<a href=#top>Go to Top</a>

<h2>Section Two</h2>
```

- **Previous Page/Document** — In document sets that follow a linear progression, for example, a book, usually only the Table of Contents and one previous chapter would point to the current document. In those cases, a Previous Page or Previous Document link should point to the previous document in the linear progression. If access to a document is likely to be random (as with, for example, man page references, municipal and other government sites, and any other nonlinear information), this navigation tool is irrelevant, often confusing, and shouldn't be used.

- **Next Page/Document** —As with the Previous Page/Document navigation tool, a Next Page or Next Document link should point to the next document in the linear progression. If access to a document can be described as random, this navigation tool is irrelevant, often confusing, and shouldn't be used.

- **Table of Contents** — If a document is three or more screen pages in length, a Table of Contents can be created at the top or left side of the document listing the sections and allowing the user to jump forward to the sections. An example of a Table of Contents (highlighted in bold in the listing) is presented in HTML Example 13-1.

HTML Example 13-1   Sample Table of Contents

```
{ Heading tags are above here}
<BODY><h1> Title of Document goes here </h1>
This chapter covers:
<ul>
<a href="#Section1">First Section</a>
<a href="#Section2">Second Section</a>
<a href="#Section3">Third Section</a>
</ul>
<a name="Section1"> <h2>First Section</h2>
{ some text }
<a name="Section2"> <h2>Second Section</h2>
{ some text }
<a name="Section3"> <h2>Third Section</h2>
{ some text }
```

The first section directly follows the table of contents, and for this reason (in theory) it might not seem important to include it as one of the entries in the table of contents. (If the user can see the contents in the browser display, he or she can probably see the start of "First Section"—so no actual link would seem necessary.) However, it should be included for consistency.

In sets of documents, it is also good to create a single document that is a generic Table of Contents for all of the other related documents. In many cases, this page is also the site's home page.

- **Index** — "Search this site"-style indexes can be placed on web pages with the Table of Contents or on the home page, or the indexes can be on a page by themselves. If you do have an index, the page with the index should be accessible from anywhere in the document structure.

- **Home** — Home can mean several things. Usually the home page is a web page at the top of the document set or even above the document set. The home page should be the starting point for a user browsing your web pages. Home, Index, and Table of Contents may all be the same page. Remember though that people can enter a site at points other than the home page—for example, when they have been given a pointer from another person who has browsed the site.

- **Site Map** — This is increasingly common as a navigational aid. In addition to the other tools for getting around your site, you also provide one page which shows and links to *every* other page. This is usually structured in some logical way, such as with a set of nested, unordered lists (`<ul>` tag) that parallel the structure of the site as a whole.

A common convention is to place a horizontal rule at the bottom of the document and to put the standard navigational tools such as Home page, Index, and Comments page links below it. (Note that some designers object to the aesthetics of the horizontal rule, arguing that its use is redundant; many other elements even of basic HTML serve the purpose of dividing a page according to type of information.)

You may also have noticed an approach that is now common, especially among sites with deeply nested content: Putting a concise Table of Contents in a colored vertical bar along the left edge of every page. We discuss this technique further later in this chapter.

Documenting for Universal Use

Just because you are creating a hypertext document in HTML doesn't mean that this information will never be needed in paper format. It is a good idea to create a document set that can be printed and read in bed as well as viewed on-line. This means that each document that you create should be at least available alternatively as a standalone article.

Standardizing Between On-Line and Off-Line Documentation

When documents that will be used both as printed documents and on-line pages are created, each page can have links to a glossary or definition page. Since the printed document does show the link with an underline, the user can be informed on the first page that underlined items can be looked up in a "glossary of links" which displays the URLs corresponding to each bit of linked text. This glossary can be printed separately and included at the end of the printed document set.

The other acceptable pointers within multiple-use documents are references to chapter or section headings when a Table of Contents is included. In this case the Table of Contents doesn't have to be at the top of each document. It can be a separate document itself that is included at the beginning of a printed document set. These references are usually noted with a "See Section *{section name}*" to indicate that the reader should refer to the Table of Contents to locate the section.

User-Controlled Granularity

In addition to making each document into a standalone article, you should decide how much information should go into a single document. For example, you may have an employee handbook that is 30 printed pages in length—six chapters, averaging six sections per chapter. When you move this normally hard-copy document on-line:

- Should it become a single 30-page on-line document?
  Not as the primary on-line copy. It might be a nice add-on feature to offer a version that is the entire document in a single file for the person who wants to print the whole thing. However, it should never be the primary method for "managing" an entire lengthy document.

- Should it become six documents, with one for each chapter?
  Maybe yes, and maybe no. Whether a document should be broken up at the chapter or section level is debatable. Ideally, no document meant primarily for on-line use should be more than about eight to ten screen pages in length. (The size of screen pages varies from system to system, so your mileage may vary.) As mentioned above, navigational controls such as Go To Top and an internal Table of Contents should be added to any document more than two screen pages in length.

- Should it become 36 documents, with one for each individual section?
  Again, maybe yes and maybe no. The question here concerns how many of the sections an average user will be likely to access at a given time. If you expect users to read three or more sections in a row or if you expect users to want to print multiple sections, they will be using the document serially and it should be divided by chapters. However, if users will refer only to specific sections, making the employee handbook more of a random-access reference source, splitting the document into sections is a better idea.

Audience Considerations

It is important to remember your audience when designing web pages. People will use different browsers and access methods.

Server Connection Speed

If you are serving only clients on a local area network, or LAN—an intranet—the speed of the server-client connection should be a consideration only if the LAN is already heavily loaded. However, if you are serving documents to the Internet, the speed of the connection—both of the server to the Internet, and of the client to the server—is an important consideration.

If the server's Internet connection is a dedicated T-1 or better, the server connection speed shouldn't be a design consideration. But if the server's connection is only a 56 kbps line and you expect to handle more than one client at a time, you should keep the volume of data sent to the client small. This is primarily true in the case of images. Images 1 to 10 KB in size don't require significant transmission activity, but a 60- or 100-KB image will take significantly more time.

Servers generally have sufficient connection speed unless they are sharing their Internet connection with other traffic. If you notice or receive reports of overall performance degradation, upgrade your connection, change web hosting providers, or construct your site with smaller "building blocks."

Client Connection Speed

The connection speed of a client to the server is a significantly more important issue than that of the server to the Internet. Client connections can be generalized into two categories: home connections and work connections.

Home connections tend to be across a modem ranging in speed from 14.4 to 33.6 kbps and often appear to be very sloooow. Some home-connection clients will use Delay Image Loading techniques for faster access to information and optionally load images only when they are interested.

If your audience contains a significant number of home connections, you should:

- Limit your images to between one and three images per page and keep the total size of all the images on a page to 30 Kbytes or less. (On a 28.8-kbps connection, *under ideal conditions* 30 KB of data take about 10 seconds to download and render. In the grand scheme of things 10 seconds is not much time, but users are notoriously and justifiably impatient.)

- List the size of the image so that users are prepared for what they are about to receive, especially if you are making pictures of your products available to a home-connection client.

- Make all of your links to other pages with text or a text/image combination. Users shouldn't have to download an image to decide if they want to follow the link.

- Avoid long, thin images such as specialty horizontal rules where the user is prone to use Delay Image Loading. That long, thin image becomes a square block that doesn't adequately separate sections of text. (The exception to this general rule is the case of background images, as noted later in this chapter.)

(On the other hand, much of the reason for the Web's explosive growth has been the eagerness of consumers for on-line multimedia experiences, including images—for entertainment rather than reference. Many such consumers do not know that Delay Image Loading is an option, and even if they did, would not use it. So to our earlier injunction about the need to know your server we must add another: Know your audience.)

Work connections are usually faster than home connections. If your audience are professionals viewing your work on higher-speed lines, then the sexy multimedia links such as images, sound, and movies can be used frequently.

Even when most of your audience is in the high-speed, work-connection category, a low-impact text mode should be available. A common technique is to offer a link on the home page to an equivalent set of pages that are text-only. Although this sounds like a doubling of your work effort, it is actually quite simple if you use web development tools that are capable of stripping the HTML from documents. (At the least, you can copy each document from your own GUI browser's window and past it into a text file.)

Client Program Configuration and Use

HTML is not displayed the same way on various client browsers—and the careful layout can be overridden with various user preferences (delay image loading, background colors, default fonts, screen resolution) even then. Unless you expect to have a captive audience viewing your pages from the same browser without overriding the settings, don't customize your pages to look perfect on only one specific browser, as this often makes them look lopsided on other browsers.

Don't assume that everyone uses the basic gray background. A black logo on the gray background will show up as a black square on a monochrome monitor. If someone sets the background to be white or purple instead of gray, a gray background will look ugly. Convert your images to use a transparent background, as described in Creating Transparent Backgrounds in Chapter 4.

Don't base the color scheme of the page elements on the default gray background, either. A beautiful, multiple-shades-of-blue horizontal rule will stand out like a sore thumb for the user who prefers an orange background.

Use common MIME types when putting images and other multimedia data out for public consumption. Making your images available as GIFs or JPEGs, of course, is the norm, despite some disadvantages of both; but PNG images, which resolve many of the problems associated with the GIF and JPEG formats, are not yet widely "readable" by most browsers. Stick with the most common formats.

Image Tricks

There are two "tricks" of some common use regarding images: background images to divide your page vertically, and the so-called single-pixel image trick.

"Barred" Backgrounds

Like other images, background images are cached by the browser. Careful consideration of this fact, together with the way in which browsers render images, has led designers almost by accident to a common look: a page with a colored vertical bar down the left edge of the page (usually with a Table of Contents arrayed vertically) and a white background (on which the headings and other text are superimposed).

In general, the way such pages are constructed is as two- or three-column tables with the `border=` attribute set to 0. The leftmost column, where the colored bar will appear, is set to a fixed width (as is the rightmost one, if three columns are used); the logo and/or Table of Contents appears in the first column (which should be sized wide enough to accommodate the widest entry without wrapping). Because its width is not specified, the second column therefore will contract or expand to occupy whatever space in the window is remaining.

(Some sites use a fixed-width frame for the bar along the left side, by the way. In this case the background of the leftmost frame can simply be a different color than that of its target frame and no image at all is required. An advantage to using frames rather than tables for this purpose is that the menu is always visible—it doesn't scroll off the top of the window when the user scrolls down in the actual text to the right.)

As for the colored bar, it is created with a simple `<body background="http://{imagesource}">` tag. The image which is pointed to is only a pixel or two in height, and x pixels wide. (More about that x in the Note, below.) The left end of what is in effect this long, thin line is a single color—a bar equal in width to that of the table's first column—and the entire rest of the line is in white (or whatever color the designer wants to use as the background of the text). The result is an extremely small image which loads almost instantaneously.

Note – How wide to make the total image—the x mentioned above—involves considering both the widest and smallest likely dimensions of the browser display, in pixels. Typically the smallest window will be 640 pixels wide; the widest, 1280 (or more). If you make x too wide, a horizontal scroll bar will be placed at the bottom of narrower windows, which may be undesirable. Worse, though, is making it too *short*. In this case the user with a wider-than-x display will see not just one vertical bar, but two or more, every x pixels across the document—quite possibly running down through the text and rendering it unreadable.

Aside from its small size, the reason the image loads quickly is that it needs to be loaded only once in order to fill the page. (Remember, as mentioned in Chapter 4, that background images are "tiled" by the browser when they are smaller than the window size.) And because once loaded, it is in the cache, succeeding pages with the same background image load the image even faster.

A further advantage of using background images is that they are treated differently than regular images. If the user has Delay Image Loading turned on, the background image is *not* replaced with a generic placeholder. The background is simply displayed in white (or the background color you've specified, or whatever the user overrides it with). Additionally, background images do not show up in printed copies of web documents.

The Single-Pixel GIF

This is one of those design tricks that HTML authors either love or hate. It is historically interesting, though, even with the availability of current-generation HTML page-layout tools such as style sheets. Without espousing one point of view or the other, we present it here together with its pros and cons.

At issue is the inability of common HTML to place elements on the page exactly where you want them. Suppose you want the first line of each of your paragraphs to be indented a half-inch or so? Suppose you want an image to appear *exactly* 75 pixels from the left margin and/or 40 pixels below the image above it, no matter how the user has configured his or her window or what the screen size is? There is no strict HTML support for indented paragraphs or "floating" images (although various things are in the works to provide such fine layout control).

One solution to this problem lies in creating a GIF image that is one pixel wide by one pixel high—and making it transparent. Place it on your site in your images directory. And whenever you want to put a piece of text or a "real" image in a precise spot, place your single-pixel GIF just before that element, sized to the exact dimension you need. The space occupied by the invisible single-pixel image will force the following element to appear where you want it.

There are two ways to size the GIF, either by using the HSPACE and/or VSPACE attributes to pad it with empty pixels or by specifying an HSIZE and/or VSIZE attribute for the image itself. These two approaches yield slightly different results, especially depending on the viewer's browser; experiment with them to see which is appropriate for your use.

On the downside, as with other images, you must be prepared for the possibility that users may suppress image loading. If you are the kind of designer who needs to have images placed just so for aesthetic reasons alone, you are probably the kind of designer who will be horrified at the thought of your page's being rendered with a host of generic image placeholders.

A more significant drawback, of course, is that the single-pixel GIF trick, although backwards-compatible with older GUI browsers, has largely been supplanted in the various style-sheet standards. That is the wave of the future, and that is the device that forward-thinking Web designers should employ for precise placement of page elements.

Tips

- **Test on multiple platforms** — Test your pages on multiple platforms before you release them to the world. What may look wonderful on the Macintosh may look horrible on a UNIX NCSA XMosaic browser. (More information on this topic is available in Chapter 15.)

- **Use statistics and logs as course corrections** — Your logs are a gold mine of information. Don't simply count the "hits": look at what percentage of the users are loading the pages but not the images in the pages. Look at which pages have never or rarely been accessed.
  - Is the wording in the link unclear?
  - Is the link broken?

  Don't wait for people to tell you that there are problems. Most people find the problem and go away without saying a thing—and may very well be discouraged from ever returning. If your logs show an average of a thousand hits per week on your home page and only ten on all the rest combined, you have some serious homework (perhaps even some soul-searching) to do.

Note – The whole issue of counting "hits" can be somewhat misleading. In the first place, your pages can be "hit" many times more than it is truly viewed; Web spiders' visits, for example, increase your hits just as real humans do. When users empty their browser caches (as smart users will do from time to time) and revisit your site, all the pages they go to again show up as hits even though they're not really newcomers. (It would be much more useful, but is rather more difficult, to count *users* instead of *hits*. You can achieve something closer to this ideal by using cookies and/or a "site registration" process to distinguish repeat visitors from true first-timers.) Use hits only as a general, relative measure of your site's success over time—if your site averages ten thousand hits a day and your nearest competitor's "only" nine thousand, that is not cause for celebration, let alone crowing about in a press release.

- Avoid the aesthetic faux pas
  - **Avoid** Click Here – The only exception to this rule is the home page of a WWW tutorial. If people are actively using a browser, they know what a link looks like and that they can click on it for more information. One alternative phrase is: "More information is available on *{descriptive word or phrase for link}*."

- **Don't use long titles** (such as ones that wrap around) — Remember that the title goes into the hotlist, where display space is limited.
- **Always use text with images that are links** — This is one thing that can't be overemphasized. There is nothing worse than encountering a home page that is a series of images without a single word on the entire page.
- **Carefully weigh the design *disadvantages* of browser- or browser-version-specific design features** — It may be tempting, for example, to use the `<font face=`*typeface*`>` tag, which in current-generation browsers from both Netscape and Microsoft specifies a particular font family (such as Helvetica, Garamond, or Bodoni) to be used in rendering text. But older versions of these browsers will continue to render the text in their defaults; and even users of the latest and greatest may not yet actually *have* these fonts on their systems.

Summary

In this chapter, you learned:

- The most important function of design and multimedia elements on a web page is supporting the content.

- Using document templates and/or SSI helps make the look and feel of your site consistent from one page to another.

- The prime consideration when designing your site is its audience.

Work-Saving Tools

Because HTML is a structured formatting language, correct syntax is important. Unfortunately, it is the little things—such as forgetting to put the closing > on a tag, or forgetting the closing tag of a container altogether—that can require debugging time. You may have existing documents from various word processing or desktop publishing programs that you want to put on-line. Tools are available to save you the rekeying and debugging time.

The first kind of tool is beyond the scope of this book: current-generation word processors, spreadsheets, databases, and presentation software with the built-in ability to save documents directly as HTML rather than in the word processors' native formats. To use such tools as WordPerfect 7, you simply put the software into "HTML mode"—this restricts you to those document features available if you were using pure HTML but otherwise displays the page in the interface and WYSIWYG format you are accustomed to for that word processor. Even embedded images in the document get transformed as required into GIF or JPEG formats.

The "built-in HTML" features of such software necessarily limit you to whatever tags the interface developer has provided. For example, you may not be able to create a framed document. Furthermore, the HTML itself is often inaccessible, so you cannot add or change optional attributes.

Other tools give you some flexibility if you need to avoid these limitations, or if you do not have access to such a word processor (or spreadsheet, etc.) at all. These specialized HTML-generating tools fall into three categories: filters, templates, and editors or authoring tools.

Filters

Filters convert documents from one format to another and are useful when the documents already exist. Some documents use basic formatting instructions, such as *make the following text bold*. It is easy to convert an instruction like this into a pair of <B> and </B> tags. In other cases, the word processor may use logical words to define a block of text. For example, in basic FrameMaker documents there is a format definition called ScreenText. When you encounter this definition, you need to provide the word processor with a cross-referenced list of format instructions, such as ScreenText, and their HTML equivalents, such as <code>.

14

Microsoft Word for Windows™ (for MS-Windows and Macintosh) and Corel WordPerfect™ are currently the most common word processors. Both Word and WordPerfect can save their documents into RTF (Rich Text Format), as well as their own native formats. Once the document has been saved as RTF, the file can be converted to HTML with a filter. (On the other hand, you can simply acquire a filter that uses the document's native format as input, and eliminate the RTF step.)

For a complete list of filters for various forms of input, check the W3C's page at:

```
http://www.w3.org/Tools/Filters.html
```

This site has links to filters for most platforms, including Macintosh, UNIX, and MS-DOS/Windows. Filters are available not only for word processor documents, but also for program language code, UNIX man pages, mail messages, and other kinds of documents.

Templates

Templates are sets of formatting instructions that can be loaded into a familiar editor. The document created with this template is then saved directly as HTML. This document is usually used for creating new documents without forcing the user to learn a new tool. In most cases, the user must still learn about tags and how they are used, although knowing the specifics of creating HTML code is generally not necessary.

As with the filtering tools described above, check the W3C *HTML Converters Page* for current information on this type of HTML-generation tool.

Authoring Tools

An authoring tool is an editor with a special role in life, creating and editing HTML and sometimes other web elements, such as boilerplate CGI or JavaScript code. Authoring tools provide an editing environment in which both text and formatting can be inserted correctly and completely. Some authoring tools offer syntax checking and correction as well; some always display the HTML and allow you to edit it freely, some never let you edit it, and some do so when you select that option.

Note – Several of these packages call themselves WYSIWYG or semi-WYSIWYG. It is important to remember that these packages can present the document with the format tags hidden and implemented, but that is no guarantee that the document will appear the same on various browsers. Take the WYSIWYG attribution with a grain of salt—not least because (as we never tire of repeating) the user, not your HTML code, controls the "what you see."

HTML for Fun and Profit

Authoring tools are available for all platforms: UNIX, Macintosh, and Microsoft Windows (all versions). Many of these products have a freeware or shareware version available on the Internet and a professional version that can be purchased.

Sample sessions with two editors, WebEdit Pro and Microsoft FrontPage, are shown below. For each of these we will create a very simple Web document from scratch, including <HEAD> and <BODY> elements and, within the latter, a heading, some text, an image, and a hyperlink. You should be aware that this will not even come close to exhausting these packages' considerable abilities.

WebEdit Pro

WebEdit is a shareware Microsoft Windows HTML editor originally developed by Ken Nesbitt and currently marketed through Luckman Interactive. WebEdit has always been of the "let users do as much HTML as they want" school of authoring tools, and for this reason has long been a favorite among experienced Windows-based HTML authors.

WebEdit has a companion professional version, which we will use here. Let's examine its operation by creating a web page. Figure 14-1 shows WebEdit Pro 2.0's main menu.

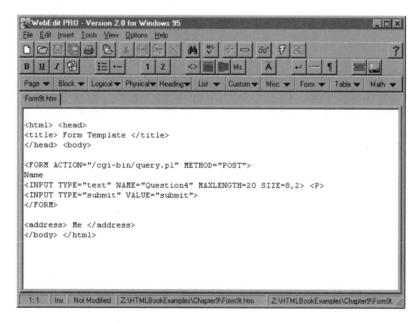

Figure 14-1   WebEdit Pro

Here is a sample session with WebEdit Pro.

1. **Create a new document.**
   If you click on the New Document button on the toolbar, you simply get a blank page. At this point you can either enter your text and HTML markup manually, or enter your text and do the markup with various toolbar buttons. Instead of using the New Document toolbar button, you can pull down the File, New... menu choice. That is the option we will choose.

2. **In the dialog box which pops open, select New Blank Page, Home Page Wizard, or Open Existing Page.**
   The Home Page Wizard walks you through various steps in creating a "typical" home page. For example, you enter a document title, select a background color or image, enter some text and headings, and so on, and then the Wizard automatically creates the necessary HTML to display the page as you requested. This is a simple way to create a page if you are creating only one, or are brand-new to HTML (which we hope you will *not* be, well before this point). A drawback of using the Wizard is that it clutters up your HTML code with (in our opinion) superfluous comments, notably a "this page created by WebEdit Pro" remark which is *not* enclosed in the comment tags <!-- and --> and therefore appears at the foot of the page when browsed. We will opt for a new blank page (the same results as if we had clicked on the New Document toolbar button in step 1.)

3. **Do a general markup, that is, HTML and HEAD/BODY.**
   WebEdit Pro, like many first- and second-generation authoring tools, allows you simply to key the tags in manually wherever you want them. Alternatively you can key in (or copy-and-paste from another document) the text you want to display and then go back and mark it up with HTML. The latter approach often makes sense for longer documents, as it frees you from having to worry about the look of the page and its individual elements until the content is in place.

   The actual markup can be accomplished either manually, or by highlighting the text you want marked up and clicking on an appropriate toolbar button (or selecting the desired tags from the menu) to enclose the text in the given tags. For simple tags like <HTML> and <BODY>, not associated with any particular text, keying the HTML in manually is generally not too hard.

   The one advantage of using the "widgets" to insert the HTML is that they will create both stop and start tags automatically, possibly preventing problems later. However, in the case of tags such as <BODY>, if you let the program do it, you will get a dialog box which lets you assign attributes (bgcolor=, background image, and the various link colors) interactively, without having to recall the correct syntax, URLs, and so on. This is particularly useful if you want to use RGB color values (e.g, #F0F0F0) instead of their mnemonic names or when the specific color combination has no mnemonic; a standard Windows color picker dialog opens.

4. Add a title.

If you've already entered the title text within the `<HEAD>` container, you can select the text and mark it up as a title using either the menu or the toolbar. (And of course, you can simply type the `<title>` and `</title>` tags by hand.) If not, using the toolbar or menu inserts the tags and puts your cursor between them, awaiting the text entry.

5. Add a heading (`<H1>`).

You have the same options for doing so as you did for entering the title: Create the text, then mark it up; or enter the tags (manually or automatically) and then the text.

6. Add a picture.

Like selecting nonstandard colors with a color-picker dialog, this is the kind of rather error-prone operation that a GUI authoring tool like WebEdit Pro excels at. The simplest way to insert an image in WebEdit Pro is to click on the Inline Image toolbar button; this pops open the dialog box shown in Figure 14-2.

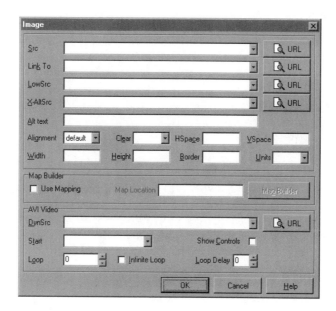

Figure 14-2 WebEdit Pro In-line Image Dialog

As you can see, adding even complex strings of attributes—even for an in-line .AVI movie—is enormously simpler than having to code it all by hand. WebEdit Pro also has an outstanding Help system, which provides detailed information on *every* HTML tag and attribute (including some esoteric ones that we have not covered).

7. **Add a few paragraphs.**

Entering text in WebEdit Pro is just like entering it into a text editor. (Just remember to include it between the correct tags!)

8. **Link to another web page.**

Adding a link to another web page is done in the same way as adding an image, except that you click on the Anchor/Link button (its icon looks like a little piece of chain) instead of the Inline Image button. A different dialog box opens which again lets you select files, URLs, and so on interactively rather than having to enter the appropriate HTML manually.

WebEdit Pro includes support for many other Web authoring tasks in addition to HTML. You can insert SSI codes and browser-specific codes (like MSIE's <marquee> tag) with the user interface. It also comes with an automatic link validation tool and an FTP upload tool, to simplify the task of publishing your pages to your server.

Microsoft FrontPage

Products which are really "Web word processors" provide an environment much closer to the WYSIWYG ideal. Unlike the templates or save-as-HTML features of general-purpose word processors, these tools were built with developing a website as their primary purpose. The assumption is that while their users will want to create a certain "look," they will not in general care *how* the look is achieved—will not want or need to learn the nitty-gritty of HTML and related minutiae.

Microsoft's FrontPage (for Windows 95/NT) was not the first such tool, but it has achieved a great deal of success on the strength of its interface and feature set.

Aside from the page-creation component, called the FrontPage Editor, the package also includes a server. This Personal Web Server (PWS) is a scaled-down version of the Internet Information Server (IIS) that ships with Windows NT. There is also a "to-do list" feature which helps ensure that you don't forget any loose ends when creating or modifying your web site.

One key notion in using FrontPage is that of the "FrontPage web." A FrontPage web is a website, which can be either on a local drive or somewhere out on the Internet on a real server. (In the latter case, of course, you will have to have administrator privileges in order to make any changes to the site.) Your FrontPage webs can be browsed with a special tool, the FrontPage Explorer, which functions similarly to the regular Windows 95/NT Explorer but is more Web-aware. Together with the Editor, PWS, and to-do features, the Explorer gives you a rich tool for creating websites that are simple to scale up to your real server.

Of main interest to us here is the Editor itself, shown open to a blank page in Figure 14-3.

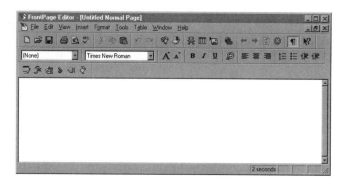

Figure 14-3 Microsoft FrontPage Editor

As with WebEdit Pro and similar tools, the interface for FrontPage consists of a blank document window and a number of toolbars and buttons along the top edge. Unlike the earlier-generation tools, though, you cannot enter HTML code directly into this window. (Indeed, if you try to do so, the HTML itself is displayed along with the page contents—probably not the effect you hope to achieve.)

In FrontPage the HTML lives behind the scenes of what you see on the screen. You simply enter your content and "mark it up" using various UI features.

Let's walk through the creation of a page using the same eight steps we did for WebEdit Pro.

1. **Create a new document.**
   As with WebEdit Pro, you can use either a toolbar button or the File, New... menu for this step. Also like WebEdit Pro, using the menu can give you other options for creating a boilerplate look, via a dialog. For this example we will use the File, New...menu.

2. **In the dialog box which pops open, select Normal Page (the default), or select a template.**
   Normal Page simply gives you a blank page. The templates and wizards displayed are standard document types that many webmasters would want to create (Employee Directory, Feedback Form, Guestbook, Hot List, Meeting Agenda, What's New, and so on); you can also create new templates for your own purposes. As with WebEdit Pro's Home Page Wizard, using the built-in templates is simple, but if you simply accept a given template's choices unaltered, your page risks looking like everyone else's who has used the same template.

Regardless which choice you make in the dialog box, including the Normal (blank) Page, your page will never be blank: it will always have HTML "built in." To view the code (and edit it, if you so choose), pull down the View, HTML... menu selection. This opens a text-editor-style window which by default displays all markup in color to distinguish it from the text itself—attributes in red, attribute values in blue, and so on.

Note – There is some markup which you *can* see in the main Editor window. Comments, for example, are by default displayed in purple. If you pass your mouse cursor over such "visible code," the cursor changes shape: It becomes a small robotlike figure. This is a sign that FrontPage has inserted what it calls a *bot* at that point. A bot—an object in the page that serves some non-HTML purpose—can be as simple as a comment or as complex as an automatically generated CGI program. When you save the page to your web, the bot is converted to a true representation of its code.

---

3. **Do a general markup, that is, HTML and HEAD/BODY.**
   This is largely automated in FrontPage, even for a "blank" document. If you view the HTML for a blank page, you will see what FrontPage considers a minimal document: a `<!DOCTYPE>` directive, the `<HTML>` and `<BODY>` containers, a `<HEAD>` and `<TITLE>`, and a couple of `<META>` tags indicating the content type and the identity of the generating software (FrontPage 2.0, in this case). The body background color is set by default to white.

4. **Add a title.**
   A title tag is automatically inserted into even the simplest FrontPage document, as explained in the preceding step. If you did not use a template or wizard to generate the page, the default title will be something like Untitled Normal Page. If you do not want to accept this default title, you can of course simply view and edit the HTML behind it. There is also a GUI-based way of editing the title (as well as other page properties): Right-click anywhere on the page. A short pop-up menu opens, one selection being Page Properties....

   Selecting Page Properties... from the pop-up opens a dialog that lets you specify not only the title but also many of the overall page characteristics (background color/image, top and left margins, default target frame, and so on).

   If you use FrontPage, right-clicking on various page and text elements is something you will quickly get used to.

5. **Add a heading (`<H1>`).**
   At the top left of the FrontPage editor toolbar is a pull-down list labeled "Change Style." Essentially, the choices in this list are equivalent to common HTML text markup codes—Heading 1, Bulleted List, Address, and so on. To create a level-one heading, select that style and simply begin typing.

As with WebEdit Pro, you can also type the text, then select what you want to change the style of before actually designating the style itself. The selected text is changed, but not the other text on the page.

6. Add a picture.

The easiest way to do this in FrontPage (just as in WebEdit Pro) is to click on a toolbar button (labeled Insert Image) to open a dialog that lets you identify the image and its properties interactively. By way of comparison with WebEdit Pro's Inline Image dialog, FrontPage's Image dialog is shown in Figure 14-4.

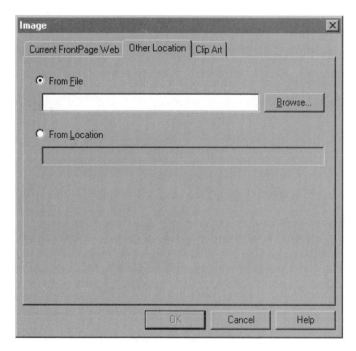

Figure 14-4 FrontPage Image Dialog

Note that this dialog box is much simpler than WebEdit Pro's—basically just a file-browsing tool. That is because the image's characteristics, like those of the page, are accessed by right-clicking on the image and selecting Image Properties... from the pop-up menu.

7. Add a few paragraphs.

Simply type in the text. Where you press the Enter key, a <P> tag is inserted. (More accurately, the text prior to the carriage return is enclosed in <P> and the seldom-used </P> tags.) To insert a <BR> tag instead, you must hold down the Shift key while pressing Enter. In the latter case, the presence of a paragraph break is signaled in the Editor by a small arrow pointing down and to the left (like the one which appears on the Enter key on most keyboards).

8. **Link to another web page.**
   As you would expect, there is a toolbar button to accomplish this task. Clicking on the toolbar opens a dialog that lets you choose the linked-to page from the current FrontPage web, another document on the local drive, or an outside location (including somewhere on the Web itself). If you have not already typed and selected some text before clicking on the Create or Edit Hyperlink button, the title of the page you choose will be entered as the hypertext itself; you can accept this or edit it without affecting the identity of the document to which the hypertext links.

More Editors

WebEdit Pro and FrontPage are by no means the only editors available. The list is changing constantly. For a list of editors, refer to:

```
http://www.w3.org/Tools/
```

See Appendix B for pointers to other resources.

Other Web Authoring Aids

Aside from tools that assist in creating the pages themselves, you may be interested in ones which perform related tasks. We mention several such auxiliary tools below; consult Appendix B for pointers to others.

FTP Tools

Although many editors come with "publish" features, not all do; and even if your editor does include such a feature, it may not do all you want.

Figure 14-5 shows the interface for CuteFTP, a shareware Windows-based FTP tool that can do nearly anything that a manual FTP session (as described in Chapter 16, *Publishing to the Web*) can do. Files are moved from local to remote machines (or back) with a simple user interface that mimics the behavior of the operating system itself. You can also create directories, change file permissions, and so on from within CuteFTP.

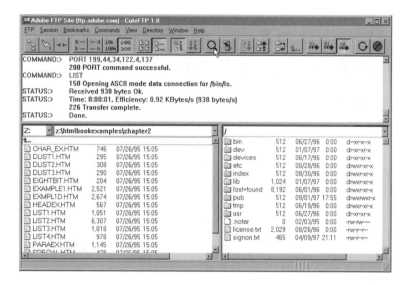

Figure 14-5   CuteFTP

Graphics Utilities

Once you have gone beyond the rudiments of page creation, including using public-domain clip art for standard images on your pages, you will probably want to experiment with creating your own. You may also need to alter the characteristics—such as size, color depth, contrast, and so on—of preexisting images. Such tasks are beyond the scope of most simple image editors.

Virtually the standard image-manipulation tool for web graphics is Adobe's PhotoShop. Nearly as powerful, but costing far less, is PaintShop Pro, a shareware utility published by JASC. PaintShop Pro can convert images from one type (GIF, JPEG, etc.) to another, add transparency to GIF images, rescale images, add a wide variety of special effects (such as embossing), and so on. The main image editing window is shown in Figure 14-6.

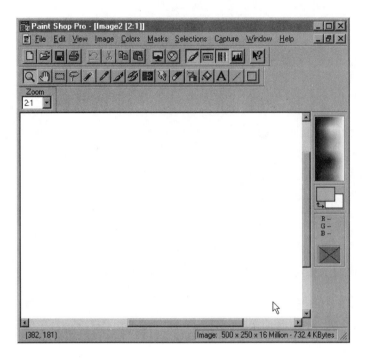

Figure 14-6 PaintShop Pro

Summary

In this chapter, you learned:

- Creation of web pages is greatly simplified by the use of filters, templates, and current-generation authoring tools.

- Besides authoring tools, various utilities exist to simplify certain ancillary tasks of the webmaster, such as FTP and graphics utilities.

Testing and Quality Assurance   15 ≡

Testing is one of the most important things any webmaster can do. There are too many variables to assume that you have everything right. Testing won't guarantee that everything is 100 percent correct. It will, though, expose the most glaring problems that aren't obvious to the person who is too close to the work (the "can't see the forest for the trees" syndrome).

Some facets of testing can be automated. Some require a human being. The ones that can be automated should be done routinely, even for small changes. Invest early in automation. It will save time and money in the long run.

Before You Go On-line

The bulk of testing can and should be done before the site is exposed to the public. You don't want to give users a bad first impression. There are too many sites available on the Web for users to remember to come back to one silly site whose designers couldn't be bothered to check their work before releasing it.

Copyedit

One of the most preventable errors with any web site is web documents that have spelling errors, punctuation errors, or grammatical problems. The website often gives a person the first view of your company, organization, product, or yourself. That impression can be marred by careless distribution of web pages without apparent concern for their professional appearance.

- **Check Spelling** — Spelling errors tend to be the most flagrant violations, since virtually every computer has a spelling checker somewhere. When all else fails, it is possible to load your web pages into a word processor, spell check them, and then save them as text files. Some HTML authoring tools even come with built-in spell checkers that ignore HTML tags and attributes.

- **Check Punctuation** — Punctuation errors such as using a comma instead of a period, or vice versa, are often undetectable on small screens. The most effective way to verify punctuation is to print out the web page and examine the paper copy or use the browser to enlarge all fonts to a distinguishable size.

- **Check Grammar** — Grammar is probably the most difficult aspect to check, certainly in English. Some software tools—none perfect—can help with this task. On the other hand, while it is important to use proper language, it is also important in many cases to retain a conversational style. If the text is made grammatically perfect at the expense of building rapport with your reader, the design suffers. Also make sure sentences are simple. A young person without a complete vocabulary or a person who doesn't speak your language as a native shouldn't get lost in the linguistic complexity.

- **Check Layout** — Do the pages meet the layout and style guidelines developed for the site? Do they have the common items required on all pages?

Note – The preceding item assumes that you have in fact established such guidelines. Doing so is one of the surest routes to a high-quality site.

Jargon Check

Checking for jargon is the most easily overlooked quality-assurance step for virtually any web page, but one of the most important. Often the designer and subject matter experts are too close to the material to determine which are understandable terms and which are jargon.

Jargon builds walls. This is a matter of critical importance. It creates the effect that the site's sponsors and desirable audience are some elite group who already know what these terms mean. Too often the potential clients will go to some other place where they don't feel foolish.

For a really eye-opening experience, gather a group of your casual customers. Don't use as your focus group the militantly devoted evangelists who already eat, sleep, and breathe your products. Take the wishy-washy, middle-of-the-road folks who could stand to be upgraded to high-quality customers and perform a test.

1. **Make a list of all potential jargon. Put these terms on index cards, one term per card. Include all of the following:**

   Brand names

   Trademarks

   Servicemarks

   Acronyms

   Technological catchwords and phrases

   Standards and specifications terminology

   Other words not contained in a standard dictionary

2. **Ask the casual customers to separate the terms that they recognize from the ones that they don't.**

3. **Then ask them to define the ones that they recognize.**

You are likely to find that your most cherished brand names and trademarks are unknown to a third (or more) of this audience. Confusing and alienating a third of any audience is a bad thing, but doing so to a third of the audience that could easily be upgraded from casual to devoted is unforgivable.

Review for Jargon

The ideal technique for screening out jargon is to get a third party to review the documents—provided, of course, that the third party is sufficiently detached from the material to give an objective opinion. Yet this option isn't always available, and it can be very time consuming.

A simpler approach, in general, is to use the spell checker. Most spell checkers have a larger vocabulary than the average person for average words, but they can expose glaring jargonitis much more easily and effectively than a human can.

Remember to disable your custom dictionary before using the spell checker for this function.

- Review every word that starts with a capital letter but isn't the start of a sentence. If it is jargon, add a glossary entry.

- Review every word that doesn't occur in a standard dictionary. If it is jargon, add a glossary entry.

- Finally, if time and other resources permit, get a third party to review the documents for jargon you may have missed in the preceding steps..

Deal with the Jargon

When you encounter jargon, either rewrite the content to explain the term when it is used, or drop the jargon altogether. Explaining everything locally can be redundant and tiresome to read, and there may be cases where marketing wants the brand name or trademark exposure everywhere. In those cases, supplement the page with links to a glossary. This can be most effective when coupled with a glossary or message frame by means of HTML frames.

- Explain or offer a glossary entry for every acronym in the documents.

- Explain or offer a glossary entry for every trademark, servicemark, or product name in the documents.

- Remember to make the glossary links similar to the regular text color. Using distinctly different colors for a page with a great many glossary links can make a page too bizarrely colorful to be readable. People can get used to the slight variation of underlining if you use it consistently to indicate that a definition is available.

Readability and Usability Check

A web page can be syntactically correct and free of jargon, but still unreadable. This is a good place to use a wide range of people representative of your expected audience, from those unfamiliar with your topic or product line to your most savvy admirers.

Offer these people an opportunity to test drive your website. Make a note of their reactions. Don't just write down their comments; watch their faces for frowns, and the way their mouse hesitates before they click on a link. People don't always say everything that is on their mind, and many of them will not admit to earlier confusion after they have figured something out. It is important to note where they are confused initially and to remedy these problems, even if they eventually figure things out for themselves. (All your users will not be so lucky as to have you sitting there with them.) Ask yourself these questions:

- Are they confused?

- Do they get frustrated?

- Do things seem to flow for them?

Use various scenarios to test the responses of this group:

- **Scavenger Hunt** — Can they find various pieces of information that are commonly asked? How many wrong turns did they take before they found the right place?

- **Exploration** — When allowed to explore the site, where do they go?

- **Graphics Limited** — Turn off graphics loading and see how they respond to your site. How much does the confusion level rise?

- **Afterward** —When they have finished viewing the site, test their comprehension. Did they get the message you wanted them to get? Did they have any problems? Is there anything that they would like you to explain to them?

Validate HTML

There are dozens of browsers and dozens of platforms and versions of each. The number of unique browser identifier strings is well over 800. With that many variations, it is impossible to test them all. When faced with such overwhelming odds, fall back to the standards. There are validation programs available for local use or via a website to verify the syntactical correctness of HTML. They include:

- HALSoft Validation Site — Offers validation of HTML 2.0 pages, Mozilla, aka Netscape, pages, and HotJava pages. They can validate pages or snippets of code, or you can download the HTML Check Toolkit.

    `http://www.halsoft.com/html-val-svc/`

    The toolkit itself is at:

    `http://www.halsoft.com/html-tk/index.html`

- Weblint — Offers validation of HTML 2.0 and Mozilla pages. Weblint is available for MS-DOS PCs. Weblint is an effective site-management tool that does more than just check syntax.

    `http://www.khoros.unm.edu/staff/neilb/weblint.html`

    For the Weblint software, look for `weblint.zip` or `weblint-1.011.tar.gz` at:

    `ftp://ftp.khoral.com/pub/perl/www/`

- Georgia Tech College of Computing Validation Service — Offers validation of HTML 2.0 and Mozilla-flavored HTML. They can validate the page for you, or you can download the scripts and do it yourself.

    `http://www.cc.gatech.edu/grads/j/Kipp.Jones/HaLidation/validation-form.html`

    The scripts are available at:

    `ftp://ftp.cc.gatech.edu/pub/people/kipp/check-html.tar.Z`

- VRMLlint — Offers validation of VRML worlds. This comes bundled in the WebSpace product.

    `http://webspace.sgi.com/`

All pages intended for general consumption should at a minimum pass HTML 2.0 validation. This will ensure that there will be few problems with older or less swiftly evolving browsers. Pages with Netscape, Internet Explorer, and/or HTML 3.2 enhancements should be validated by the appropriate program.

Note – Many current-generation HTML authoring tools include an HTML syntax-validation feature.

Verify Links

Ensuring that the web page can be rendered adequately on a standards-based browser is one thing. Verifying that other errors that can interfere with your site's usefulness don't occur is another. The most common error message is the dreaded "File not found." This happens frequently on design projects with many content providers. The webmaster, or whoever wears the on-line editor hat, should check that the pieces come together properly.

Link-checking programs aren't really state of the art yet. New ways of referencing URLs, such as in style sheets and Java- or frames-enhanced pages, take a while to be incorporated into these tools. Keep on top of link-checking updates.

Link checking should ideally also include checking for orphans. (Orphans are files that don't have any web pages pointing to them, so they cannot normally be accessed unless the user magically knows their exact URLs.) When web pages are removed, it is important to know which pages they point to and provide alternate means of getting to these downstream, orphaned pages.

Some of the tools currently available include:

* EIT's Webtest Toolkit — This is a customizable link checker. It offers many nice features like incremental checking.

    `http://www.eit.com/wsk/dist/doc/admin/webtest/verify_links.html`

    Alternatively, you can download the toolkit directly at:

    `ftp://ftp.eit.com/pub/wsk/doc/webtestdoc.tar`

* Webxref — A Perl program.

    `http://www.sara.nl/cgi-bin/rick_acc_webxref`

    `http://www.sara.nl/Rick.Jansen/Web/webxref/`

* HTMLchek — This offers both syntax checking and link checking.

    `http://uts.cc.utexas.edu/~churchh/htmlchek.html`

Browser and Platform Check

Validating HTML does not, alas, ensure that everything on your site is functionally perfect. It is just a shotgun approach to take care of many nonobvious problems. Now comes the human element. Set up a group of systems with various browsers and have people load the pages and look at them. Your testing hardware should always be low-end systems. Don't use the top-of-the-line systems here; they will warp your perspective by leading you to think your snazziest pages will be trouble free for all users.

Following are some recommended testing configurations.

Hardware and OS

- **A laptop with Microsoft Windows 3.11 or Microsoft Windows for Workgroups** —This is a good test platform because it exposes problems with low graphics systems. Many older laptops are limited to a 640 x 480 pixel resolution. With the older Microsoft Windows products, the colormap can be limited to 256 colors quite easily. Do this. This platform will expose problems with pages where the logo is overpowering, the graphics become too grainy, and colormap problems occur. Note that testing under Microsoft Windows 95 is *not* a substitute for testing your site's behavior on older Windows platforms.

- **Macintosh with small screen** — Don't get a 17" monitor for the Mac; use a small screen. Macintosh browsers open the smallest windows and tend to display things smaller than anyone else. This platform will expose problems with image width and other sizing problems. Don't resize the browsers! Leave them at the default size. Also, compare the colors to those on the laptop. If your colors seem to wash out or get too dark from platform to platform, massage your images (by altering the gamma values) to look reasonably good on both.

- **Monochrome X-terminal served by a UNIX system** — The $600-800 X-terminals are the choice of many companies for their employees' home use. Some companies even put these on the office desktop. Using a monochrome monitor is a good way to make sure both that the site as experienced by monochrome users isn't too washed out and that your colorblind users won't have a problem. Colorblind people can still distinguish saturation and brightness, even if they do have some problems identifying the hue.

Rendering HTML may seem straightforward enough that it should be platform independent. Yet graphics aren't always the same from platform to platform. Other multimedia types definitely vary between platforms. With the addition of VRML and, in a few rare cases, Java, a little extra checking is always in order.

15

Software

It is good to test on a wide variety of browsers, but it is not always practical. If you have to cut corners, at least test on browsers that make up more than 5 percent of the site's expected audience. "Browsers" here refers to products by a given company, of a specific version, and on a specific platform. UNIX browsers can be lumped together, but don't consider PC or Mac browsers together even if the "brand name" is the same. Check with the main browser statistics sites to learn which browsers, versions, and platforms you *must* account for and which ones you *might* be able to ignore. A good place to start is Yahoo's List of Browser Statistics sites, at:

```
http://www.yahoo.com/Computers_and_Internet/Internet/
        World_Wide_Web/Browsers/Browser_Usage_Statistics/
```

If you have an Internet audience, always include at least two of the main commercial on-line services such as CompuServe, AOL, or Prodigy. The main on-line sites don't always have accurate numbers in the browser statistics areas, and they do include a larger percentage of novice users than full service Internet service providers.

(Note, though, that the on-line services have generally formed alliances with browser vendors for their Web interfaces. America OnLine, for instance, includes a version of Internet Explorer as its default browser.)

Speed Check

Always verify the speed of your pages. If you don't, others might do so, and tell the public—not just you. Below is a real-world example of a post to an Internet discussion group (names were deleted or changed to protect those still learning).

> After Melanie's post (29 June) I decided to visit some sites. I'm not a developer (yet) but I am a communicator learning about this medium. Here is the woman-on-the-net's viewpoint, ok? (and I have a 28.8 modem & 7100 Power Mac, by-the-by)
>
> - *[site name deleted]* : Don't know about content because my first "click" took so d--n long to load that I aborted. Too many separate trips between my computer & host.
>
> - *[site name deleted]*: Same complaint. I waited 60, count-em, 60 seconds and it still hadn't finished loading! Abort time, particularly since at that time I had not a clue what the page was going to look like.
>
> So ... Remember!!!! We real-world folks don't have a lot of patience. The coolest graphics won't mean anything if we abort before they load! (in fact, I usually load with graphics OFF, but made an exception for this experiment)

The importance of speed cannot be overemphasized. Speed (and by extension, byte size) is especially important to users outside the United States. Many ISPs in New Zealand, for example, charge their users by the amount of traffic rather than at a flat rate per month, and other countries follow the same practice. Most European countries have more expensive telecommunications, thus lower average bandwidth. Speed is also important to users of commercial on-line services where by-the-hour charges are incurred. Most importantly, speed is critical to the novice user who gets confused and frustrated easily and thus requires a faster response.

To test for speed, test in the real world.

- If the site will go on the Internet, test from a remote spot on the Internet, not from the same Internet service provider. Ask your system administrator to verify that your test site is at least eight hops from your web server.

- For U.S. sites, test during the peak time, usually 11 a.m. to 2 p.m. Pacific time (8 to 11 a.m. Eastern). Outside the United States, adjust the peak time accordingly.

- If even 20 percent of your audience will be home or nomadic users, test with a 14.4-kbps or 28.8-kbps modem.

- Make sure your pages load in less than a minute maximum, ideally less than 30 seconds.

After the Site Goes On-line

After the site goes on-line, your job is not complete. There is no test that can replace real-life usage. Your pool of testers has now grown to encompass your entire audience community.

Feedback — Comments from Users

Feedback from your customers is important for many reasons. Part of the perception of interactivity is the response from the webmaster following reports of problems.

User comments are valuable in that they give insight into areas that the design team may be oblivious to, as mentioned earlier, because the latter are too close to the material and the design.

Nonetheless, take user comments with a grain of salt. It takes all kinds to make up the Internet and there is always one person with a really skewed perspective—and probably adamant about flaunting it. If the complaint or comment seems unreasonable, wait until more than one person comments on it before taking action.

However, it should take only one complaint about a page having too noisy a background, being too heavy on graphics, or suffering from other design detriments covered in this book, before you take at least investigative action.

15

Logfile Analysis

Logfiles are gold mines of information. Always review the error log. This is the first place to find problems. Problems are neatly recorded here for you. Investigate these errors in particular:

- "File not found" errors can indicate that a link checker needs to run. It can also indicate that you are listed improperly in a Web index somewhere. Your web doesn't end at the boundary of your server. All links coming into and leaving your site also need to be maintained.

- "Server not available" errors indicate that the server is overloaded. Hardware upgrades may be needed, and it is important when these appear to rerun your speed tests. Start monitoring system resources at the first occurrence of this error message, if you aren't monitoring already. Of course, if you are not running your own server, this may not be feasible—but it may let you know that it's time to shop for another web hosting provider.

- "Invalid METHOD" or "Invalid request" errors can indicate that network bandwidth problems are mangling requests. This can be on your side of the Internet or on the client's side. Make sure that you know which side it is on before panicking; if on yours, don't panic unnecessarily, but do take corrective action.

- Research all other errors that occur regularly.

The activity logs tell the story of where people do go and where they don't go. Check the following:

- Prepare a list of web pages that are expected to be requested regularly. When they aren't, find out why. Have links to them been removed, leaving them orphans?

- Check the commonly accessed pages. Are they three clicks or fewer from the home page?

- Check to see if images are loaded when their pages are loaded. Rule out the images that are stored in proxies. The remaining pages represent the percentage of your audience that is running without graphics. Are you adequately meeting the needs of the graphics-less population?

- Check times; some log files list start and end transfer times for each request. This is a very valuable resource to make sure that your pages, including images, will transfer in the recommended 30-second time frame.

Test after Upgrade

Static sites aren't very popular. Thus, change should often be occurring on your website, but you don't need to go through a full-blown test for every little change.

Copyedit, validate HTML, and run the link checker after every update. If you are a creative hacker, create an orphan checker. This is the one significant automation tool lacking from a typical webmaster toolkit. Run these automated tests after every update.

After every significant publishing cycle, whether it be weekly, monthly, or just every time a new product is added, run a full-blown test on all new material including all human-intensive testing.

Test all new potential jargon with a sample of your middle-of-the-roaders.

Final Note

Testing isn't always seen as a part of design in most media. In many media, it doesn't need to be. On the Web, however, testing is a vital function. The Web is half aesthetic creation, half technical creation. The technical half does require an investment in quality similar to any software project.

An intelligent design shop will dedicate at least 5-10 percent of resources for this activity.

Summary

In this chapter, you learned:

- Testing allows you to find errors before the user can, which would otherwise be cause for some (perhaps acute) embarrassment.

- Testing has many phases including:

- copyediting

- jargon checking

- HTML syntax checking

- link checking

- browse/platform checking

- speed checking

- Testing doesn't stop when the site goes on-line.

≡ *15*

HTML for Fun and Profit

Publishing to the Web 16 ≡

No, that's not publishing *on* the Web—put away your aspirations to write the Great Twentieth-Century Novel (at least for now). It's publishing *to* the Web.

If you have been following along in *HTML for Fun and Profit* to this point and experimenting with developing your own working web documents, you have a more or less substantial body of material to be shared with the world. Chances are though that your material is on your local PC or computer; now you want—perhaps even need—to put it out *there* for the world to see. That's what this chapter is about: the mechanics of moving your documents, scripts, images, and perhaps multimedia files from here to there.

You may not need to read this chapter if you:

- are developing web documents just for your own enlightenment; or

- are producing documents only for an intranet—a closed LAN-type web that is available only to users of your own company or other organization; or

- already have experience moving files over a TCP/IP connection from one computer to another, especially using FTP; or

- are the administrator of the server on which your web documents are to be hosted.

In any of these cases, feel free to skip ahead to Chapter 17—where you will learn details of site management, promoting your website to the world, and so on. Otherwise, read on.

Note – Whether you jump ahead to Chapter 17 or read this one first, you should be aware that there is a minimal amount of overlap between the two. They are related but not identical topics.

The "Here" and the "There"

You should be familiar with the "here" by now. You should have been placing your documents and other web-development files in a standard directory, or somewhere in an organized tree of directories and sub-directories. When we refer to "your cgi-bin directory," you know exactly where to find it.

Somewhere out on the Web is the "there"—your target machine, the one that a user will be contacting when he or she types `http://www.yourserver.com` into the browser's URL field. It's a machine run by your Internet service provider (ISP) or other Web hosting service. Assuming you do not want to mail floppies to that site's administrators to be copied as and when they see fit, how do you get your content onto their machine? In nearly all cases, you use the File Transfer Protocol, or FTP.

FTP: The Internet's Pack Animal

FTP was one of the Internet's first general-purpose tools. Effectively, it connects a source computer to a target computer via a standard login/password dialog. Once connected to the remote, you can perform a limited subset of commands, usually UNIX based, to accomplish basic tasks related to moving files from the source to the target.

To accomplish an FTP transfer, you can use a simple set of shell commands (if your local computer understands FTP, as nearly all UNIX and Windows/NT boxes do) or any of a number of GUI-based tools, including some current-generation HTML editors and software specifically designed for FTP work. We will cover the ins and outs of "manual FTP" here, with occasional reference to the GUI versions; one example of GUI-based FTP was covered in Chapter 14.

Note – FTP has many uses beyond the fairly narrow ones discussed here, such as getting files *from* a remote computer *to* your local one. We will focus here on the process of "putting" files, however. For more information about all aspects of FTP, check Appendix B.

Transfer Types

Regardless of which method you use for FTP—manual or GUI—it is important to understand the available types of file transfer which FTP supports. There are two basic types: ASCII and binary.

ASCII transfers are for files containing plain text only—the letters of the alphabet, digits 0–9, punctuation, and a handful of special characters such as tab and newline. This will be the preferred method of transferring HTML files, text files, Perl scripts, simple e-mail messages, uuencoded files, and the like. Files transferred as ASCII are not necessarily bit-for-bit identical at both the sending and the receiving ends, although the files as displayed on the two systems will look identical. Different operating systems differ subtly in the specific bit patterns used to represent even simple text; specifying ASCII as the transfer type ensures that the translation from one operating system, or OS, to another will be correct. (You might say that the *meaning* of the file as received is identical to its meaning as sent, even if their *forms* differ.)

Binary transfers are for nontext files—images, sound files, and other multimedia objects, as well as compiled CGI programs. (Note that if you are sending compiled CGI or other programs, the compilation must have occurred on the same kind of machine, the same OS, and probably the same OS version as the remote machine runs; otherwise the program will probably not execute correctly, if at all.) If you were to open such a file in a text editor, your display would fill with meaningless garbage characters—the bit patterns are meaningful to a computer but not to the human eye and mind. In a binary transfer, the FTP software makes no attempt to analyze the data; it simply copies it bit for bit to the target.

If running your FTP session manually, as through a UNIX shell, you can specify the transfer mode explicitly. You can also set the transfer explicitly with most GUI FTP packages. However, in the latter case there is usually an "auto" option as well. With this option turned on, you don't have to worry (at least in theory) about the transfer type—the software package determines what is appropriate based on the file's contents or its extension, or by some other means.

Be careful, though: This automatic determination may not always work as advertised. (One of our web hosting services, for example, requires that Perl scripts be uploaded in ASCII mode, as you might expect. However, with auto mode on, this transfer does not work—that is, the transfer itself occurs, but the scripts are not executable. Explicitly transferring Perl scripts as ASCII always works.)

Manual FTP

This FTP technique will primarily be of interest if you have been keeping your web files on a computer for which you cannot run a GUI FTP client—for example, if you have been using a dumb terminal connected to a UNIX machine. It may also be of interest for general-information purposes.

Making the FTP Connection

To open an FTP connection to a remote computer—if you do not already have an open FTP connection—simply enter the command:

```
ftp remote
```

For *remote*, substitute the domain name of the target computer. For example, if your website is hosted on a computer known as www.nobodys.com, enter:

```
ftp www.nobodys.com
```

If you *are* already connected to one remote computer with FTP, you can break the connection with this computer without leaving FTP by typing:

```
close
```

In this case, you can then connect to a different machine by typing:

```
open newremote
```

Logging In

Once connected to a remote computer, you will be prompted for a username and password. A sample login sequence might look like this:

```
Name (www.nobodys.com:yourname): yourname

331 Password required for yourname.

Password:

230 User yourname logged in.
```

If prompted for the name as in the above fashion, with the : followed by a username, the username so specified is the default. If that is the username you want to use, you can simply enter a carriage return to accept the default. What you type following the Password: prompt is masked (not displayed).

You are probably familiar with the concept of "anonymous FTP." This lets you access files on a remote computer without having a specific username: You enter anonymous as the username and, usually, your e-mail address as the password. Obviously, this approach cannot be used for servers accepting web documents from webmasters—anyone in the world could delete or replace a site's critical data, requiring no more information for access to the site than the domain name. For this reason, your web host administrator should issue you a specific username and password.

Aside from identifying you as a user with authorization to add and remove files, your login will also set such options as the default working directory on the remote machine, the set of commands to which you have access, and so on.

Moving Around

After logging in, you need to be sure that you are in the correct directory and if not, move to the correct one. Determining where you are depends on whether the remote computer is UNIX or NT based. If the former, simply type pwd (for "print working directory"); if the latter, cd (by itself). Changing directories is done with the cd command followed by the path you want to move to, regardless of the remote computer's OS. A sample follows, on a UNIX host:

```
ftp> pwd
```

```
/wwwdocs/
```

```
ftp> cd images
```

(The "ftp>" is simply this machine's command prompt string.)

Note that the path (images in this example) is relative to the current working directory unless it begins with one of the special characters identified in Table 16-1.

Table 16-1 Special Path Identifiers

Identifier	Meaning
/	The path is relative to the host computer's root directory. Access to this directory may be forbidden altogether by the administrator, or it may be controlled in various ways—such as mapping the initial / character in pathnames to a "virtual root" which will vary from one user to the next.
./	The path is relative to the current working directory. Same as not specifying any special characters at all, although it is useful in some limited cases.
../	The path is relative to the parent directory of the current working directory. You can chain these together, so that a path beginning ../../ specifies a directory relative to the parent of the current directory's parent. As with the /, there may be restrictions placed on your access to directories above those actually assigned to you.

If you do a significant amount of moving around from one directory to another, it may be a good practice to always confirm that you are in the correct directory by entering a pwd or cd command (depending on the operating system) after each move. Note that on many UNIX systems, the lcd command positions you in your starting directory. This can be useful if you've lost your place or simply want to "go home" without entering a lengthy pathname prefixed by a chain of ../ identifiers.

Finding What's There

To list the files in a directory on an NT remote computer, use the dir command (optionally followed by a file specification, such as *.shtml to list all files with the .shtml extension).

On a UNIX box, the command is `ls` (followed by an optional file spec and/or various command-line options). If used without any command-line options, the `ls` command simply displays the appropriate filenames. Using the `-l` (for "long format") command-line option will provide additional information, such as the file's permissions, size, and date last modified. A sample UNIX session might look like this:

```
ftp> ls *.*html
150 Opening ASCII mode data connection for file list.
index.html
page1.shtml
page2.shtml
orderform.shtml
ftp> ls -l *.*html
150 Opening ASCII mode data connection for file /wwwdocs/.
total 112
-rw-r--r--  1  yourname admin  2010 Jul 31 12:12  index.shtml
-rw-r--r--  1  yourname admin 35890 May  9  1996 page1.shtml
-rw-r--r--  1  yourname admin 12542 Jul  1 06:52 page2.shtml
-rw-r--r--  1  yourname admin 17651 Jun 10 08:03 orderform.shtml
```

The seven columns of data in the file list itself are:

- File type and permissions (mode) flags. The first flag typically indicates whether the indicated file is a normal file (value –) or a subdirectory (value d). Following this are three sets of three flags, each set indicating the read/write/execute permissions for (respectively) the file owner, the file owner's group, and all other users. If a permission is –, that user (or class of users) does not have that permission; otherwise it will be r, w, or x, respectively. In the above listing all files can be read and written to by the owner, and only read by the owner's group and all others.

- Number of links to the file. This is "links" in the UNIX sense, roughly, of aliases for the filename, *not* in the HTML sense of hyperlinks!

- Username of the file's owner.

- Owner's group. All usernames (other than that of the file's owner) in the same group as the owner will share the "owner's group" permissions.

- Size in bytes.

- Date and time last modified. (Note that the time appears only if the file was last modified in the current calendar year; otherwise it is replaced by the year.)

- Name of the file.

Of these, the most important elements for a webmaster are the permissions, owner, and of course the filename itself. (Other information may be of interest, especially when trying to determine if a file is the most current version available.) If you are not the file's owner, you probably don't have permission to modify it.

Creating New Directories

As we'll explain in Chapter 17, a well-organized directory structure can prevent much confusion and difficulty, especially if your website contains many documents. (Your web hosting provider may have certain requirements of its own, such as requiring you to put all CGI scripts in a cgi-bin directory off the document root. Such directories may have already been set up for you.)

Regardless of whether the remote computer is UNIX or NT based, the command for creating a new directory is the same:

```
mkdir directoryname
```

As with the cd command to move to a different directory, *directoryname* here can be either relative to the current working directory, or specified as an absolute pathname. The following are examples of valid commands to create new directories:

`mkdir images`	Creates a subdirectory (named images) of the current working directory
`mkdir ../templates`	Creates a subdirectory (templates) of the current working directory's parent directory (i.e., creates a "sibling" of the current working directory)
`mkdir ../templates/headers`	Creates a subdirectory (headers) of a sibling of the current working directory
`mkdir /wwwdocs/forms`	Creates a subdirectory (forms) off the absolute path /wwwdocs, regardless of the current working directory

"Putting"

To this point, all commands (once the initial FTP connection has been made) have been used to navigate the directory structure of the remote computer. The specifics often vary by the operating system under which the remote computer runs. Actually moving your files to the remote machine is standard, however, starting with the specification of the file transfer mode (as described earlier in this chapter). To set a particular mode, simply type `ascii` or `binary` (note all lowercase). This puts the FTP software on the remote machine into the correct state for receiving the data. If you have files of more than one kind to transfer, they must be transferred in separate steps, each preceded by the appropriate mode-setting command.

To send the file(s), use the `put` and `mput` commands. The former sends a single file, for example:

```
put orderform.shtml
```

The mput command is used for transferring multiple files:

```
mput orderform.shtml mailform.shtml *.hdr user*.txt
```

As you can see, you simply list the files to be transferred one at a time, on the same line as the `mput` command itself without commas or other delimiters. You can use wildcard characters if files to be transferred have similarly constructed filenames.

Default behavior for the `mput` command is to prompt you for verification before transferring each file that matches those in your file list. This can become rather tedious (especially when using wildcards, which can match many files on your system). In order not to be prompted this way, use the `prompt` command *before* issuing the `mput`; this turns off prompting. Transfer your files and then use the `prompt` command again to restore the default prompting behavior.

How does FTP know where to put the files? It puts them into your current working directory, which is why it's important to know where you are on the remote machine before initiating the transfer. (It is possible to move files if placed incorrectly, but this can be tedious and error-prone if the number of files is large.) Also note that there is no way to specify a target filename: The transferred files will have exactly the same names on the remote computer as on the local one. If files by the same names already exist in the current working directory, they will be overwritten.

Changing File Permissions

Once you've got your files where you want them, you need to be sure that they are accessible to the world. On a UNIX host, the `ls -l` command (as described above) will tell you their current permissions. To change a file's permissions, use the `chmod` command:

```
chmod  who permission filespec
```

Here *who* is any or all of the letters u, g, or o (for user, group, or other, respectively) and *permission* is either a + or - followed by the permission(s) (r, w, or x) you want to add or remove. If you omit the *who*, ugo is assumed (i.e., the permission is being set for all users). (Note that user and permission should not be separated by a space on the command line.) As with most other commands discussed here, *filespec* can be a single file or multiple files and specified with a path (relative or absolute) if desired. The following are valid chmod commands:

`chmod o+rx /wwwdocs/cgi-bin/*.pl`	Adds, to all Perl scripts in the cgi-bin directory, read and execute permission for "all other users"
`chmod go-w basicform.html`	Removes, from the basicform.html file, write permission for all but the user

Windows NT is somewhat simpler, as files can be marked only read-only or not. (There is neither an explicit write permission, nor execute permission.) Use the attrib command to set or unset this attribute:

> attrib *permission filespec*

In this case *permission* can be either +r or -r (to make the file read-only or not, respectively.) There is no equivalent to the UNIX chmod command's *who* option.

Removing

Occasionally, you may need to remove files from a remote machine. (For example, you may have decided to reconfigure your site to use SSIs instead of straight HTML files, requiring that all files with the .htm and .html extensions be removed. No point in paying for all that extra disk space!)

Removing files is accomplished with the delete command:

> delete olduserinfo.txt
>
> delete *.shtml

Use wildcards with the delete command with care, as you can easily end up deleting more than you intended.

Logging Out

To end your FTP session, enter quit on the line by itself. (Some machines may include a bye command for the same purpose.) If you want to remain in FTP but connect to a different remote site, enter:

> close
>
> open *newremote*

Replace *newremote* with the name of the new site.

Summary

In this chapter, you learned:

- How to establish and end an FTP session with a remote host.

- How to navigate around the directory structure on the remote host and create new directories.

- How to move files from the local to the remote host, change file permissions if necessary, and remove files that are no longer needed.

Table 16-2 FTP Commands

Command	Command Line Option	Description
ftp *remote*		Establish an FTP connection with the indicated host (UNIX/Windows NT hosts)
close		Close the connection with the current host but remain in FTP in order to establish a new connection with a different host (UNIX/NT)
open *newremote*		Establish an FTP connection with a new remote host over a previously opened and closed connection (UNIX/NT)
pwd		Display the current working directory's name (UNIX)
cd		Display the current working directory's name (NT)
cd *path*		Move to the indicated directory (UNIX/NT)
ls *filespec*		Display files matching *filespec* (UNIX)
	-l	Display file names, permissions, sizes, modification dates, and so on, for files matching *filespec*
dir		Display file names, sizes, and modification dates for files matching *filespec* (NT)
mkdir *directoryname*		Create a new directory (UNIX/NT)
ascii		Specify ASCII file transfer mode (UNIX/NT)
binary		Specify binary file transfer mode (UNIX/NT)

Table 16-2 FTP Commands (continued)

`put` *filename*	Copy file named *filename* from the local machine to the current working directory on the remote (UNIX/NT)
`mput` *filespec*	Copy all files matching *filespec* from the local machine to the current working directory on the remote (UNIX/NT)
`prompt`	Toggle verification prompting for all files matching *filespec* in an `mput` operation (UNIX/NT)
`chmod` *who permission filespec*	Assign/Remove *permission* to specified user(s) for all files matching *filespec* (UNIX)
`attrib` *permission filespec*	Assign/Remove read-only attribute for all files matching *filespec* (NT)
`delete filespec`	Removes from the system all files matching *filespec* (UNIX/NT)
`quit`	End the FTP session (UNIX/NT)

16

HTML for Fun and Profit

Putting Data on the Internet 17 ≡

Not everyone will want to put his or her creations on the Internet, but most people will. This chapter covers what is involved in putting data on the Internet. If you have a large and complex site configuration, you may want to have your own server. However, having your own server means that you provide both system and WWW server administration, security maintenance, and Internet connectivity. That is a major undertaking for many small organizations (even some big ones), and it is beyond the scope of this book. Appendix B lists some resources for researching this subject in depth.

Service Providers

One of the many booming areas of Internet commerce is providing both the servers on which user web pages can be located and the maintenance of those servers. These *web hosting providers* vary widely in services offered and cost, so it is important to shop around.

Different service providers charge for different things. The most common things to charge for are:

- **Disk Space** — Many service providers charge by how many megabytes of data you store on the WWW server. Some services are more granular than that and charge by the kilobyte instead of by the megabyte.

- **Traffic** — Every time someone requests your pages from the WWW server, the server must use a little processor time and a little bit of its connectivity bandwidth. Each connection alone is very little overhead. However, if you have 1000 people checking out your pages every day, the processing adds up.

- **Extra Services** — Processing forms, using clickable images, doing WAIS searches, and running other CGI scripts and Server Includes take processing power. WAIS databases also take up disk space. Special server-side features such as streaming RealAudio and FrontPage extensions are not available on all hosting services. Many service providers charge extra for these and other capabilities, and some don't provide these services at all.

- **Server Index or Company Listing** — Some service providers offer an index or company listing to link your pages into. If you are expecting added value from this listing, it is a good idea to browse prospective service providers' own websites before making your decision. Some service providers may have a hundred different web page listings, with minimal descriptions or organization. If your listing doesn't explain itself well enough to tempt people to look at the page, the additional listing isn't worth the cost. On the other hand, service providers may have a hundred listings or more, but have them grouped intelligently. In this case, your listing may stand out for the people who are looking for what you provide.

Other Considerations

Local or National?

You may want to consider whether to have your site hosted on a local or regional Internet service provider (ISP), or on a server provided by a nationwide or international host. In some respects the answer to this question doesn't matter at all: Regardless of who hosts your site, it will be more or less equally available to visitors. (There is only one Web, after all.)

But there are subtler issues involved. Local ISP staffs are often more accessible and more willing to help you with setting up your site. They can be much more helpful than the big guys when it comes to resolving problems with your own connection, especially if you have special requirements (such as setting up a dedicated or ISDN (integrated services digital network) line to your home or office). And many webmasters—like consumers in general—simply feel more comfortable dealing with someone who lives around the corner. (Indeed, this can be a very big consideration if your site itself is local or regional in scope and purpose.)

On the other hand, a larger web hosting provider is more likely to support some of the more advanced features, and less likely to require that your CGI programs be cleared with their staffs before you install them. (They put you in a cgi-bin of your own, where you assume responsibility for your own behavior—or misbehavior, as the case may be.) They will probably provide greater redundancy (see below), and perhaps will offer around-the-clock technical support versus the more "small-town" business hours (9 to 5 on weekdays, 9 to noon on Saturdays, closed Sunday) that you may encounter with the local ISPs. If your site will have huge bandwidth requirements, a national provider may be your only choice (although you may pay a premium for it).

Redundancy

In this context, redundancy is the ability of a web hosting provider to supply sufficient resources to its customers so they do not have to worry about their site's availability to the Web community. There are two kinds of resources to be considered: physical plant and network.

Does the provider serve its pages from a single computer, or are there multiple servers running "in sync" with one another and able to pick up the slack should one or two be inoperable for whatever reason? How often do they do backups? (This may not be an issue if all you are keeping on their server are your web documents themselves—assuming you've had the foresight to keep your own copies of them—but it can be critical if you are storing regularly updated databases of information there, and there only.) Are their servers physically colocated in one building?

(None of these questions may be important if your business does not depend on the Web for its lifeblood.)

As for network redundancy, the bulk of the Internet's traffic volume is not provided by lines connecting one city to those adjacent to it, let alone within a city. Rather, enormous "pipelines," called backbones, carry it across countries and oceans. Most web hosting providers are not backbone providers as well: They contract with other parties for that service, which brings the Internet into their own servers. (The backbones may be operated by national or international phone companies, for example.)

You may wish to review therefore how many and which backbones or other Network Access Points (NAPs) serve any ISP you are considering. This has become increasingly important as the Internet has grown not only in size and volume, but also in complexity. A breakdown in service or other unavailability of one backbone will not cripple an ISP with more than one "on-ramp." The *Boardwatch* ISP directory (see below, Finding a Web Hosting Provider) identifies the backbone providers for all ISPs that it lists.

E-mail Aliases

If you already have Internet service either with the web host provider you ultimately select or with another ISP, you probably do not need another account just for maintaining your website. (You will receive an FTP login and password that will enable you to move web documents and other files from your local system to the server.)

However, particularly in the case of organizations with several e-mail contacts, each for a specific purpose (sales, support, webmaster, and general corporate information, for example), you may wish to establish a pool of e-mail addresses that share a common "brand name." For instance, mail sent to you might be addressed to webmaster@nonprofit.org, and to your board of directors, board@nonprofit.org. This can easily be accomplished by most ISPs without actually needing to set up new e-mail accounts; they simply provide a translation table so that mail to webmaster@nonprofit.org actually gets routed to yourname@yourownisp.net, and so on. However, some ISPs put a limit on the number of e-mail aliases you will receive with your web hosting account, which may be an important consideration for sites with many possible contacts.

17

How Much Will It Cost?

It is difficult to make generalizations, since there are so many regional variations in the costs of things (web hosting service as well as anything else). Market and regulatory forces can also drive costs up or down.

As a point of reference, though, in the spring of 1997 one of us undertook a cost comparison for a client. We considered both the total cost and the unit cost (for example, cost per megabyte of disk storage), and we looked at local ISPs and nationals (a total of 16 different providers, 6 locals and the other 10 nationals).

In general, there are two kinds of costs: one-time and recurring. For the one-time costs we included fixed setup fees and domain-name registration (see below for more information on the latter); recurring costs included monthly per-megabyte disk storage fees. (This particular client did not have particularly high bandwidth requirements. You should be aware though that if your site *does*, your web hosting provider may charge you either on a straight-line basis—X amount per megabyte transmitted—or on a sliding scale, and may even set a maximum bandwidth threshold.)

The one-time costs for the 16 providers ranged from zero to $450, with $125–150 being typical. The annual recurring costs ran the gamut from $192 to $6000 (average just over $1000, with a median of about $750). On an annual per-megabyte basis, this worked out to a range of $1.92/MB (for a host offering a minimum of 100 MB storage) to about $215/MB (for 5 MB storage).

As you can see, in web hosting costs as in almost all else on the Internet, your mileage may vary greatly.

Finding a Web Hosting Provider

First, of course, if you already have an ISP (you probably do, if you are building your own pages!), consider them first. They are a known quantity, after all, and if you are satisfied with their regular Internet service you may well be satisfied with them as a web host.

Second, consider contacting the webmasters of sites you visit regularly or otherwise admire. Most sites have a webmaster mailto: link, and most webmasters will be happy to tell you who provides their service.

If you don't know of any places that are renting web space, there are two common references:

* *Boardwatch Magazine* is a monthly publication nominally for ISPs and bulletin-board system (BBS) administrators. However, it also provides copious information and solid opinion on many topics of interest to web developers and even technologically savvy (or just curious) consumers. *Boardwatch* publishes a quarterly listing of ISPs (at last count, including nearly 4000 of them) organized geographically (currently covering

only the United States, Canada, and Brazil, although other countries are in the process of being added). The directory, about 475 pages long, is available in hard copy (from booksellers or direct from the magazine, at `http://www.boardwatch.com`), and on-line in condensed form at:

```
http://www.boardwatch.com/isp/index.htm
```

• "The List," frequently updated, is found at MecklerMedia's *internet.com* site. At the time of this writing, The List included over 3000 ISPs in a wide number of countries. The information provided about each ISP is somewhat more detailed (though still certainly not comprehensive) than that in the on-line *Boardwatch* directory. The List is located at:

```
http://thelist.internet.com/
```

No matter what your source(s) of information, once you've got your list of candidate web hosts, visit their own websites for pricing and service details. Sometimes it is difficult to compare, because not all hosts provide the same information or provide it in the same way. In such cases to not hesitate to contact the provider's sales department with specific questions.

Acquiring a Domain Name

If your site is small and personal, or otherwise set up with a very limited audience in mind, there may be no need for you to acquire a domain name. In this case you simply use the URL assigned to you by your ISP or other web hosting provider; chances are that this will be something like:

`http://{host's domain name}/path/~youraccount`

On the other hand, many organizations prefer to establish a "brand name" that not only uniquely identifies their site but is also easy for potential new visitors to locate and for potential return visitors to recall. Furthermore, if at some future date you change ISPs, you take the domain name with you—so there's no risk of its becoming an unknown address.

A registered domain name is a site's brand name. It includes at least two parts; a high-level domain and a subdomain. The high-level domain is the "extension" to the URL—the portion that follows the last dot in the server name. These include standards such as `.com` (for commercial sites), `.org` (nonprofits), `.edu` (schools and colleges), and so on, as well as country codes for sites outside the US (`.fr` for France, `.jp` for Japan, etc.). The subdomain is what uniquely distinguishes your site from all the others sharing the same high-level domain—typically the company or other organization name. When you acquire a domain name, you acquire the rights to those two pieces *plus* any other components that may be used for various services. Once you acquire `bookshelf.org`, for example, no one else can establish an FTP site known as `ftp.bookshelf.org` or such e-mail addresses as `webmaster@bookshelf.org`.

Currently, domain names are administered by one organization, the InterNIC, to ensure that no duplication exists, that trademarks are protected, and so on. The cost is $100 for initial setup of the domain name and the first two years' use; thereafter you will be billed $50 annually.

The InterNIC has come under fire recently for not anticipating, let alone keeping up with, the eruption in demand for domain names. This has led to reports of lost payments and/or registrations, ugly legal battles over who has the right to domain names, and other problems. In consequence various proposals are afloat to decentralize the authority currently concentrated in the InterNIC. In fairness, though, it is unlikely that *any* organization could have foreseen what has happened to the Web in the last few years; also, far more registrations are processed without problems than with them. (Of course, if yours is one of the latter, it may be difficult for you to appreciate this average rate of success.)

If you are considering acquiring a domain name, usually your ISP will be willing to handle the process for you (including acting as a go-between for future dealings you have with the InterNIC, such as the annual payment). Filling out the various required forms is not very burdensome, however, and you may opt to handle it yourself.

In any case, you should make it a point to visit the Internic's site at `http://www.internic.net` in order to keep up with the current status of and future developments in the domain registration process.

Announcing a WWW Page

Once your web pages have been created, people need to use them. This will happen only if people know about them. There are a few things to consider when creating and posting an announcement.

Netiquette

On the Internet it is important to remember that everything is content based. Hype is viewed as very poor taste at best, counterproductive at worst. Your announcement should be a simple, matter-of-fact description of your site's URL, its contents, and the intended audience. Don't include any subjective descriptions such as "great" or "unique." *Never* use exclamation marks. An example announcement is:

> Announcing. The Website for the Clueless, an unusual look at those trapped on the Information Superhighway without a road map. On the site you can find some information about the latest Internet disease, Information Overload, some tips for

travelers, and news about the development and construction of the Infobahn. Get snapshots, full reports, the latest news releases, and the current traffic reports of participating on-ramps. Our URL is:

http://www.withoutaclue.com/

<a href="http://www. withoutaclue.com/"> The Website for the Clueless </a>

Places to Tell the World about Your Web Pages

Blatant and intrusive advertising is also in poor taste, and netizens, or net citizens, will acquaint you with this fact if you overstep social propriety. They may acquaint you with this fact by flaming you, that is, by sending you a very heated note, or they may send you hundreds of copies of your announcement, a practice called mailbombing. Fortunately, there are some places that you can go to announce your addition to the web.

- **Net-Happenings Mail List** — An announcement area for all types of events on the Internet. The subject line usually starts with an all-capital-letter word that describes the type of item. Web pages are usually announced with a WWW> at the start of the subject line. Send announcements to:

    net-happenings@is.internic.net

- **Directory of Directories ("dirofdirs")** — An index of pointers to key resources on the Internet. The DofD is maintained by the InterNIC. Send e-mail to admin@ds.internic.net to obtain the template for submitting your entry, or visit:

    http://ds2.internic.net/dod/dodform.html

- **Open Market's Commercial Sites Index** — A list of commercial websites. Add an entry by completing the form found at:

    http://www.directory.net/dir/submit.cgi

- **WWW Virtual Library** — A subject-oriented index of websites. Various people maintain each subject area. To contact the person who manages the area to which you want to submit your entry, refer to:

    http://celtic.stanford.edu/vlib/Maintainers.html

    If you can't find an area that covers your entry, send e-mail to:

    www-request@dubois.fisk.edu.

- **What's New Announcements** — There are various "What's New" lists on the Net. One such is NCSA's What's New Page. To add an entry to this list, fill out the form found at:

    http://www.ncsa.uiuc.edu/SDG/Software/Mosaic/Docs/whats-new-form.html

- **Registering with the spiders** — Several organizations canvass the Net and record new websites. These programs are called spiders. When you register with these sites, it means that you want your site added to the list the next time the spider investigates the Net. This investigation may occur the next day or two months later. The spider's site on the Web is not for short-term announcements; instead, it is more of a long-term index where people can find you through indexes. Some of the more successful indexes for probing that you can register with are:

  - **Lycos** — To register with the Lycos spider, complete the form found at:

    ```
    http://www.lycos.com/addasite.html
    ```

  - **Yahoo!** — Technically, Yahoo! is not a spider but an index. It is, though, the starting point for many Web searches, especially those that begin with a category of information. To register with it, visit the page at:

    ```
    http://add.yahoo.com/fast/add?
    ```

  - **WebCrawler** — Register with this spider, once independent but now a subsidiary of America OnLine and also affiliated with Excite!, at:

    ```
    http://www.webcrawler.com/WebCrawler/Help/GetListed/HelpAddURL. html
    ```

  - **AltaVista** — Register with this popular and comprehensive search tool by completing the form located at:

    ```
    http://www.altavista.digital.com/av/content/addurl.htm
    ```

  - **HotBot** — This search engine provided by *Wired* accepts new registrations at:

    ```
    http://www.hotbot.com/addurl.html
    ```

  - **ALIWEB** — To register with the ALIWEB spider, complete the form found at:

    ```
    http://www.nexor.com/aliweb/doc/registering.html
    ```

    (Note that unlike many other spiders and search engines, ALIWEB requires you not simply to fill out a registration form but also to build a site index file in a special format. Details are available at the ALIWEB site.)

  - **World Wide Web Worm** — The World Wide Web Worm, or WWWW, is like Yahoo!, an index of websites rather than a true spider. Add an entry by completing the form at the following link:

    ```
    http://www.goto.com/WWWWadd.html
    ```

- **Netnews (Usenet) groups** — It is important to limit your announcements to relevant groups. Following is a list of Netnews groups that would be interested in websites related to their focus. Also, review * . announce groups and, if your website has a local focus, consider posting to *{local area}*. announce, for example, ba . announce for San Francisco Bay Area announcements.

- **comp.newprod netnews** group — If you have new computer products on your web page, announce it here.

- **comp.infosystems.announce** — This is a fairly generic announcement area.

- **biz.*** — If your website has a business focus, you may want to post to the appropriate group here.

There are literally hundreds of search engines available on the Web now, including 10 or 20 top ones. Registering with them all is probably not possible, and even doing so with just the top ones can test your commitment to your site's success.

An outstanding resource for promoting your website is Jim Rhodes' *The Art of Business Website Promotion*. This site explains much about how spiders and other search engines work, how to leverage this into successful placement in the lists of "hits" returned by the engines when a user is searching for information, which search engines to focus on, and so on. We don't necessarily endorse all of Rhodes' suggestions, some of which verge on the controversial to put it mildly, but it is an excellent all-in-one-place introduction to the process. (Note: Rhodes has also developed a software program to register your site and keep the registrations up-to-date. You do not need to buy the software in order to use the information on his site, however.) *The Art of Business Website Promotion* can be found at:

```
http://www.deadlock.com/promote/
```

Site Management

It is all very exciting, getting your site on-line for the first time. But eventually you will have to worry about care and feeding—keeping the site healthy. Here is a grab-bag of things to keep in mind:

- **Keep your site organized.** We are not speaking here of an organizational or navigational scheme to help your users get around the site. Here we mean keep it organized for *your* purposes. Don't put all your documents and other files into the same directory on the server; for example, in your root directory you might simply have an `index.html` (the default document for a directory if no other is specified in the URL). From the root directory might hang `documents`, `salesinfo`, `products`, and perhaps `images` subdirectories. This is more work upfront but it pays huge dividends over the long run. (However, be sure to read the next tip as well.)

- **Use `index` documents in all subdirectories**. These documents are the defaults that will be opened automatically should someone simply enter a pathname as a URL on your site without supplying a document name. The exact name to be used for these index documents varies from server to server and from one Web host to another, but common names include `index.html`, `index.htm`, and `default.html`. If you have not provided an index document, a user who supplies a path but no document name will see what looks like an FTP directory listing: a list of all the files (HTML documents and anything else) in that directory. This may merely confuse the user. It is also a potential security hole, as there may well be files that you don't *want* to be seen by users.

- **Use relative URLs for all links to other documents within your site.** We covered this to some extent in Chapter 3. It bears repeating here because of the potential impact on your workload should you ever need to move the site to a different host or domain name.

- If permitted by your web host's policies and configuration, **use Server Includes and style sheets.** This will minimize redesign efforts.

- **Test everything before making it public.** Site testing and quality assurance were covered in Chapter 15. It is a relatively simple matter to set up a test area of your site (unlinked to by any of your real pages, of course) which mirrors the directory structure of the production area. Also, if you have used relative addresses for your links, moving the documents from the test to the production area is greatly simplified. Testing CGI and other programs is especially critical.

- **Periodically check all links to external sites.** If the number of such links is fairly small, it is easy to do this manually—by visiting your site yourself and just clicking on the links. Larger sites are simpler to check by using software agents which sniff out all the links and report back to you if any of them are no longer active.

- **Use discretion in legal matters.** If you want to use text or an image from someone else's site, *always* get permission if they have not explicitly made the data available for copying. Provide appropriate disclaimers, copyright notices, and so on, for any material on your own site. Also, note that even the Web's time-honored open permission just to link to sites is facing legal challenges; be very careful about this, as it may become even more the norm, and acquire permission if you have any doubts.

Note – The case that publicized this issue was brought against Microsoft by TicketMaster, a retailer of tickets to concerts and other events. Microsoft had provided links, on framed pages, to pages deep within the TicketMaster site. This enabled visitors to the Microsoft Network (MSN) effectively to bypass the advertisements and other information that they would normally have had to view if visiting TicketMaster directly—thereby wasting the considerable resources that the ticketing company had spent to develop the higher-level pages.

- **Don't forget Netiquette.** Be patient with your web host's staff; reply promptly and courteously to e-mail messages to you from visitors to your site; treat requests-to-link and requests-to-be-linked-to from other webmasters with professionalism and tact. Everyone has bad days (you're allowed to have them, too)—but one hallmark of the Web, as of the Internet in general, is that we are truly in this together.

Summary

In this chapter, you learned:

- How to evaluate potential web hosting providers.

- How to acquire a domain name.

- Steps you can take to publicize your website.

- Some guidelines for site management.

Future Directions 18 ≡

A wide variety of Web-related technology initiatives are underway among a number of organizations around the world. While they may all eventually have an impact on web developers, several seem of importance in the not too distant future:

- future generations of HTML and related technologies;
- solutions to the bandwidth crisis; and
- improvements in the security and privacy of Web-based transactions.

This chapter provides a brief overview of these areas of concern.

The Future of HTML

HTML was created by refining SGML to a small set of simple tags. HTML 1.0 can best be described as a pidgin language. HTML 2.0 added interactivity tools (notably forms) to the HTML standard. With HTML 3.2, the specification has become a platform for documents and other media both closer to what users have come to expect from more traditional forms, and closer to what designers have learned about the nature of the "ideal" user interface.

Expected in the near- to mid-term are a number of further refinements in the ways that web resources are presented to users.

HTML 4.0 (Neé Cougar)

Perhaps a bit gun-shy after the experience with what was supposed to have been the revolutionary HTML 3.0, the drafters of the HTML 4.0 specification seem to have tempered their ambitions. The new version appears to be an incremental improvement over 3.2—a significant increment, to be sure, but not an attempt to incorporate every new technology currently being pushed by vendors.

Still in draft form as of this writing, the new specification concentrates its improvements in four main areas:

- **Tables:** Here the spec calls for new tags and attributes to permit decimal alignment (i.e., alignment of text on " . " and " : " characters), enhanced border and rule styles (such as dotted lines), and some improved control over column and cell properties. A new `<COLGROUP>` tag is proposed, which will enable multiple adjacent columns to behave as a unit. There are also two slightly more esoteric table features outlined in the spec: "scrollable" tables (i.e., able to be scrolled independently of the browser display), and incremental display of large tables—kind of a streaming table feature.

- **Forms:** To the existing table model, HTML 4.0 is expected to add a number of ·improvements primarily in the area of user interface. These improvements include an "access key" attribute to permit various form elements to be controlled entirely using keyboard shortcuts (e.g., Ctrl-S might be a shortcut to submit the form); read-only and dynamically disabled/enabled form fields; a feature that permits the form designer to assign a tab order to form elements; and true image-based buttons.

- **Internationalization:** There is a growing recognition of (and discomfort with) the fact that what is nominally the World-Wide Web has a marked English-language bias. HTML 4.0 addresses this in several ways, notably by adding explicit support for multiple character sets.

- **Accessibility:** The media have not made much of this development, but a key to the Internet's (particularly the Web's) long-range success is how well it can support the needs of users who cannot see, hear, and/or type at a keyboard. Recently we have seen the introduction of browsers based not on text, but on Braille and speech. A blind user, for example, can have a document read aloud to him or her. In order for such an interface to work well, audible cues must be embedded in the HTML to indicate the document structure and other elements—a particularly complicated task when it comes to converting forms and tables to speech. Access keys, described above, are one such improvement under HTML 4.0 (pressing a particular keystroke in order to submit a form is much easier for a blind user than trying to hit a Submit button with a mouse). There is also a new tag, `<ACRONYM>`, which basically instructs a speech-based browser to read the letters *as letters* rather than trying to pronounce them as a word.

HTML 4.0 also adds improvements in other areas. For example, new `<INS>` and `<DEL>` tags indicate that the text which they enclose has been, respectively, added to or removed from an earlier version of the document. An HTML 4.0-aware browser might render the inserted text in bold or a different font, and the deleted text as strike-through. Additionally, much work has also been done to standardize in some areas that until now have been subject to vendor-specific solutions—such as full style and embedded-object support.

Extensible Markup Language: XML

Yes. Just when you thought you had a handle on HTML, here comes this new beast.

Like HTML, XML (still under development at this writing) is a child of the Standardized General Markup Language, SGML. One thing that SGML can do, which was not carried over into its greatly simplified HTML offspring, is that it allows you to define your own tags, attributes, and other markup elements. XML will let you do so.

What use might this be to you? Think of it as a logical extension of the still fairly recent notion of style sheets. (Indeed, style sheets will be integrally affiliated with XML.) Better, think of it like the styles associated not with a web document, but with a word-processing document: You're given a standard base of styles in Word or WordPerfect, and the software gives you the ability to create your own styles that employ all of the word processor's display capabilities, and named whatever you want. If you aspire to be a standup comedian and want to share your routines with fellow would-be Seinfelds, Rudners, and Sinbads, you can define one style for witty repartée and another for rambling shaggy-dog stories.

Similarly, in XML you could define your own `<RIPOSTE>` and `<COMEBACK>` tags, and different ones to handle `<BUILDUP>` and `<PUNCHLINE>`. You could set up your own website capable of being browsed by anyone with a comic-aware browser.

That is the catch, of course: How to make these specialized markup elements recognizable and renderable by a browser. To some extent this will be handled by style sheets, and to some extent it will be handled by building into your XML code itself the Data Type Definitions (DTDs) of any new tags. But it is also envisioned that specialized areas of interest might develop their own browsers. (The XML FAQ mentions "music, chemistry, electronics, hill-walking, finance, surfing, linguistics, knitting, history, engineering, rabbit-keeping etc." all in one breath, as it were. A heady mix, true—on the other hand, right now all those groups must use the same markup tools to communicate their very different messages. Rather like trying to represent the full range of spoken Mandarin Chinese in the 26 letters of the Roman alphabet!)

Bandwidth Fixes

To a naïve user of the Web, bandwidth—more accurately, response time—seems like the weather in that everyone complains about it but no one ever fixes it. But in fact several efforts are underway that *do* speak to the general perceived cloggage of the Internet's pipes. These will be of interest to web developers because of their implications for how much and what kind(s) of content can be reasonably be delivered to its audience.

We will not cover it in any greater detail here, but one such effort—the so-called Internet2—is just moving beyond the talking stage. Internet2, at this writing scheduled for implementation by the end of 1997, will be an extremely high-speed alternative Internet operating at speeds measured in hundreds of megabits per second. Unfortunately it is intended to be available only to government scientists, universities, and other researchers; *fortunately*, this should still speed things up for other users as well, since the research organizations will no longer be competing for the same main Internet bandwidth.

HTTP 1.0+

By far, the least common denominator among Web content-delivery protocols is still HTTP 1.0. A new version, HTTP 1.1, was officially released in mid-1996, although its use is still not as widespread as the earlier one's. This new version attempts (and by and large, succeeds) to resolve three main areas of concern with HTTP 1.0: inefficient use of TCP; weak support for caching; and extreme limits on the number of IP addresses. The next version of HTTP, dubbed HTTP-NG, is still in the very early stages of planning and design. HTTP-NG is expected to radically overhaul many of the underpinnings of what is still effectively a decades-old technology. Caching in particular seems to be of interest to the HTTP-NG developers; like disk caching on client machines, Internet caching would put data in the pipeline before it's needed.

Portable Network Graphics (PNG)

This new graphic format was briefly mentioned in Chapter 4. It avoids the licensing difficulties associated with the GIF format, but like GIF it is a "lossless" technology. (That is, although compressed, the image quality is not compromised. JPEG by contrast is "lossy": At very high compressions, the image quality degrades.) PNG also enhances the GIF89a format's transparency feature and expands the number of colors able to be represented.

Significantly, PNG graphics are better compressed (smaller) than their GIF counterparts, and because of a unique interlacing algorithm display much faster.

PNG became a formal W3C recommendation in late 1996. As of this date, however, browser support is extremely limited—notably, both Internet Explorer (through version 3.x) and Netscape Navigator can handle PNG graphics only through the use of plug-ins. This is expected to change in the near future. (MSIE version 4.0, recently introduced, *does* provide native support for the PNG format.)

(One interesting sidelight to the PNG format: PNG images are accompanied, as are GIFs, with a header that incorporates basic information about the image—transparency characteristics and so on. PNGs, though, can include true metadata in their headers, which means that search engines can index PNGs by their descriptions instead of just their filenames.)

"Push" Technology

Frequently touted as a service both to users and to information suppliers, "push" technology *may* (depending on how it is implemented over time) help to reduce bandwidth blockages. To the extent that a server already knows who is interested in its content, for example, it can deliver that content without needing the users to submit HTTP requests for it—roughly halving the number of transactions required for the delivery.

Unfortunately, in many cases what is called "push" technology (and the reason why we keep putting it in quotation marks) is actually a kind of passive *pull* technology. The user specifies his or her area(s) of interest and the server is periodically polled by software (a user agent) to see if there is any new content. This actually increases the number of transactions, and if the users set their agents on a hair-trigger—"Check the *Wall Street Journal* and *Le Monde* every 30 seconds for new content"—the increase can be enormous.

Security and Privacy

We expect these issues to be lingering for some time to come. For now, though, there are a few areas that web developers might want to stay abreast of.

Digital Signatures

You have probably already encountered these in some form or another. The general question is: "How do I know who this [downloadable shareware, Java applet, file, HTML document, whatever] came from, and how do I know that it does what it's supposed to and no more?"

Although the exact answer has not yet been settled on, the trend seems to be to answer this two-pronged question as follows:

- You will know that it came from the stated source because only that source can provide you with a key that unlocks it and/or identifies the source. (This "key" is the digital signature.)

- The key itself might conceivably be forged or otherwise misrepresented. But you can verify both the source and the purpose of the downloaded object by getting the blessing of a trusted (by you, anyhow) third party. For example, you trust that shareware downloaded from a computer magazine's website has been evaluated, virus checked, and so on by the magazine's staff. (Of course, this can lead to a hall of mirrors: How do you know that the magazine's website is secure? That's where the parenthesis in "trusted (*by you*) third party" comes in.)

Firewalls and Proxy Servers

Typically, a corporate intranet is secured from incursion by placing some technical barrier—hardware, software, or a mixture of both—between the intranet and the outside world. In an extreme case, the barrier would allow only outgoing traffic. In practice this extreme case would render an Internet connection virtually useless to those inside the firewall, since they couldn't even receive a requested HTML document from outside. (The only completely safe Internet connection is a completely *dis*connected Internet—an oxymoron if we've ever heard one.)

Vendors are hard at work developing practical solutions to this dilemma, and perhaps we will soon see some kind of breakthrough. It should be pointed out, though, that according to a recent interview with an investigator with the National Security Agency, over 70 percent of the security breaches in corporate networks originate *inside* the firewall.

Content Ratings

Although not specifically a matter of security or privacy issue, this is a related issue.

There are two approaches to preventing access to "objectionable" websites. One of these is simply to incorporate (in the browser or an add-on package) a list of forbidden sites, which a parent, teacher, or other authority can add to or subtract from. (The list might also be in the form of objectionable words in the document's content.) Alternatively, websites can be self-rated—not as good, bad, or indifferent, but as "safe for viewers of age or moral sensibility" X, Y, or Z. At this time, the major independent initiative seems to be W3C's PICS (Platform for Internet Content Selection).

In general, PICS is a self-rating system: As webmaster, you assign to your site any of various standard content labels (with a <META> tag) that enable content-blocking or -filtering software to work properly. The client program (such as Cyber Patrol, SurfWatch, Cyber Snoop, and Microsoft's Internet Explorer) notices whether the site has a PICS rating in the document head and if so, permits or forbids access to the site based on the self-rating and the level of control that the client is operating under. (If there is no self-rating at all, whether access to the site will be permitted likewise depends on the current setting of the client.) Different client packages have different rating "vocabularies," so the <META> tag has to take this into account by including separate ratings for SurfWatch, for MSIE, and so on.

Detailed information on PICS, including format of the tag, lists of client software supporting the PICS standard, and so on, is available from W3C at:

```
http://www.w3.org/PICS/
```

Conclusion

They say that dog years are seven times faster than people years. And now there are Internet years. Internet years don't seem to pass at a constant rate, but they are definitely even faster than dog years. Things created on the Internet experience a very fast evolutionary rate, and the WWW is no exception. The topics discussed here will possibly be passé by 1998, and a new future as yet undreamed will be evolving.

18

Reference

Appendix A lists HTML tags, environment variables, special characters, hexadecimal RGB values for common colors, and so on.

HTML Tag Reference

Tags for formatting and processing the following elements are tabulated below:

- Documents
- Paragraphs
- Characters
- Lists
- Anchors
- Images
- Tables
- Frames
- Server includes
- Forms
- Input form elements
- Index pages

Tags, attributes, and other items that have been introduced or changed under HTML 3.2 or since the previous edition of *HTML for Fun and Profit* are presented in **boldface**.

A

Document Formatting

Tag	Description
<!doctype>	**HTML document type directive**
<html>	HTML document indicator
<head>	Document head
<body>	**Document body**
<div>	**Document section/division**
<address>	Owner/contact
<h1>...<h6>	**Headings**
<title>	Title
<!-- -->	Comment

Paragraph Formatting

Tag	Description
<blockquote>	blockquote
<p>	**paragraph**
**
**	**line break**
<hr>	**horizontal rule (horizontal line)**
<pre>	preformatted text

Character Formatting

Tag	Description
`<em>`	emphasized
`<var>`	variable
`<cite>`	citation
`<i>`	italics
`<strong>`	strong
`<b>`	bold
`<code>`	code
`<samp>`	sample
`<kbd>`	keyboard entry
`<tt>`	teletype
`<key>`	keyword
`<dfn>`	**dfn**
`<strike>`	**strikethrough**
`<basefont>`	**document base font**
`<font>`	**font size/color**
`<big>`	**enlarge font**
`<small>`	**reduce font**
`<sub>`	**subscript**
`<super>`	**superscript**
`<u>`	**underline**

List Formatting

Tag	Description
\<li>	**list item**
\<ul>	**unnumbered list**
\<ol>	**ordered list**
\<menu>	menu list
\<dir>	directory list
\<dl>	description list
\<dt>	data term
\<dd>	data description

Anchor Formatting

Tag	Attribute	Description
\<A>		Anchors hyperlinks.
	HREF	Points to destination of link.
	NAME	Defines a named anchor so that a link can point to a place in a document, not just to the document itself.

Image Formatting

Tag	Attribute	Description and Notes
\<IMG>		Incorporates images in a document.
	SRC	The href for the image.
	ALIGN	Text can be aligned to start at the top, middle, or bottom of the side of an image.
	ALT	A name that can be displayed on browsers that don't have image capabilities.

HTML for Fun and Profit

Table Formatting

Tag	Attribute	Description and Notes
<TABLE>		Defines the table.
	BORDER	Adds borders to separate rows and columns in tables.
	ALIGN	Defines the overall alignment of the table itself within the browser window. Also affects text flow.
	CELLSPACING	Sets the amount of space between adjacent cells, in pixels.
	CELLPADDING	Sets the amount of space within cells, in pixels, measured from the edge of the cell to the edge of the closest text.
	WIDTH	Specifies the width of the table as a whole, either in absolute pixels or as a percentage of the browser display's width.
<TR>		Marks the end/start of a table row.
	ALIGN	Specifies the default horizontal alignment for cells in that row.
	VALIGN	Specifies the default vertical alignment for cells in that row.
<TD>		Encloses a cell of table data.
	COLSPAN	Modifies the number of columns a cell will span.
	ROWSPAN	Modifies the number of rows a cell will span.
	ALIGN	Defines the horizontal text alignment within a cell.
	NOWRAP	Declares that the cell text cannot be broken up to wrap from one line to the next.
	HEIGHT	Specifies the height of a cell.
	VALIGN	Defines the vertical text alignment within a cell
	WIDTH	Specifies the width of a cell.

A

Table Formatting *(continued)*

Tag	Attribute	Description and Notes
<TH>		Encloses a cell of a table heading.
	COLSPAN	Modifies the number of columns a cell will span.
	ROWSPAN	Modifies the number of rows a cell will span.
	ALIGN	Defines the horizontal text alignment within a cell.
	NOWRAP	Declares that the cell text cannot be broken up to wrap from one line to the next.
	HEIGHT	Specifies the height of a cell.
	VALIGN	Defines the vertical text alignment within a cell
	WIDTH	Specifies the width of a cell.
<CAPTION>		Creates a title for the table, outside of the table.
	ALIGN	Specifies the placement (top or bottom) of the caption, relative to the table.

A ≡

Frames

Tag	Attribute	Description
`<FRAMESET>`		Encloses the individual frame definitions (requires a `</FRAMESET>` stop tag)
	`ROWS=`	Defines the number of rows in the frameset
	`COLS=`	Defines the number of columns in the frameset
`<FRAME>`		Defines the start of a new window (frame) within a frameset
	`SRC=`	Defines the source file to be loaded into the window
	`NAME=`	Names the window (frame)
	`MARGINHEIGHT=`	Defines the vertical margin around the window
	`MARGINWIDTH=`	Defines the horizontal margin around the window
	`SCROLLING=`	Defines whether scrolling should be employed
`<A>`		
	`TARGET=`	Identifies the specific window into which the HREF document will be loaded

A

Server Includes

Tag	Attribute	Description and Notes
`<!--#CONFIG>`		Used in conjunction with the `<!--#FLASTMOD>` and `<!--#FSIZE>` to customize time and date displays. Also used alone to configure error messages.
	ERRMSG	Defines the error message string.
	TIMEFMT	Defines the date and time format returned.
	SIZEFMT	Defines the size format returned.
`<!--#ECHO>`		Returns a variable value.
	VAR	Defines the variable to return.
`<!--#EXEC>`		Executes a script or program.
	CMD	Defines the name of the program or script to be executed and that the program can be anywhere on the system.
	CGI	Defines the name of the program or script to be executed and that the program can exist only in an area defined as executable by the access.conf file.
`<!--#FLASTMOD>`		Displays the last modified date of a file.
	FILE	Defines the location of the document, based on the calling document.
	VIRTUAL	Defines the location of the document, based on the DocRoot variable.
`<!--#FSIZE>`		Displays the size of a file.
	FILE	Defines the location of the document, based on the calling document.
	VIRTUAL	Defines the location of the document, based on the DocRoot variable.
`<!--#INCLUDE>`		Adds the contents of a file to the document returned from the server.
	FILE	Defines the location of the document, based on the calling document
	VIRTUAL	Defines the location of the document, based on the DocRoot variable.

Forms

Tag	Attributes	Description and Comments
`<FORM>`		
	`ACTION=`	Defines the cgi-bin script or program to execute with the incoming data.
	`METHOD=`	Defines whether the incoming data will be stored in the environment variable `QUERY_STRING` (GET method) or standard input (POST method).
	`ENCTYPE="multipart/form-data"`	**Identifies the form as able to accept HTTP file uploads as well as regular form data.**
`<INPUT>`		
	`TYPE`	Defines the type of input field. (See Table 9-2.)
`<TEXTAREA>`		
	`ROWS`	Defines the height of the text area.
	`COLS`	Defines the width of the text area.
	`NAME`	Defines the variable name.
`<SELECT>`		
	`NAME`	Defines the variable name.
	`SIZE`	Defines the number of items displayed.
	`MULTIPLE`	Indicates that more than one item can be selected.
`<OPTION>`		
	`SELECTED`	Makes the item selected by default.

Input Form Element Formatting

Input Type	Attributes	Description and Notes
submit		
	VALUE	Alters the text on the submit button.
reset		
	VALUE	Alters the text on the submit button.
image		
	SRC	Defines the URL for the image.
	NAME	Defines a variable name to be prepended to x and y when returning coordinates.
hidden		
	NAME	Defines the variable name.
	VALUE	Defines the value of the variable listed in NAME.
radio		
	NAME	Defines the variable name.
	VALUE	Defines the value of the variable listed in NAME.
	CHECKED	Indicates selected by default
checkbox		
	NAME	Defines the variable name.
	VALUE	Defines the value of the variable listed in NAME.
	CHECKED	Indicates selected by default.
text		
	NAME	Defines the variable name.
	VALUE	Defines the value of the variable listed in NAME.
	SIZE	Defines the number of characters in the returned value.

HTML for Fun and Profit

Input Form Element Formatting *(continued)*

Input Type	Attributes	Description and Notes
file	MAXLENGTH	Controls the display size of the text box.
	NAME	Defines the variable name.

Index Pages

Tag	Attribute	Description
<ISINDEX>		Creates a prompt to gather a request for searching.
	ACTION	Defines the script or program called to complete the search.

Cookie Processing

CGI Directive/Element	Option	Description
Set-Cookie		
	name=value	Gives the cookie a name and assigns its value.
	expires=date	Sets the expiry date for the cookie.
	path=path	Defines the path on the designated domain for which the cookie can later be retrieved.
	domain=domain	Identifies the server permitted to retrieve the cookie.
	secure	Indicates whether the cookie is to be transmitted only via a secure socket connection. (Value **secure**, or omitted.)
HTTP_COOKIE		Environment variable containing semicolon-delimited list of all cookies available on the current page.

A

JavaScript Elements

JavaScript Element	Option	Description
`<script>`	`language=` `"JavaScript"`	Opens a JavaScript code block.
`</script>`		Closes a JavaScript code block.
`;`		JavaScript statement terminator.
`document`		The JavaScript object corresponding to the currently open Web document.
	`.write`	Returns a line of text (possibly with HTML) to the user's browser.
	`.bgColor`	The background color for the current Web document.
`Date()`		The JavaScript object corresponding to the current date/time.
`//`		Marks an in-line JavaScript comment.
`onClick=`*`eventhandler`*		The name of the JavaScript event handler which reacts to a user mouse-click on a given object.
`onMouseOver=` *`eventhandler`*		The name of the JavaScript event handler which reacts to the presence of the user mouse cursor when placed over a given object.
`function `*`name()`*		Defines the start of a JavaScript function.
`var `*`varname`*		Defines a JavaScript variable.
	`=value`	Initializes a JavaScript variable.

JavaScript Elements *(continued)*

JavaScript Element	Option	Description
	new	Establishes a new instance of a JavaScript object.
dateobject	**.getHours**	Returns the "hours" portion of the indicated date object.
	.getMinutes	Returns the "minutes" portion of the indicated date object.
	.getSeconds	Returns the "seconds" portion of the indicated date object.
=		JavaScript assignment operator.
+		JavaScript add/concatenate operator (depending on whether processing numeric or string date).
+=		Add/concatenate the following value to that of the current value of a variable.
!		JavaScript negation operator (e.g., != interpreted as "is *not* equal to").
(condition) ? truevalue : falsevalue		If *condition* is true, use *truevalue*; otherwise use *falsevalue*.
return		Ends a function.
	value	With return statement, passes the indicated value back to the JavaScript code which invoked the function.

Environment Variables

This table lists (in alphabetical order) common CGI environment variables and their applicability to various servers.

Variable Name	SSI Only?	Description
AUTH_TYPE		Protocol-dependent authentication method used to validate the user (if running the script requires authentication, of course).
CONTENT_LENGTH		Length of the content (provided by the client, not calculated or otherwise determined by the server).
CONTENT_TYPE		When a query has other information attached to it (e.g. data passed from a POST operation), this shows that information's content type.
DATE_GMT	Yes	Current date and time, based on Greenwich Mean Time.
DATE_LOCAL	Yes	Current date and time, based on the local time zone.
DOCUMENT_NAME	Yes	The name of the current document.
DOCUMENT_ROOT		The value of DocRoot for this server.
DOCUMENT_URI	Yes	The full Universal Resource Indicator (URI) for the current document.
GATEWAY_INTERFACE		Version number of the CGI specification that this server complies with.
HTTP_ACCEPT		Content (MIME) types this server can process
HTTP_COOKIE		Value of the cookie returned from the client.
HTTP_REFERER		URL that issued the particular request (the "link-from" document).
HTTP_USER_AGENT		Browser name and version number (use with care — there are nearly 1000 valid values).
LAST_MODIFIED	Yes	Date and time that the current document was last changed.
PATH		Path(s) for CGI executables on this server

Variable Name	SSI Only?	Description
PATH_INFO		The "extra information" following the actual path to and name of the particular CGI script as represented in the URL.
PATH_TRANSLATED		PATH_INFO, translated as necessary (including virtual-to-physical file mapping) by the server.
QUERY_STRING		Information following the ? in a URL which executes the particular script. (URL-encoded, e.g. with each space replaced by + and carriage return/line feed combinations represented as %0D%0A.)
REMOTE_ADDR		IP (Internet protocol) address of the host machine from which the particular request originated.
REMOTE_HOST		Name of the host machine from which the particular request originated. May not be available in all cases, and if it's not, it is supposed to be set to REMOTE_ADDR.
REMOTE_IDENT		Dependent on functionality installed on the server, this is the "remote user name" returned from the server.
REMOTE_USER		Authenticated user name (assuming that running the script requires user authentication, of course).
REQUEST_METHOD		The method employed by the particular request, e.g. GET, POST, etc.
SCRIPT_NAME		Virtual path (URI) to the script.
SERVER_NAME		Server's host name; may appear either as a domain name, e.g. servername.domain.com, or as an IP address, e.g. 111.11.111.
SERVER_PORT		Port number to which the particular request has been directed (usually 80 by default)
SERVER_PROTOCOL		Name and version of the protocol associated with the particular request.
SERVER_ROOT		Directory where the server resides
SERVER_SOFTWARE		Name and version of the server software.

Note: Not all the environment variables mentioned in the previous table will be available on every server, or for every request. Items marked "Yes" in the "SSI Only?" column are available only if using server-side includes; other items (if valid on a particular server and for a particular request) are available both to SSI and to CGI scripts.

8-bit ASCII Characters

Items in this table are used for rendering characters that are not part of the standard Roman alphabet (letters a-z and A-Z, digits 0-9, and punctuation), that is, the ISO Latin-1 character set.

To display any of these special characters in your own HTML, simply enter either the corresponding string name or 8-bit ASCII value where you want the character to appear. (Remember to enter the surrounding & and ; characters in either case.)

Display Character	String Name	8-bit ASCII	Description
			nonbreaking space
¡	&iexcl;	&#161;	inverted exclamation mark
¢	&cent;	&#162;	cent sign
£	&pound;	&#163;	pound sterling sign
¤	&curren;	&#164;	general currency sign
¥	&yen;	&#165;	yen sign
¦	&brvbar;	&#166;	broken (vertical) bar
§	&sect;	&#167;	section sign
¨	&uml;	&#168;	umlaut (dieresis)
©	&copy;	&#169;	copyright sign
ª	&ordf;	&#170;	ordinal indicator, feminine
«	&laquo;	&#171;	angle quotation mark, left
¬	&not;	&#172;	not sign
	&shy;	&#173;	soft hyphen
®	&reg;	&#174;	registered sign
¯	&macr;	&#175;	macron
°	&deg;	&#176;	degree sign

Display Character	String Name	8-bit ASCII	Description
±	&plusmn;	&#177;	plus-or-minus sign
2	&sup2;	&#178;	superscript two
3	&sup3;	&#179;	superscript three
´	&acute;	&#180;	acute accent
µ	&micro;	&#181;	micro sign
¶	&para;	&#182;	pilcrow (paragraph sign)
·	&middot;	&#183;	middle dot
¸	&cedil;	&#184;	cedilla
1	&sup1;	&#185;	superscript one
º	&ordm;	&#186;	ordinal indicator, masculine
»	&raquo;	&#187;	angle quotation mark, right
1/4	&frac14;	&#188;	fraction one-quarter
1/2	&frac12;	&#189;	fraction one-half
3/4	&frac34;	&#190;	fraction three-quarters
¿	&iquest;	&#191;	inverted question mark
À	&Agrave;	&#192;	capital A, grave accent
Á	&Aacute;	&#193;	capital A, acute accent
Â	&Acirc;	&#194;	capital A, circumflex accent
Ã	&Atilde;	&#195;	capital A, tilde
Ä	&Auml;	&#196;	capital A, dieresis or umlaut mark
Å	&Aring;	&#197;	capital A, ring
Æ	&AElig;	&#198;	capital AE diphthong (ligature)
Ç	&Ccedil;	&#199;	capital C, cedilla
È	&Egrave;	&#200;	capital E, grave accent
É	&Eacute;	&#201;	capital E, acute accent
Ê	&Ecirc;	&#202;	capital E, circumflex accent

Display Character	String Name	8-bit ASCII	Description
Ë	&Euml;	&#203;	capital E, dieresis or umlaut mark
Ì	&Igrave;	&#204;	capital I, grave accent
Í	&Iacute;	&#205;	capital I, acute accent
Î	&Icirc;	&#206;	capital I, circumflex accent
Ï	&Iuml;	&#207;	capital I, dieresis or umlaut mark
Ð	&ETH;	&#208;	capital Eth, Icelandic
Ñ	&Ntilde;	&#209;	capital N, tilde
Ò	&Ograve;	&#210;	capital O, grave accent
Ó	&Oacute;	&#211;	capital O, acute accent
Ô	&Ocirc;	&#212;	capital O, circumflex accent
Õ	&Otilde;	&#213;	capital O, tilde
Ö	&Ouml;	&#214;	capital O, dieresis or umlaut mark
x	&times;	&#215;	multiply sign
Ø	&Oslash;	&#216;	capital O, slash
Ù	&Ugrave;	&#217;	capital U, grave accent
Ú	&Uacute;	&#218;	capital U, acute accent
Û	&Ucirc;	&#219;	capital U, circumflex accent
Ü	&Uuml;	&#220;	capital U, dieresis or umlaut mark
Ý	&Yacute;	&#221;	capital Y, acute accent
þ	&THORN;	&#222;	capital Thorn, Icelandic
ß	&szlig;	&#223;	small sharp s, German (sz ligature)
à	&agrave;	&#224;	small a, grave accent
á	&aacute;	&#225;	small a, acute accent
â	&acirc;	&#226;	small a, circumflex accent
ã	&atilde;	&#227;	small a, tilde
ä	&auml;	&#228;	small a, dieresis or umlaut mark
å	&aring;	&#229;	small a, ring

A ☰

Display Character	String Name	8-bit ASCII	Description
æ	&aelig;	&#230;	small ae diphthong (ligature)
ç	&ccedil;	&#231;	small c, cedilla
è	&egrave;	&#232;	small e, grave accent
é	&eacute;	&#233;	small e, acute accent
ê	&ecirc;	&#234;	small e, circumflex accent
ë	&euml;	&#235;	small e, dieresis or umlaut mark
ì	&igrave;	&#236;	small i, grave accent
í	&iacute;	&#237;	small i, acute accent
î	&icirc;	&#238;	small i, circumflex accent
ï	&iuml;	&#239;	small i, dieresis or umlaut mark
ð	&eth;	&#240;	small eth, Icelandic
ñ	&ntilde;	&#241;	small n, tilde
ò	&ograve;	&#242;	small o, grave accent
ó	&oacute;	&#243;	small o, acute accent
ô	&ocirc;	&#244;	small o, circumflex accent
õ	&otilde;	&#245;	small o, tilde
ö	&ouml;	&#246;	small o, dieresis or umlaut mark
÷	&divide;	&#247;	divide sign
ø	&oslash;	&#248;	small o, slash
ù	&ugrave;	&#249;	small u, grave accent
ú	&uacute;	&#250;	small u, acute accent
û	&ucirc;	&#251;	small u, circumflex accent
ü	&uuml;	&#252;	small u, dieresis or umlaut mark
ý	&yacute;	&#253;	small y, acute accent
þ	&thorn;	&#254;	small thorn, Icelandic
ÿ	&yuml;	&#255;	small y, dieresis or umlaut mark

A

Common Color Names and RGB Equivalents

Most places where a color is called for in HTML (e.g., the `bgcolor=` attribute of the `<body>` tag), you can use either the mnemonic name or the hexadecimal RGB value to produce the desired color. Using the mnemonics is certainly simpler, but using RGB values permits you to produce up to 256 different colors. (Also, on occasion Microsoft Internet Explorer will not display the mnemonic correctly, but it always handles the RGB values the right way.) Netscape accepts many more mnemonics than those displayed here, including some quite exotic ones (such as `BlanchedAlmond`, `NavahoWhite`, and `LavenderBlush`).

Mnemonic Name	Hex RGB Value
Black	"#000000"
Navy	"#000080"
Blue	"#0000FF"
Teal	"#008080"
Green	"#008000"
Lime	"#00FF00"
Aqua	"#00FFFF"
Maroon	"#800000"
Purple	"#800080"
Olive	"#808000"
Gray	"#808080"
Silver	"#C0C0C0"
Red	"#FF0000"
Fuchsia	"#FF00FF"
Yellow	"#FFFF00"
White	"#FFFFFF"

More Information

Appendix B includes information on books, Usenet newsgroups, and Web sites that we have found useful. Of course there is a lot more information than this out there (FTP sites, mailing lists, Internet Relay Chat (IRC) channels, and so on) — but if you check these resources, you should eventually get just about all your questions answered.

Note that the newsgroups and HTML links appear in HTMLized form on the CD-ROM for easy use. Open the file `Docs/AppendixB/appendxb.html` to see it.

Books

This edition of *HTML for Fun and Profit* covers HTML 3.2 itself completely and also establishes a foundation in many related technologies. By now, though, you should have an appreciation of how very much more there must be to know about developing a web site. Good new books on these subject are being published with a frequency that rivals the rate of change of the Web itself. But here are some outstanding references to keep an eye open for (listed in alphabetical order by author's name).

Asbury, Stephen, et al.: *CGI How-To*. Waite Group Press, 1996. Subtitled "The Definitive CGI Scripting Problem-Solver," this book takes an interesting question-and-answer approach to solving many of the intricacies of CGI programming. Both C and Perl code is provided for all the examples.

Breedlove, Bob, et al.: *Web Programming Unleashed*. Sams.net Publishing, 1996. Covers Java, HTML, CGI, Perl, Visual J++, JavaScript, VBScript, and ActiveX.

Kooros, Paul, and Michele DeWolfe: *JavaScript*. Prima Publishing, 1996. An excellent introductory text.

McComb, Gordon: *JavaScript Sourcebook*. John Wiley & Sons, Inc., 1996. McComb is probably best-known as the guru of the WordPerfect macro language in all its forms. In this outstanding reference, he turns his attention to covering all you need to know about JavaScript, with copious sample code.

Pesce, Mark: *VRML: Browsing & Building Cyberspace*. New Riders Publishing, 1995. The Virtual Reality Modeling Language, or VRML, was co-developed by Mark Pesce. If you need to know something about this tool for creating on-line 3D worlds that users can "walk" or "fly" around in, you should hunt down a copy of this excellent book. (*Note: Apparently there were some last-minute production problems with this book, especially regarding the CD-ROM which accompanied it. If you do acquire a copy of Pesce's VRML book, be sure to visit the web site at* `http://www.mcp.com/newriders/internet/vrml_update.html` *to bring your software up to date.*)

343

Schwartz, Randal L., and Tom Christiansen: *Learning Perl*, 2nd edition. O'Reilly & Associates, Inc., 1997. The so-called "Llama Book" (for the picture on its cover), this is considered the definitive introduction to the Perl language.

Siegel, David: *Creating Killer Web Sites*. Hayden Books, 1996. Although many of its design techniques have been largely supplanted by the CSS1 style-sheet specification, it has a great deal to teach you about page design and graphics.

Swank, Mark, and Drew Kittel: *World Wide Web Database Developer's Guide*. Sams.net Publishing, 1996. Want to hook your web site up to a database? Here's the place to start.

Tittel, Ed, et al.: *Foundations of World Wide Web Programming with HTML and CGI*. IDG Books Worldwide, Inc., 1995. Includes coverage of Perl, Java, C, and UNIX shell programming. Very good reference material on SGML and DTDs (Document Type Definitions).

Wall, Larry, Tom Christiansen, and Randal L. Schwarz: *Programming Perl*, 2nd edition. O'Reilly & Associates, Inc., 1997. The companion to the "Llama Book" (see above, *Learning Perl*), this "Camel Book" explains *everything* about the nuances and scope of the Perl language. Perl was developed by Larry Wall, and he should know. (Note that the emphasis is *not* on CGI programming, but on Perl as a powerful general-purpose language.)

Wong, Clinton: *Web Client Programming with Perl*. O'Reilly & Associates, Inc., 1997. This provides detailed information on what might seem to be a dubious enterprise: building your own web client using nothing but Perl. (Most people, after all, are content using their browsers as their sole web client.) But if you take time to read and understand it, you will come away with a solid understanding not only of the nominal subject, but also of HTTP and what makes a browser tick.

Newsgroups

You won't find a newsgroup on every single topic in every single chapter, so we haven't grouped these by the chapter they're relevant to. Instead, we've grouped them by general topic. Also, note that both Microsoft and Netscape operate public newsgroups on topics of interest to their specific product lines (for example, a Microsoft group on VBScript). Check these companies' websites for current information.

Background/Basics/HTML

```
comp.infosystems.www.authoring.html
comp.infosystems.www.authoring.stylesheets
comp.infosystems.www.authoring.images
comp.infosystems.www.authoring.misc
comp.infosystems.wais
comp.mail.mime
```

Browsers

```
comp.infosystems.www.browsers.ms-windows

comp.infosystems.www.browsers.x

comp.infosystems.www.browsers.mac

comp.infosystems.www.browsers.misc
```

Servers

```
comp.infosystems.www.servers.ms-windows

comp.infosystems.www.servers.unix

comp.infosystems.www.servers.mac
```

CGI/Perl

```
comp.infosystems.www.authoring.cgi

comp.lang.perl.misc

comp.lang.perl.announce

comp.lang.perl.modules
```

JavaScript

```
comp.lang.javascript
```

Java

```
comp.lang.java.announce

comp.lang.help

comp.lang.java.programmer

comp.lang.java.setup

comp.lang.java.security

comp.lang.java.gui

comp.lang.java.advocacy
```

B

Websites

Chapter 1: Getting Started

Internet History/Background

Vint Cerf's concise history of the Internet and related networks:

`http://www.simmons.edu/~pomerant/techcomp/cerf.html`

Internet Valley's History of the Internet and WWW:

`http://www.internetvalley.com/intval.html`

The Web, Specifically

The Web History Project:

`http://www.webhistory.org/`

CERN:

Where it all started. CERN's home address on the Web is at `http://www.cern.ch`. Note that the principal activity at CERN is particle physics, not the Web. If you're interested primarily in their involvement in the latter, check instead `http://www.cern.ch/CERN/WorldWideWeb/WWWandCERN.html`.

World-Wide Web Consortium (W3C):

`http://www.w3.org`

HTML 3.2:

Full specification: All the tags, attributes, and so on are gathered in the document located at `http://www.w3.org/TR/REC-html32.html`.

Differences between HTML 2.0 and 3.2: If you're already familiar with the earlier standard, check `http://www.w3.org/pub/WWW/Journal/5/s3.musciano.html` for a convenient shortcut reference to the newer one.

National Center for Supercomputing Applications (NCSA):

This computer science institute has long been a focal point for Internet developments. Their home page is at `http://www.ncsa.uiuc.edu/`; for their Internet-related resources, jump directly to `http://www.ncsa.uiuc.edu/Indices/Outreach/online-resources.html`.

Mosaic:

    http://www.ncsa.uiuc.edu/SDG/Software/Mosaic/

Netscape Communications Navigator browser:

    http://www.netscape.com/products/

Microsoft Internet Explorer browser:

    http://www.microsoft.com/ie/

Wide Area Information System (WAIS):

Probably the simplest route to information about WAIS is via Yahoo!. Check the page `http://www.yahoo.com/Computers_and_Internet/Internet/Searching_the_Net/WAIS/` for current links.

HTML 4.0/Cougar:

The press release announcing the first public working draft of the next-generation HTML specification is at `http://www.w3.org/Press/HTML4`.

Chapter 2: The Basics

HTML 3.2 reference specification:

The authoritative ("official") version of HTML current as of this writing is at `http://www.w3.org/TR/REC-html32.html`.

NCSA's Beginner's Guide to HTML:

This outline of building basic web documents can be found at `http://www.ncsa.uiuc.edu/General/Internet/WWW/HTMLPrimer.html`.

Netscape's HTML Reference Guide:

    http://developer.netscape.com/library/documentation/htmlguid/
      intro.htm

Microsoft HTML references:

Most of these are collected in the Microsoft SiteBuilder Network site's Authoring section, at `http://www.microsoft.com/workshop/author/default.asp`. There's a good beginner's introduction to HTML coding at `http://www.microsoft.com/workshop/author/plan/novice-f.htm`.

B

Builder.Com's tutorial on basic HTML:

C I Net's Builder.Com site is a great place to, er, browse around if you're looking for basic information on all sorts of web authoring technologies. Their introductory HTML tutorial is at
`http://www.cnet.com/Content/Builder/Authoring/Basics/?bl.fd.start1`.

HTML and Internet Assistance:

Although not a reference in itself, this page provides many valuable links to other pages which are. Find it at `http://www.kern.com/~samt/htmlhelp.htm`.

Donnie Garvich's Teach Me HTML tutorial:

A simple introduction to most of what you need to know. The top level of this site, at `http://www.geocities.com/Athens/Forum/4977/index.html`, includes links to information about the Netscape and Microsoft browsers, and of course to the tutorial itself.

HTML Writer's Guild:

You need to join this organization (currently tens of thousands of members, so you're not alone) in order to use their resources, but the basic membership is free. Their page of links to HTML resources is at
`http://www.hwg.org/resources/html/intros.html`.

Chapter 3: Hypertext—Linking Documents

W3C's HTTP reference page:

`http://www.w3.org/Protocols/`

W3C's hypermedia reference page:

`http://www.w3.org/WhatIs.html`

NCSA's Beginner's Guide to URLs:

`http://www.ncsa.uiuc.edu/demoweb/url-primer.html`

David W. Baker's Guide to URLs:

`http://www.netspace.org/users/dwb/url-guide.html`

Chapter 4: Multimedia—Beyond Text

Usenet MIME FAQs:

```
http://www.cis.ohio-state.edu/hypertext/faq/usenet/mail/mime-
faq/top.html
```

W3C's graphics reference page:

```
http://www.w3.org/Graphics/
```

The Portable Network Graphics (PNG) home page:

```
http://www.wco.com/~png/
```

Bovine Design's Help Pages on use of Web graphics:

```
http://www.bozine.com/helppages.html
```

Creating Web Graphics:

```
http://www.widearea.co.uk/designer/
```

Imagemap Help Page:

```
http://www.ihip.com/
```

Real Networks (RealAudio/RealVideo)

```
http://www.realaudio.com/index.html
```

Royal Frazier's GIF Animation on the WWW

```
http://members.aol.com/royalef/gifanim.htm
```

Chapter 5: Tables

Builder.com's guide to creating "seamless table layouts":

```
http://www.cnet.com/Content/Builder/Authoring/Htmltips/ss02i.html
```

Microsoft SiteBuilder Network's guide to tables:

```
http://www.microsoft.com/workshop/author/newhtml/
```

B

Netscape's guide to tables:

`http://developer.netscape.com/library/documentation/htmlguid/`
`tags3.htm#1087856`

"Webmaster's Tips": Tables Everywhere:

`http://www.cio.com/WebMaster/wm_previous_tips.html#tables`

Urb LeJeune's HTML Table Tutorial:

`http://www.charm.net/~lejeune/tables.html`

Chapter 6: Frames

Sharky's Netscape Frames Tutorial:

`http://www.newbie.net/frames/menu.html`

Neil Johan's Introduction to Frames:

`http://www.geocities.com/SiliconValley/Park/7476/frame.htm`

desktopPublishing.com's page of links to frames information:

`http://desktopPublishing.com/framesweb.html`

Webmonkey series on frames:

Jill Atkinson wrote a series of three features on the topic of frames, using an entertaining "Midwestern picnic" metaphor. The last in the series, at `http://www.hotwired.com/webmonkey/html/96/36/index2a.html`, has pointers to the earlier parts.

The WDVL page of links to frames resources:

Includes some good references on the *cons* of using frames as well. Find it at `http://WWW.Stars.com/Location/Navigation/Frames/`

Chapter 7: Introduction to CGI

CGI "master site":

NCSA hosts what are considered the authoritative references on CGI. The top page of this valuable site is at `http://hoohoo.ncsa.uiuc.edu/cgi/`.

University of Leeds (UK) CGI tutorial:

`http://agora.leeds.ac.uk/nik/Cgi/start.html`

WDVL's page of CGI resource links:

`http://www.charm.net/~web/Vlib/Providers/CGI.html`

Perl references:

The Perl Language Home Page:

`http://language.perl.com/`

Comprehensive Perl Archive Network (CPAN):

`http://www.perl.com/CPAN-local//CPAN.html`

Far More Than Everything You've Ever Wanted to Know... (FMTEYEWTK):

`http://www.perl.com/CPAN-local/doc/FMTEYEWTK/index.html`

Perl documentation (including man pages):

`http://www.perl.com/CPAN-local/doc/manual/html/index.html`

University of Florida Perl Archive:

`http://www.cis.ufl.edu/perl/`

Perl Meta-FAQ:

`http://www.cre.canon.co.uk/~neilb/perl/metaFAQ/home.html`

Carnegie-Mellon's on-line Perl manual (searchable):

`http://www-cgi.cs.cmu.edu/cgi-bin/perl-man`

Chapter 8: Server Includes

NCSA server-side includes information:

Emphasis on use with the NCSA HTTPd server, but also of good general usefulness. Find it at `http://hoohoo.ncsa.uiuc.edu/docs/tutorials/includes.html`.

Apache server SSI:

`http://www.apache.org/docs/mod/mod_include.html`

Matt Kruse's Server-Side Includes tutorial:

`http://mkruse.netexpress.net/www/info/ssi.html`

Step-by-step guide to server-side includes:

`http://www.webtools.org/counter/ssi/step-by-step.html`

Webmonkey on XSSI:

A clear, concise description of XSSI in general can be found at `http://www.hotwired.com/webmonkey/geektalk/97/26/index3a.html`.

Yet another WebMonkey feature on XSSI:

`http://www.hotwired.com/webmonkey/html/97/36/index1a.html`

Howard Fear's introduction to XSSI:

`http://www2.informatik.uni-erlangen.de:8081/IMMD-II/Services/xssi/index.html`

University of Missouri XSSI information page:

`http://www.cclabs.missouri.edu/things/instruction/www/html/xssi.shtml`

Computer Shopper SiteBuilder feature on SSI:

`http://www.zdnet.com/cshopper/content/9704/cshp0051.html`

Chapter 9: Creating Forms

WebCom Forms Tutorial:

```
http://www.webcom.com/html/tutor/forms/intro.shtml
```

Inter-Link 2000 Web Services guide to creating forms:

```
http://www.mercury.2kweb.net/guide-to-publishing-html/creating-
  forms.html
```

Netscape's guide to creating forms:

```
http://developer.netscape.com/library/documentation/htmlguid/
  forms.htm
```

Joe Barta's forms tutor:

```
http://junior.apk.net/~jbarta/tutor/forms/index.html
```

Carlos Peros's forms tutorial:

```
http://robot0.ge.uiuc.edu/~carlosp/cs317/cft.html
```

Digital Equipment Corporation's (DEC) on-line forms testing utility:

```
http://www.research.digital.com/nsl/formtest/home.html
```

Chapter 10: Processing Data from Forms

NCSA's guide to forms processing with CGI:

Includes a link to the cgi.pm Perl5 module. This module has largely supplanted cgi-lib.pl (see below) as the standard not for just processing forms data, but also performing dozens of other common Perl5 tasks. It's at http://hoohoo.ncsa.uiuc.edu/docs/cgi/forms.html.

University of Kansas Academic Computing Services "Instantaneous Introduction to CGI Scripts and HTML Forms":

```
http://kufacts.cc.ukans.edu/info/forms/forms-intro.html
```

MIT's cgiemail Home Page:

A freeware forms-to-e-mail package for use on UNIX servers only. The home page is at `http://web.mit.edu/wwwdev/cgiemail/`.

Rick Osborn's wcgimail Home Page:

The Windows 95/NT answer to cgiemail (above). Find it at `http://www.spacey.net/rickoz/wcgimail.stm`.

cgi-lib.pl Home Page:

`cgi-lib.pl` (as the page asserts) "has become the de facto standard library for creating Common Gateway Interface (CGI) scripts in the Perl language." The library contains a ton of routines for forms and other common processing. Don't reinvent the wheel — find one that's already been invented, at `http://www.bio.cam.ac.uk/cgi-lib/`. Note: `cgi-lib.pl` is for use with Perl4 only. If you're using Perl5, a better resource is `cgi.pm`, at NCSA's site (above).

FormMail:

Matt Wright's FormMail is a popular form-to-e-mail CGI tool. You don't need to pay anything for it. Just go to `http://www.worldwidemart.com/scripts/formmail.shtml` to get it.

Joe Walker's guide to creating forms and processing forms data:

`http://www2.ncsu.edu/bae/people/faculty/walker/hotlist/forms.html`

Chapter 11: Client-Side Processing

Cookies:

Cookie Central:

`http://www.cookiecentral.com/index2.html`

RFC 2109 - HTTP State Management Mechanism (the Cookie and Set-Cookie headers):

Slightly different from Netscape's proposal, but interoperable with it. The RFC is at `http://ds.internic.net/rfc/rfc2109.txt`.

Netscape's cookie specification:

Note that this has been superseded by the "official" RFC 2109 (above). Find it at `http://www.netscape.com/newsref/std/cookie_spec.html`.

Andy Kington's HTTP Cookie Info pages:

```
http://www.illuminatus.com/cookie.fcgi
```

Malcolm's Guide to Persistent Cookies:

```
http://www.emf.net/~mal/cookiesinfo.html
```

Jasmin Consulting's guide to cookies:

```
http://www.jasmin.com/cook0696.html
```

JavaScript:

Netscape's links to JavaScript resources:

```
http://cgi.netscape.com/comprod/products/navigator/version_2.0/s
cript/script_info/
```

Builder.com's JavaScript for Beginners:

```
http://www.cnet.com/Content/Builder/Programming/Javascript/
```

Gamelan/Developer.com's JavaScript site:

```
http://javascript.developer.com/
```

24-Hour JavaScript.com (formerly Kurt's JavaScript Archive):

An enormous repository of prewritten JavaScripts, at
```
http://www.javascripts.com.
```

Tradepub.com a2z JavaScript Yellow Page:

```
http://www.tradepub.com/javascript/m_main2_0.htm
```

Gordon McComb's guide to using JavaScript with forms:

```
http://www.javaworld.com/javaworld/jw-06-1996/jw-06-
javascript.html
```

Java:

Sun Microsystems Java FAQ:

```
http://java.sun.com/products/jdk/faq.html
```

comp.lang.java Java FAQ:

```
http://sunsite.unc.edu/javafaq/javafaq.html
```

Sun Microsystems Java tutorial:

`http://java.sun.com/docs/books/tutorial/TOC.html`

Digital Focus Java Developer site:

`http://www.digitalfocus.com/digitalfocus/faq/`

Gamelan:

The premiere resource for Java applets, at
`http://www.gamelan.com/index.shtml`.

Trevor Harmon's "The Coffee Grinder" Java resources site:

`http://www.trevorharmon.com/coffeegrinder/`

The Mining Company's Focus on Java e-zine:

`http://java.miningco.com/`

VBScript:

Note: Many of the items in this list require either the use of Microsoft's Internet Explorer browser, or a VBScript plug-in for Netscape. See the NCompass Labs link below for the Netscape plug-in.

Microsoft's VBScript home page:

`http://www.microsoft.com/vbscript/`

Microsoft VBScript FAQ:

`http://www.microsoft.com/vbscript/us/techinfo/vbsfaq.htm`

Microsoft VBScript tutorial:

`http://www.microsoft.com/vbscript/us/vbstutor/vbstutor.htm`

VBScripts.com:

`http://www.vbscripts.com/`

Scribe: The VBScripter's Resource:

`http://www.km-cd.com/scribe/`

NCompass Labs, Inc.:

Makers of the ScriptActive plug-in (and others) that lets users of the Netscape browser enjoy the advantages of VBScript, ActiveX, and other Microsoft-centric web technologies. NCompass is at `http://www.ncompasslabs.com/`.

Chapter 12: Style Sheets

W3C's style sheet resources site:

```
http://www.w3.org/Style/
```

Builder.com's "Get Started with Cascading Style Sheets":

```
http://www.cnet.com/Content/Builder/Authoring/CSS/
```

(Note especially the great CSS Reference Table at
`http://www.cnet.com/Content/Builder/Authoring/CSS/table.html`.)

Microsoft User's Guide to Style Sheets:

```
http://www.windows.com/workshop/author/css/css-f.htm
```

NetscapeWorld comparison of CSS to JavaScript style sheets (JSSS):

```
http://www.netscapeworld.com/netscapeworld/nw-07-1997/nw-07-
css.html
```

Norman Walsh's introduction to cascading style sheets (WWW Journal):

```
http://www.w3.org/Journal/5/s3.walsh.html
```

Jakob Nielsen's Alertbox—Effective Use of Style Sheets:

```
http://www.useit.com/alertbox/9707a.html
```

HotWired—Simson Garfinkel on the advantages of CSS over tables (etc.):

```
http://www.hotwired.com/packet/packet/garfinkel/97/10/
index2a.html
```

WebMonkey—Positioning with Style Sheets:

```
http://www.hotwired.com/webmonkey/html/97/25/index2a.html
```

Web Design Group's CSS Quick Tutorial:

```
http://www.htmlhelp.com/reference/css/quick-tutorial.html
```

Web Review's Style Sheets Reference Guide:

http://www.webreview.com/guides/style/

Chapter 13: Style Guide

Art and the Zen of Web Sites:

http://www.tlc-systems.com/webtips.shtml

Wide Area Communications' Creating Graphics for the Web:

http://www.tlc-systems.com/webtips.shtml

Sun Microsystems website interface guide:

http://www.sun.com/sun-on-net/uidesign/

Danny Goodman's JavaScript and User Interface Design:

http://developer.netscape.com/news/viewsource/goodman_ui.html

Heather Champ's take on good web design:

http://www.webdeveloper.com/categories/design/design_site_
critiques.html

WebDeveloper—tuning graphics for performance:

http://www.webdeveloper.com/categories/design/design_performance
_tuning_rww.html

WDVL's page of links to web style resources:

http://www.stars.com/Vlib/Authoring/Style.html

Builder.com on design:

http://www.cnet.com/Content/Builder/Graphics/Design/

(Also check their Secrets of the Web Design Masters page,
http://www.cnet.com/Content/Builder/Graphics/Masters/.)

Chapter 14: Work-Saving Tools

Unlike the links provided for other chapters of this edition of HTML for Fun and Profit, *this category changes almost too rapidly to keep a handle on. Probably the best approach here is to visit one or more of the following sites, using its site-specific search engine to find the kind of tools on the platform that you're working in.*

Shareware.com:

```
http://www.shareware.com
```

TUCOWS:

```
http://www.tucows.com
```

Forrest Stroud's Consummate Winsock Apps: (Win 3.x/95/NT only):

```
http://cws.internet.com/
```

Free Software Foundation (GNU) software archives:

```
http://www.gnu.org/software/software.html
```


As for the packages we specifically covered in this chapter (all Win 3.x/95/NT):

WebEdit Pro:

```
http://www.luckman.com/webeditpro/index.html
```

Front Page:

```
http://www.microsoft.com/frontpage/
```

CuteFTP:

```
http://www.cuteftp.com/
```

PaintShop Pro:

```
http://www.jasc.com/psp.html
```

Chapter 15: Testing and Quality Assurance

HTML and VRML validation:

HALSoft Validation Site:

```
http://www.webtechs.com/html-val-svc/
```

Weblint:

```
http://www.khoros.unm.edu/staff/neilb/weblint.html
```

Georgia Tech College of Computing Validation Service:

```
http://www.cc.gatech.edu/grads/j/Kipp.Jones/HaLidation/
validation-form.html
```

Doctor HTML:

```
http://www2.imagiware.com/RxHTML/
```

VRMLlint:

```
http://vrml.sgi.com/Tools/vrmllint.tar.Z
```

Links validation:

EIT's Webtest Toolkit:

```
ftp://ftp.eit.com/pub/eit/wsk/
```

Webxref:

```
http://zoutmijn.bpa.nl/rick/Web/index2.html
```

HTMLchek:

```
http://uts.cc.utexas.edu/~churchh/htmlchek.html
```

MOMSpider:

```
http://www.ics.uci.edu/pub/websoft/MOMspider/
```

lvrfy (UNIX shell-based links checker):

```
http://www.cs.dartmouth.edu/~crow/lvrfy.html
```

Browser statistics:

Yahoo!'s list of browser statistics sites:

```
http://www.yahoo.com/Computers_and_Internet/Software/Internet/
World_Wide_Web/Browsers/Browser_Usage_Statistics/
```

BrowserWatch:

```
http://www.browserwatch.com
```

Chapter 16: Publishing to the Web

Electronic Frontier Foundation (EFF) guide to FTP:

```
http://www.eff.org/papers/eegtti/eeg_137.html#SEC138
```

Zen and the Art of the Internet—FTP:

```
http://www.cs.indiana.edu/docproject/zen/zen-1.0_5.html#SEC17
```

NetTrain FAQ on FTP resources:

```
http://www.fau.edu/rinaldi/nettrain/ftp.html
```

Chapter 17: Putting Data on the Internet

Finding a web hosting provider:

Boardwatch Magazine:

```
http://www.boardwatch.com/ISP/index.ihtml
```

The List:

```
http://thelist.internet.com/
```

Budgetweb.com's list of budget web hosting providers:

```
http://www.budgetweb.com/budgetweb/index.html
```

Acquiring a domain name:

InterNIC:

```
http://www.internic.net
```

AlterNIC (alternative domain-name registration service):

```
http://www.alternic.net/
```

Builder.com - How to Get Your Own Domain Name:

```
http://www.cnet.com/Content/Features/Howto/Domain/
```

Site promotion:

Builder.com - How to Promote Your Site:

```
http://www.cnet.com/Content/Builder/Business/Promote/
```

Net-Happenings mail list:

```
net-happenings@is.internic.net
```

InterNIC Directory of Directories ("dirofdirs"):

```
http://ds2.internic.net/dod/dodform.html
```

WWW Virtual Library:

```
http://celtic.stanford.edu/vlib/Maintainers.html
```

NCSA's What's New page:

```
http://www.ncsa.uiuc.edu/SDG/Software/Mosaic/Docs/whats-new-
form.html
```

Jim Rhodes' The Art of Business Website Promotion:

```
http://www.deadlock.com/promote/
```

Spiders/Search engines:

Lycos — `http://www.lycos.com/addasite.html`

Yahoo! — `http://add.yahoo.com/fast/add?`

WebCrawler —

```
http://www.webcrawler.com/WebCrawler/Help/GetListed/
HelpAddURL.html
```

AltaVista — `http://www.altavista.digital.com/av/content/addurl.htm`

HotBot — `http://www.hotbot.com/addurl.html`

ALIWEB — `http://www.nexor.com/aliweb/doc/registering.html`

World-Wide Web Worm — `http://www.goto.com/WWWWadd.html`

Site management:

Netscape LiveWire guide to site management:

Although its focus is on the Netscape LiveWire product line, this paper's recommendations are broadly applicable across platforms. Find it at `http://developer.netscape.com/library/documentation/livewire/sitemgr2.htm`.

Managing server content:

`http://www10.netscape.com/comprod/server_central/support/fasttrack_man/content.htm`

SunWorld OnLine—Securing Your Web Server:

`http://www.sun.com/sunworldonline/swol-07-1996/swol-07-webmaster.html`

Chapter 18: Future Directions

W3C's HTML 4.0 ("Cougar") specification (working draft):

`http://www.w3.org/TR/WD-html40-970708/cover.html`

The XML FAQ:

`http://www.ucc.ie/xml/`

Jon Bosak's paper on XML, Java, and the future of the Web:

`http://sunsite.unc.edu/pub/sun-info/standards/xml/why/xmlapps.htm`

PC Magazine's page of links to XML information:

`http://www8.zdnet.com/pcmag/iu/toolkit/xml.htm`

Official Internet2 home page:

```
http://www.internet2.edu/
```

HTTP-NG:

```
http://www.w3.org/Protocols/HTTP-NG/Activity.html
```

W3C overview of the Portable Network Graphics (PNG) format:

```
http://www.w3.org/Graphics/PNG/Overview.html
```

W3C's page of information on the PICS content-rating mechanism:

```
http://www.w3.org/PICS/
```

Bonus Links: Certification

DePaul University's Web Developer Program:

```
http://www.cs.depaul.edu/institute/brochure/webp.html
```

NJIT's WebMaster Certification Program:

```
http://www.njit.edu/CPE/webmaster/Webmaster.html
```

USWeb Professional Certification Program:

```
http://www.usweb.com/certification/2.0.html
```

Index

containers, 12
empty elements, 12
future of, 6, 315-17
HTML 4.0, 315-16
security/privacy, 319-20
  content ratings, 320
  digital signatures, 319
  firewalls/proxy servers, 319-20
standard, 4-5
tables, 5
tags, 11, 12, 323-33
  case sensitivity of, 15
  defined, 15
validation, 283-84
version 4.0, 6
versions of, 4
XML (extensible markup language), 316-17
HTTP 1.0+, 318
http, 4, 48
HTTP cookies, 182, 207-15
  defined, 208-10
  retrieving, 212-15
  setting, 210-11
HTTP file upload, 183-85
HTTP-NG, 318
Hyperlink color attributes, 23
Hypertext, 3, 47-58
  addressing variations, 51-57
  anchor tags, 47
  elements of, 47-49
  links, 47
    adding, 49-51
  mailto link, 57
  URLs (Universal Resource Locators), 47,
    48-49

—I—

`<i>` and `</i>`, 18, 44
id Software home page, 64
`IF` element, 151
image, 187
Image formatting, 326
Imagemaps, 71-73
  client-side, 72-73
  server-side, 71-72
Image tricks, 262-65
`<img>` tag, 66, 68, 71-73, 77, 326

`border=` attribute, 71
  `usemap=`*mapname* attribute, 72
Inches, 243
`INCLUDE` directive, 140
  `FILE` attribute, 140, 143-44
  `VIRTUAL` attribute, 140-41, 143-44
Indenting text, 250
index.html, 313
Index (link), 258
Index pages, 333
Inheritance, 239
In-line images, 63-71
  adding, 66
  aligning, 66-67
  alternatives to, 67
  "barred" backgrounds, 263-64
  design considerations, 64-65
  filler images, 64
  image efficiencies, 67-69
  links, adding to simulate buttons, 71
  single-pixel GIFs, 264-65
  transparent backgrounds, 69-70
    giftrans utility, 69
    listing colormap of image, 70
    setting by color, 70
    setting by colormap cell, 70
`<INPUT>` tag, 156, 158
  `NAME` attribute, 160-61
  `TYPE="checkbox"` attribute, 163
  `TYPE="file"` attribute, 183
  `TYPE="hidden"` attribute, 165-66
  `TYPE="image"` attribute, 158
  `TYPE="radio"` attribute, 160-61
  `TYPE="reset"` attribute, 178-81
  `TYPE="submit"` attribute, 156
  `TYPE="text"` attribute, 166-69
  `VALUE` attribute, 160
Interlaced GIFs, 68
Internal style sheets, 235-37
Internet, 1-2
  domain name, acquiring, 307-8
  home page, announcing, 308-11
  Internet service providers (ISPs), 55, 303-7
  netiquette, 7, 308-9
  putting data on, 303-13
  site management, 311-13

Metacharacters, 37-38
METHOD= attribute, <FORM> tag, 156, 186
Microsoft FrontPage, 272-76
Microsoft Internet Explorer, 7, 183, 283,
   286, 320
  and cookies, 210
Microsoft Network (MSN), 312
Microsoft Windows, 5
MIDI format, 62
MIME formats, 60-62
  AVI, 61
  Basic Sound, 61
  filename extensions for, 62-63
  GIF (Graphics Interchange Format), 60
  JPEG (Joint Photographic Experts Group), 60-61
  MIDI, 62
  MPEG (Motion Picture Experts Group), 61
  PDF (Portable Document Format), 61
  PNG format, 61
  PostScript, 61
  QuickTime, 61
  RealAudio, 62
  TIFF (Tagged Image File Format), 61
  VRML (Virtual Reality Modeling
    Language), 62
  WAV format, 61
mkdir *directoryname* command, FTP, 297, 300
Monospace font display, 29
Mosaic, 5-6, 7
MPEG (Motion Picture Experts Group), 61, 137
mput *filespec*, FTP, 298, 301
Multimedia, 59-77
  animated GIFs, 74-75
  browser-specific, 76
  imagemaps, 71-73
  in-line images, 63-71
  MIME formats, 60-62
  multimedia links, adding, 62-63
  preloading of images, 69
  RealAudio files, 75-76
Multiple forms, 182-83
Multiple radio buttons, 162-63
Multiple spaces, 28
Multithreading, 225

—N—

NAME= attribute:
  <a> and </a> tags, 50
  <INPUT> tag, 160-61
Named anchors, 50-51
Named frames, 105-7
Naming documents, 20-21
Navigation, 256-59
  Go to Top link, 257
  Home link, 259
  index, 258
  Next Page/Document link, 257
  Previous Page/Document link, 257
  site map, 259
  Table of Contents link, 258
NCSA (National Center for Supercomputing Activ-
  ities), 5
Nested frames, 102-4
Nested lists, 39-40
Net-Happenings Mail List, 309
Netiquette, 7, 308-9
Netnews (Usenet) groups, 310
Netscape Communicator 4.0, 208
Netscape Navigator, 5, 7, 23, 33, 42, 48, 283
  changing font size in, 15
Network Access Points (NAPs), 305
Next Page/Document link, 257
<NOFRAME> tag, 110-11
No-frame clients, 110-11
noshade= attribute, <hr> tag, 30
NOWRAP attribute, <td> tag, 87-88
Numbered lists, 38

—O—

Oblique typeface, 238
<ol> and </ol> tags, 38, 41, 45
  type= attribute, 41
OLE (Object Linking and Embedding), 227
open command, FTP, 294
Open Market's Commercial Sites Index, 309
<OPTION> tag, 175-77, 186
  SELECTED attribute, 176-77
Ordered lists, 38
Orphans, 284

Typeface, changing, 238-39
TYPE="file" attribute, <INPUT> tag, 183
TYPE="hidden" attribute, <INPUT> tag, 165-66
TYPE="image" attribute, <INPUT> tag, 158
TYPE="radio" attribute, <INPUT> tag, 160-61
TYPE="reset" attribute, <INPUT> tag, 178-81
TYPE="submit" attribute, <INPUT> tag, 156
TYPE="text" attribute, <INPUT> tag, 166-69

—U—

<u> and </u> tags, 35, 45
<ul> and </ul> tags, 38, 45
UNIX grep tool, 203
Unordered lists, 38
URLs (Universal Resource Locators), 47, 48-49
    absolute URLs, 48
    components of:
        directory path, 49
        filename, 49
        port, 48
        search components/variables/location
            pointer, 49
        service type, 48
        system name, 48
    relative URLs, 48, 51
    setting background by, 249-50
Usability check, 282
usemap=mapname attribute, <img> tag, 72
User-controlled granularity, 260
uucp (UNIX-to-UNIX copy program), 2

—V—

valign= attribute, <tr> tag, 91
value= attribute, <li> tag, 41
VAR attribute, ECHO element, 147
Variables, echoing, 147-48
<var> tag, 34, 44
VBScript, 6, 207, 227-28
VIRTUAL attribute:
    FLASTMOD element, 144
    INCLUDE directive, 140-41, 143-44
Virtual hosts, and document root, 54-56
vlink= attribute, <body> tag, 23, 50
VRML (Virtual Reality Modeling Language), 62
vspace=pixels attribute, 66

—W—

WAV format, 60, 61
WebCrawler, 310
WebEdit Pro, 269-72
Web hosting service, 55
Weblint, 283
Webmaster, 26
Web page, announcing, 308-11
Web publishing, 291-301
    FTP, 292-99
Webxref, 284
What's New Announcements, 309
White space, controlling, 28-31
width= attribute, <hr> tag, 30
width=pixels attribute, 68-69
width=value attribute, <td> tag, 87
WordPerfect, 11, 267
Word processing, formatting text in, 11-12
Word wrapping, 86-88
Work-saving tools, 267-78
    authoring tools, 268-77
        editor list, 276
        Microsoft FrontPage, 272-76
        WebEdit Pro, 269-72
    filters, 267-68
    FTP tools, 276-77
    graphics utilities, 277-78
    templates, 256, 268
World-Wide Web Consortium (W3C), 4
    HTML Converters page, 268
    PICS, 320
World Wide Web Worm (WWWW), 310
World Wide Web (WWW), 5-6
    culture, 7
    emotags, 7
    interactive nature of, 6
    miscellany, 6-9
    naming, 7
    page format philosophy, 8
    people, 8-9
    profiting from, 9
    publishing to, 291-301
    See also Web publishing

WWW browsers:
  and document naming, 20-21
  and WYSIWYG, 15
WWW Virtual Library, 309
WYSIWYG, 8, 11, 267, 268
  and WWW browsers, 15

—X—

XML (extensible markup language), 316-17
XMosaic, 20
X-Windows, 5

—Y—

Yahoo!, 286, 310

Company does not warrant that the SOFTWARE will meet your requirements or that the operation of the SOFTWARE will be uninterrupted or error-free. The Company warrants that the media on which the SOFTWARE is delivered shall be free from defects in materials and workmanship under normal use for a period of thirty (30) days from the date of your purchase. Your only remedy and the Company's only obligation under these limited warranties is, at the Company's option, return of the warranted item for a refund of any amounts paid by you or replacement of the item. Any replacement of SOFTWARE or media under the warranties shall not extend the original warranty period. The limited warranty set forth above shall not apply to any SOFTWARE which the Company determines in good faith has been subject to misuse, neglect, improper installation, repair, alteration, or damage by you. EXCEPT FOR THE EXPRESSED WARRANTIES SET FORTH ABOVE, THE COMPANY DISCLAIMS ALL WARRANTIES, EXPRESS OR IMPLIED, INCLUDING WITHOUT LIMITATION, THE IMPLIED WARRANTIES OF MERCHANTABILITY AND FITNESS FOR A PARTICULAR PURPOSE. EXCEPT FOR THE EXPRESS WARRANTY SET FORTH ABOVE, THE COMPANY DOES NOT WARRANT, GUARANTEE, OR MAKE ANY REPRESENTATION REGARDING THE USE OR THE RESULTS OF THE USE OF THE SOFTWARE IN TERMS OF ITS CORRECTNESS, ACCURACY, RELIABILITY, CURRENTNESS, OR OTHERWISE.

IN NO EVENT, SHALL THE COMPANY OR ITS EMPLOYEES, AGENTS, SUPPLIERS, OR CONTRACTORS BE LIABLE FOR ANY INCIDENTAL, INDIRECT, SPECIAL, OR CONSEQUENTIAL DAMAGES ARISING OUT OF OR IN CONNECTION WITH THE LICENSE GRANTED UNDER THIS AGREEMENT, OR FOR LOSS OF USE, LOSS OF DATA, LOSS OF INCOME OR PROFIT, OR OTHER LOSSES, SUSTAINED AS A RESULT OF INJURY TO ANY PERSON, OR LOSS OF OR DAMAGE TO PROPERTY, OR CLAIMS OF THIRD PARTIES, EVEN IF THE COMPANY OR AN AUTHORIZED REPRESENTATIVE OF THE COMPANY HAS BEEN ADVISED OF THE POSSIBILITY OF SUCH DAMAGES. IN NO EVENT SHALL LIABILITY OF THE COMPANY FOR DAMAGES WITH RESPECT TO THE SOFTWARE EXCEED THE AMOUNTS ACTUALLY PAID BY YOU, IF ANY, FOR THE SOFTWARE.

SOME JURISDICTIONS DO NOT ALLOW THE LIMITATION OF IMPLIED WARRANTIES OR LIABILITY FOR INCIDENTAL, INDIRECT, SPECIAL, OR CONSEQUENTIAL DAMAGES, SO THE ABOVE LIMITATIONS MAY NOT ALWAYS APPLY. THE WARRANTIES IN THIS AGREEMENT GIVE YOU SPECIFIC LEGAL RIGHTS AND YOU MAY ALSO HAVE OTHER RIGHTS WHICH VARY IN ACCORDANCE WITH LOCAL LAW.

ACKNOWLEDGMENT

YOU ACKNOWLEDGE THAT YOU HAVE READ THIS AGREEMENT, UNDERSTAND IT, AND AGREE TO BE BOUND BY ITS TERMS AND CONDITIONS. YOU ALSO AGREE THAT THIS AGREEMENT IS THE COMPLETE AND EXCLUSIVE STATEMENT OF THE AGREEMENT BETWEEN YOU AND THE COMPANY AND SUPERSEDES ALL PROPOSALS OR PRIOR AGREEMENTS, ORAL, OR WRITTEN, AND ANY OTHER COMMUNICATIONS BETWEEN YOU AND THE COMPANY OR ANY REPRESENTATIVE OF THE COMPANY RELATING TO THE SUBJECT MATTER OF THIS AGREEMENT.

Should you have any questions concerning this Agreement or if you wish to contact the Company for any reason, please contact in writing at the address below.

Robin Short

Prentice Hall PTR

One Lake Street

Upper Saddle River, New Jersey 07458

About the Software

Contents

The disc that accompanies this book contains many tools that we hope you will find useful. Some of these tools are trial versions, others shareware or freeware and still others that are created by the author to help you with your experience with this book. There may be minor discrepancies in the final CD. If so, we apologize for any deletion. This is a list of those tools:

A 30-day trial version of O'Reilly's WebSite server software, version 2.0, for Win32
The full Apache server software, version 1.2, for Unix
Perl for both Win 32 and Unix platforms
Example code from chapters 2 though 12 from the book
Appendix B from the book in HTML form

Utilities for Win32
CuteFTP
Sheet Stylist
FTPEdit
PaintShop Pro
Map This!
GIF Construction Set
giftrans executable
giftrans readme
WebEdit Pro

Utilities for Unix
ImageMagic
giftrans executable
giftrans readme
xhtml-1_3.zip (HTML editor for Unix)

System Requirements

Windows 95, Windows NT, SunOS, or Solaris platforms

Technical Support

Most of the software mentioned above is created by third parties and we have provided it because we feel that the software utilities are excellent. Please pay careful attention to the registration instructions provided. Prentice Hall does not offer technical support for this software. However, if you have a damaged disk that needs replacement, email us at:

discexchange@prenhall.com